Women on the Right

Conservative Gender Movements in Japan

By
Ayaka Suzuki

Women on the Right

Conservative Gender Movements in Japan

By
Ayaka Suzuki

TRANS
PACIFIC
PRESS

Women on the Right: Conservative Gender Movements in Japan
© 2024 by Ayaka Suzuki
Originally published in Japanese 2019 *Joseitachi no Hoshu Undo: Ukeika suru Nihon Shakai no Jenda* (Women's Conservative Movement: Gender in Japanese Society that Shifting to the Right) by Jimbun Shoin.
This English edition published 2024 by Trans Pacific Press.

Trans Pacific Press Co., Ltd.
PO Box 8547
#19682
Boston, MA, 02114, United States
Telephone: +1-6178610545
Email: info@transpacificpress.com
Web: http://www.transpacificpress.com

Copyedited by Dr. Karl E. Smith, Melbourne, Australia
Layout designed and set by Ryo Kuroda, Tsukuba-city, Ibaraki, Japan
Cover designed by Klassic Designs

Distributors

USA, Canada and India
Independent Publishers Group (IPG)
814 N. Franklin Street,
Chicago, IL 60610, USA
Email: frontdesk@ipgbook.com
Web: http://www.ipgbook.com

Europe, Oceania, Middle East and Africa
EUROSPAN
1 Bedford Row,
London, WC1R 4BU
United Kingdom
Email: info@eurospan.co.uk
Web: https://www.eurospangroup.com

Japan
MHM Limited
3-2-3F, Kanda-Ogawamachi, Chiyoda-ku,
Tokyo 101-0052
Email: sales@mhmlimited.co.jp
Web: http://www.mhmlimited.co.jp

China
China Publishers Services Ltd.
718, 7/F., Fortune Commercial Building,
362 Sha Tsui Road, Tsuen Wan, N.T.
Hong Kong
Email: edwin@cps-hk.com

Southeast Asia
Alkem Company Pte Ltd.
1, Sunview Road #01-27,
Eco-Tech@Sunview
Singapore 627615
Email: enquiry@alkem.com.sg

Library of Congress Control Number: 2023924175

All rights reserved. No reproduction of any part of this book may take place without the written permission of Trans Pacific Press.
ISBN 978-1-920850-17-3 (hardback)
ISBN 978-1-920850-18-0 (paperback)
ISBN 978-1-920850-19-7 (eBook)

Table of Contents

List of Figures vi

List of Tables vi

Acknowledgements vii

Preface x

Introduction 1

Part I A History of the Japanese Conservative Movement 17

    1 Conservatism, the conservative movement, and the right-wing 19

    2 Lineage of the conservative movement in postwar Japan 31

Part II The Conservative Movement and the Family 65

    3 Changes in the family discourse: Image of the 'suffering mother' 71

    4 The politics of 'family values':
       An analysis of conservative magazine articles 97

    5 The women's movement against gender equality 121

Part III The Conservative Movement, Women's Lives and Sexuality ... 147

    6 The contentious comfort women issue 155

    7 Women who cannot sneer at comfort women:
       Interaction and gender in the action conservative movement 191

Conclusion: The women's conservative movement in Japan:
Its difficulties and prospects 211

Bibliography 227

Appendix: Translations of organization names 247

Index 251

List of Figures

0.1 Types of U.S. right-wing movements 10

1.1 Political awareness in postwar Japan 24

2.1 Signature-collecting for formalization of Yasukuni Shrine visits (1977) 42

2.2 Changes in feelings of affinity towards South Korea 59

3.1 Changes in numbers of articles for analysis 77

3.2 Statue of a mother 85

3.3 'Our mother, who tried her utmost to raise and protect us' 88

3.4 Mother and child walking through burnt ruins, Tokyo 91

4.1 The structure of conservative 'family' discourse 115

6.1 On-screen caption from a Flower Clock demonstration march 173

6.2 Scene of a Flower Clock street propaganda event 175

6.3 Number of videos mentioning comfort women 177

6.4 Protest against an anti-Osprey-deployment demonstration 178

6.5 Protest against a memorial day for comfort women 179

List of Tables

4.1 Number of articles analyzed 102

5.1 Respondent profiles 131

6.1 Number of videos per group 164

6.2 Breakdown of types of activity 165

6.3 List of activities analyzed 166

7.1 List of menus for cookery classes 200

Acknowledgements

This book is a significantly expanded and revised version of a doctoral dissertation I submitted in 2016 to the Graduate School of Human Sciences, Osaka University, entitled 'The phenomenon of rightward drift and the women's conservative movement in contemporary Japanese society.' I received funding for its publication in the form of a Grant-in-Aid for Scientific Research from the Japan Society for the Promotion of Science (JSPS) (JP19HP5158). Moreover, the research summarized in this book was made possible by funding from JSPS grants (12J00489, 15J04286, and 16H06926). I received funding from JSPS grants (22HP6008) to translate this book into English for publication.

I received guidance from many academics in advance of the publication of this book. Over long years, I was the recipient of stringent but warmhearted guidance from my supervisor at Osaka University Graduate School, Professor Muta Kazue. Every time she read my thesis draft, I was presented with questions about three steps higher than the stage I had then reached, and I feel that she nurtured me to this point as a scholar as I feverishly endeavored to address them. I cannot thank her enough. My secondary supervisor Associate Professor Tsuji Daisuke astutely pointed out that value judgements tend to creep in unintentionally when anyone studies conservative movements from the perspective of gender, teaching me the importance of firmly maintaining a value-free stance (*Wertfreiheit*). I do not know how many times I was rescued by him inviting me out to coffee and lending an ear when I felt that my research had hit a brick wall. My other secondary supervisor, Professor Tomoeda Toshio, taught me the importance of pursuing the novel topic of conservative movements in the discipline of sociology. The one word, 'Interesting!' that he uttered at the public hearing for my doctoral dissertation still gives me encouragement.

From Professor Okano Yayo from Doshisha University, my undergraduate supervisor and host researcher for my JSPS Research Fellowship for Young Scientists (Postdoctoral Fellow), I learned of the richness of knowledge that emerges from connecting empirical research in sociology with philosophical and political thought. If I had not taken her classes in 'History of modern political thought', I probably would not have thought to follow the path of a researcher.

Both in and out of seminars, I received much advice from my seniors in the Social Environment Studies Course in the Graduate School of Human Sciences, Osaka University. From Professor Kubota Hiroyuki of Nihon University, I received many suggestions from the beginning of writing the paper that became the first iteration of the chapters in this book. Associate Professor Takamatsu Rie of Ritsumeikan University frequently offered advice on both public and private matters, and always helped me. Both have continued to look out for me since I moved away from Osaka, where we spent time as graduate students.

I am very grateful to my friends from graduate school who engaged in cordial rivalry, especially Associate Professor Tamashiro Fukuko of Meio University. The presence of 'Fuku-chan,' as I call her, enabled me to keep my eyes on the future during graduate school, which tended to be lonely.

Not only for this book, but on an everyday basis, I have had much advice from Notre Dame Seishin University's Professor Hamanishi Eiji about social movement theory, for which I thank him.

In this way, I received guidance and suggestions from many individuals leading up to the publication of this book, but I reiterate that all responsibility for the content discussed in this volume remains with me.

The Japanese-language version of this book was published by Jinbun Shoin. I am greatly indebted to Mr. Matsuoka Takahiro, Editor of Jinbun Shoin, ever since I was approached to publish my doctoral dissertation. He read my manuscript multiple times and provided detailed advice not only on wording but also on content. I am very honored to have been able to produce my first monograph with Mr. Matsuoka, and it was an excellent learning experience. I thank him wholeheartedly.

After the publication of the Japanese version of this book, I received numerous invitations from study groups and book review circles. My thanks to the academics who arranged and hosted these occasions, too. In particular, I extend thank to my learned colleagues in the Institute of Humanities and Social Sciences at the University of Tsukuba who later welcomed me as an Associate Professor, especially Professors Okuyama Toshio and Doi Takayoshi. I am also very grateful to be colleagues with Professors Akane Meguro and Hajime Akiyama. The discussions I had with students who attended my seminars in the School of Social and International Studies in Tsukuba University's College of Social Sciences were something to look forward to each week. Due to the pandemic

Acknowledgements

which began in 2020, their campus life became quite different from what they had imagined, and I am sure they were disappointed. However, I personally learned a great deal from the attitude of those female students who continued to learn and think as their curiosity dictated, even under such difficult circumstances.

In anticipation of publication of this English version, I also convey my gratitude to Ms. Uematsu Yuko and Emeritus Professor Sugimoto Yoshio of Trans Pacific Press Co., Ltd., the translator Dr. Leonie Rae Stickland and especially the editor Dr. Karl Smith for giving this book the opportunity to be read by a much wider audience.

And finally, I give thanks for my precious friends; for my father, who continued to support my academic endeavors no matter when; for my mother who gave me birth and raised me, and always worries about me; for my life with my husband, Kato Makoto, my friend and good rival, who for a long time has shared our irreplaceable everyday existence that overflows with laughter at the silliest things; and our beloved daughter, Hana, who has Makoto and me wrapped around her little finger, but always gives us her smiles.

February, 2024
Suzuki Ayaka

Preface

In this book, I discuss the grassroots women's conservative movement that has appeared in Japan since the 2000s. When I began to seriously consider becoming a researcher, I never imagined I would end up pursuing such a study. My career as a scholar began with studies of the opposition to gender equality which I discuss in Part II of this volume. However, I did not experience that movement contemporaneously. The nationwide expansion of this movement was seldom reported in the mass media, and that opposition movement had already ended before I first learned of it. It should go without saying that not every woman has the same political views as other women. However, as an emerging scholar, I naively found it curious that there were women who would oppose policies for gender equality. When I entered graduate school and had to decide upon a topic for my Master's dissertation, although it was obvious that my research life would be fraught with many difficulties, I chose this topic.

Similar to many scholars around the world studying right-wing civic movements such as ultraconservatism, I encountered a variety of barriers to my research. It was an arduous daily struggle. What gave me the greatest trouble was that so little research had been done on right-wing civic movements in Japan. At the time, interest in these movements was growing both academically and socially, and articles alluding to right-wing civic movements frequently appeared in commercial media, but no adequate surveys had been conducted of their activities or activists. Chapter Five of this book is based on my first published paper in an academic journal. That paper demonstrated, based on textual analysis of the claims of the women – especially those who self-identified as 'homemakers (*shufu*)' – that this movement differed from the mainstream in terms of not making too many political statements. Although they were opposed to gender equality policies, these women were not criticizing the government or local authorities, but were simply making the case that the family is a "good thing" through the description of their own family episodes. Reactions to the paper varied. Some critics claimed that such women did not actually exist, and that I had been taken in by a feminist discourse claiming that 'homemakers were opposed to gender equality policy.' To address this critique, I conducted interviews for my next research project.

There have been several factors behind the focus on right-wing civic movements since the late 2000s. First, at that time social movements had not completely emerged from a 'winter period' that followed the collapse of the student movement. The Japanese student movement had met its heyday in the 1960s. What clearly marked the end of the student and left-wing movements in Japan was the so-called 'Asama Sanso Incident' in 1972, when infighting in the most radical student group led to twelve members being lynched, including pregnant women. They took a hostage and barricaded themselves in a mountain lodge called Asama Sanso. Scenes of police negotiating and attacking the lodge with a crane and wrecking ball were broadcast live on television, with about eighty percent of Japan reportedly watching. This incident conclusively destroyed the image of left-wing social movements. Subsequently, large-scale collective action ceased in Japan, and civic activities such as volunteerism NPOs and NGOs that did not foreground their political positions became more widely accepted. Notably, the student movement (mostly males) had expressed outrage at both university authorities and the government that signed the Japan–U.S. Security Treaty; but despite proclaiming radical ideals and ideas, once they graduated from university they found corporate jobs, as normal, and went on to form the core of the Japanese labor market. Today, when I talk to university students, they are clearly resigned to the belief that society and politics will not change through social movements.

Amid the dampening of left-wing civic movements, right-wing versions took shape and expanded their activities, assertively embracing new communication technologies such as the Internet. In Japan, right-wing civic movements have been the more proactive among social movements that utilized the Internet. This was the second reason for my study. I recall organizing a feminist demonstration march with friends in 2015 without any foreknowledge or guidance on how to do so. In Japan in 2022, both left- and right-wing were assertively engaging in collective action, but at the time, this was not the case. Knowledge and skills had not been effectively passed down from previous generations, and we had no idea what we needed to do to hold a demonstration march. How would we decide on a route? If we started and ended at parks, would we need permission to use those parks? In that case, what procedures would be necessary at the police station? Ultimately, one of my friends was given the information by an acquaintance, and we were able to put our plans into practice without a hitch, but when we were searching the Internet for information, most of the web pages displayed at the top of the search results belonged to right-wing civic movements.

Knowhow about activities, such as where to apply for a permit to demonstrate, or what route would be best to follow to appeal to more people, was shared online. Members connected with one another through already established networks.

Part III of this book explores right-wing civic movements in the age of social media. Underpinning the emergence of these movements in Japan in the 2010s was the rapid spread of hostility and antagonism towards South Korea and China. This was not simply an ideological dispute, but a tension that had become part of the everyday life of people living in Japan. Let me illustrate this by talking about a friend who has been away from Japan for a long time. We met in Tokyo when she was home temporarily after a long absence. She had found life in Japan wearisome and living overseas appeared to suit her, as she was considerably more energetic than when we had last met.

Over coffee, she told me about her visit to a hair salon before our meeting. While chatting with the hairdresser, somehow the topic shifted to South Korea. Around that time, the Japanese government's removal of South Korea from 'Group A' of its preferred export controls was frequently in the news in Japan, and my friend was astonished to hear the hairdresser suddenly declare with no logical connection: 'I think that was only natural.'

My first thought was: 'This society is drifting to the right;' but something bothered me, and for several days this story stuck in the corner of my mind. To get to the point, what bothered me was that a person involved in the service industry like a hairdresser said such a thing to someone they had met for the first time, and a customer, no less. Talk of politics is easily divisive and regardless of the impetus, a hairdresser speaking of politics to a new customer risks a complaint being made about the hair salon, or a negative review posted online; and unless the hairdresser's skill was outstanding, an offended customer would be unlikely to become a regular patron. Despite that, the hairdresser in question clearly expressed his view on Japan–South Korea relations, an extremely sensitive topic, and, moreover, with an implied assumption that the customer would agree. That was what made me uncomfortable.

He perhaps did not understand that discussing Japan–South Korea relations was 'political' in the sense that people's opinions might differ. Perhaps he saw this topic as relatively harmless and inoffensive, akin to small talk, like: 'This year's rainy season is long, isn't it?' or common gossip, like celebrity scandals that cause a furor on television chat shows. In fact, it was widely reported that more than fifty percent of respondents in a public opinion poll run by major newspaper companies and television channels at the time said they 'agreed' with the removal of South Korea from 'Group A,' so it is not surprising that the hairdresser should hold this view.

All the examples discussed in this book are, in one sense, 'readily understandable.' The experts, politicians, political organizations, civic groups and others who take a firm stance under their own names are visible and easy to identify. However, to understand the Japanese 'conservative swing,' it will not suffice to examine only the most conspicuous targets. Our neighbors, hairdressers, taxi drivers and others we come into contact with every day voice discriminatory opinions about South Korea and China as if engaged in small talk; cyberspace overflows with hatred and anger; and politicians, authorities and the mass media make no attempts to curb the situation. How can sociology, my academic discipline, grasp, interpret and respond to these circumstances? I do not want to pass on to the next generation a society filled with hatred that has been fanned to the utmost extent, which is already past the point where anybody knows where it originated.

When I conduct fieldwork, respondents continually ask both explicitly and implicitly whether I am right or left. When I present my research at conferences and study groups, I am asked: 'Do you side with them?' As there are very few scholars in Japan researching right-wing civic movements, my presentations on social movements are often met with the impression of being out of place. When I began this research, I was quite troubled by this, but I have started to think that it is all right now. Nothing would give me more pleasure than if what I have learned about Japan thus far could make even a small contribution to worldwide studies of the extreme right.

Introduction: The new conservative movement and gender

The new conservative movement in contemporary Japan

Until quite recently, the conservative movement was not a topic of academic research in Japan. One reason for this is probably that until the 1960s in Japan, 'social movements' referred to progressive movements that were diametrically opposed to 'conservatism,' principally the labor movement. For example, although 'social movements' is in the title, Akamatsu Katsumaro's 1952 book *A History of Japanese Social Movements* mainly discusses socialist movements. The social movements of the time aimed for social change through class struggle, with workers as their agents.

In Japan, 'new social movements' appeared from the 1970s onwards as the student movement, women's movement, environmental movement, and those driven by ethnic minorities began to flower. According to Hasegawa Koichi, the foremost scholar of social movements in Japan, these 'new social movements' have two distinguishing characteristics: first, their agents were fumbling to form a collective identity as something other than workers; and second, they emphasized self-determination as a 'need by a social minority to seek democratic substantiation and consistency' (Hasegawa 1990: 21). Since then, these are typically the kinds of social movements that first come to mind, and the historians of postwar Japanese social movements have focused on those that support the democratic system and pursue social justice and rights for the marginalized.[1] One exception is Katagiri Shinji's (1995) history of Japanese social movement theory, which alludes to right-wing movements, but only those of the 1950s which were examined in the context of postwar fascism studies.

And yet, the conservative movement has been continuous throughout the postwar era. Although it has not been subject to much academic research, the conservative movement has been intermittently and critically mentioned in commercial media and news reports. In postwar Japan, there have been numerous debates about Japanese responsibilities for the Asia-Pacific war, as well as recurring friction with neighboring

---

1 Examples include Shakai undo ron kenkyukai (ed.) (1990), and Yazawa (ed.) (2003).

Introduction

countries of East Asia. Examples of flash points include official visits to Yasukuni Shrine by the emperor and prime minister, the history textbook saga that triggered a diplomatic crisis with South Korea and China for downplaying or ignoring acts of aggression by the Japanese military, and the use of the term 'invasion/aggression' (*shinryaku*). Groups and individuals who support official visits to Yasukuni Shrine, call for acts of aggression by the Japanese military to be removed from history textbooks, and take a hardline stance towards Korea and China have been called the 'conservative faction' (*hoshuha*) or 'right-wing' (*uyoku*). Although journalists have reported a 'conservative swing' (*ukeika*) or 'backlash' (*handoka*), coverage has been sporadic, with interest in such groups evaporating once disputes settle down.

However, since the 2000s academics have begun to research conservative movements, perhaps drawn by the increasingly conspicuous groups that have assumed a new movement style and had some influence both socially and politically. In 1997, for example, the Japanese Society for History Textbook Reform (Atarashii rekishi kyokasho o tsukuru kai) (hereafter, 'Textbook Society') was formed, and their activities aimed at the compilation of junior high school history and civics textbooks based on historical revisionism that repudiated such historical facts as the Nanking massacre and military 'comfort women' and increasing the uptake of that textbook. Oguma Eiji and Ueno Yoko are pioneers in studying conservative movements in Japan with their 2003 book, '*Iyashi' no nashonarizumu* (Nationalism of 'healing'), reporting the results of a survey which Ueno conducted at the History Circle (Fumi-no-kai), a group of interested persons from the Kanagawa Prefecture branch of the Textbook Society. Oguma observes that the History Circle had a similar style to traditional civic movements and that participants called themselves 'ordinary' citizens. He further observed a 'fluidization phenomenon' which arose from the collapse of the Cold War system and globalization, and which formed the backdrop for the grassroots expansion of the conservative movement in Japan (Oguma and Ueno 2003: 5). Oguma's hypothesis that people who harbor anxiety about the 'fluidization phenomenon' are drawn towards nationalism became influential not only in academic research, but more broadly,[2] and has

---

2   Using the keyword 'social fluidization,' Takahara (2005) also considers Japanese, Chinese and South Korean nationalism in the 2000s.

been a touchstone for discussing the conservative movement since the Textbook Society was formed.

In the late 2000s, a succession of activist groups called the 'Action Conservative Movement' (Yamaguchi 2013a) began to form, emphasizing direct action such as streetside speeches, demonstrations and protest marches. Among these groups, the Association of Citizens against the Special Privileges of resident-Koreans (Zainichi tokken o yurusanai shimin no kai) (hereafter, 'the Association of Citizens') established in 2007 has been conspicuous for its aggressive streetside speeches abusing and smearing resident Koreans and its activities expressing intense hostility to Korea and China. Yasuda Koichi's publication, *The Internet and Patriotism* (2012), is superior reportage based on painstaking research on the Association of Citizens and the groups linked with the action conservative movement. Yasuda, who attended the Association's activities all around Japan and interviewed its activists, says of people attracted to the group that 'the horizon where they ended up in their search for somewhere to direct the anxiety and dissatisfaction which they felt in their everyday life just happened to be the battleground called patriotism' (Yasuda 2012: 313). Here, again, we see Oguma's argument that people turn to chauvinistic nationalism because of 'anxiety' and 'dissatisfaction.'

However, the shortcomings of this explanation have also been noted. Higuchi Naoto, for example, points out: 'It would, however, be unreasonable to see the movement as being made up *exclusively* of "stressed people"' (Higuchi 2016: 13, emphasis original). He draws on resource mobilization theory to elucidate the factors behind the Association of Citizens' emergence and the characteristics of those in the Japanese anti-foreigner movement. Based on life history interviews of thirty-four activists from the association and affiliated groups, Higuchi argues that we must consider two levels of explanation, namely, the individual and social. First, on an individual level, in the process of political socialization, activists have already formed an ideology friendly to the anti-foreign movement, learning of the expression 'Special privileges for Japan-residing' Koreans (*Zainichi tokken*) through the Internet, and proceeding to connect with others who oppose foreign residents. Next, at the social level, Higuchi cites 'the geopolitical structure of East Asia' (2016: 5), which from the late nineteenth until the mid-twentieth centuries was characterized by 'empires' and 'colonies'. Squaring accounts from

Introduction

the age of colonialism is yet to be achieved. Moreover, since the 1990s, the former empire and its former colonies have become equal players in a globalized economy. Thus, Higuchi argues, a compositional arrangement has come about in which antagonistic feeling arising from the historical connection between Japan and the nations of East Asia is directed at ethnic minorities in Japan, including resident Koreans.

However, not only is there no consensus on whether to characterize the various groups in the action conservative movement, including the Association of Citizens, as 'conservative,' there is no consensus on the definition of the term itself. Higuchi referred to these groups with the expression *haigai shugi undo*, which in the 2016 English translation of his book, is rendered as 'nativist movement,' although *haigai* could also be translated as anti-foreign; exclusivism; chauvinism; or xenophobia. Importantly, Higuchi observed that his informants expressed '[m]ajor differences in standpoint concerning the central issues of diplomacy and defense, which have been the focus of political confrontation in the postwar Japanese political opposition axis' (Higuchi 2016: 73), including some whom he situates further right than conservative (Higuchi 2016: 73), but he does not fully distinguish the concepts of 'nativism,' 'conservative' and 'right-wing.' In Chapter One, I will clearly define the term 'conservative movement' used in this book, but I take it to mean all groups in the action conservative movement, including the Association of Citizens.

The women who participate in the conservative movement

Most participants in the Japanese conservative movement are male, but there is no shortage of women, either. Otsuki Takahiro, who served as executive director of the Textbook Society until 1998, interviewed participants of a symposium that the group held in 2000, and four out of the ten respondents were women (Otsuki 2000). Some women who participated in such events went on to launch their own groups. Women commonly appear in descriptions of study groups – the main activities of the History Circle – and the social gatherings which followed. The occupations of study-group attendees, in order of numerical prevalence, were company employees, retirees, housewives, and students. Ueno states that 'housewives in their thirties and female company employees' also participated (Oguma and Ueno 2003: 80).

4

The new conservative movement and gender

Conservative movement groups with the word 'women' in their title reportedly began to form in the 2000s. The greatest trigger for this was opposition to gender equality policies. The Basic Act for Gender-Equal Society enacted in 1999 sought to achieve equal social participation of men and women in all fields. From 2000 until about 2006, opposition to the Basic Act expanded into a nationwide movement. Following the Basic Act's enactment, gender equality ordinances were passed by local government bodies as well, and groups who opposed these ordinances started to emerge. There were groups in Ube City in Yamaguchi Prefecture, for example, called the Yamaguchi Women's Forum Ube (Yamaguchi josei foramu Ube), and Ube Women's Group to Think about Gender Equality (Danjo kyodo sankaku o kangaeru Ube josei no kai) (Koshiba 2008).

As we have seen, women also participated in the Association of Citizens, which expresses animosity towards resident-Koreans in an extremely aggressive tone. Women were among the speakers at the Association of Citizens' protest rally held in Tsuruhashi in Osaka Prefecture, where there is a concentration of Korean residents. Yasuda depicts that scene as follows:

> The one interjecting in a particularly shrill voice was a young woman wearing an above-the-knee skirt with a flimsy cardigan around her shoulders. Her modest appearance, which gave the impression of a female office clerk who had raced there on her way home from work, combined with her regular features, made her even more distinctive among the participants in that political rally. (Yasuda 2012: 5)

Among groups called the action conservative movement, some have formed centered on women. Groups such as Japan Women's Group Gentle Breeze (Nihon josei no kai Soyokaze) (hereafter, 'Gentle Breeze'), Patriotic Women's Gathering Flower Clock (Aikoku josei no tsudoi Hanadokei) (hereafter, 'Flower Clock'), Japanese Women for Justice and Peace (Nadeshiko Action), Citizens' Group that will not Permit Invasion of Japan (Nihon shinryaku o yurusanai shimin no kai), and Bracing Wind Yamato (Rinpu Yamato) have developed vigorous activities both in conjunction with male-centered groups and independently. Like the Association of Citizens, these women's groups declare their hatred of

5

Introduction

resident-Koreans and make speeches condemning countries of East Asia. They also frequently mention the comfort women issue.

In the 2010s, a succession of books were published by women associated with the action conservative movement. Sanami Yuko (2013), *Joshi to aikoku* (Women and patriotism); Kawasoe Keiko et al. (2014), *Kokubo joshi ga yuku* (National defense women on the go); Yamamoto Yumiko (2014), *Josei ga mamoru Nihon no hokori* (Japan's pride that women preserve); Sugita Mio (2014), *Nadeshiko fukkatsu: josei seijika ga dekiru koto* (The revival of Nadeshiko: What female politicians can do)[3] are examples whose titles emphasize 'women,' 'patriotism' and 'Japan.' Meanwhile, women were widely sharing information in conservative forums.

A framework for understanding the women's conservative movement

As we can see, the conservative movement in contemporary Japan has been supported by large numbers of women, but the gender perspective is missing from academic studies of the movement. Oguma and Ueno's research on the Textbook Society (2003) describes women participating in its activities, but does not analyze their participation. Moreover, although female activists are included in Higuchi's interviews from the Association of Citizens and activists of the action conservative movement, and although Higuchi himself observed that 'research that employs the perspective of gender is necessary' (Higuchi 2012: 159), his analysis (2016) does not provide such a perspective.

There are two reasons for investigating the women of the Japanese conservative movement from a gender perspective. First, participants' experiences within the movement can be assumed to differ according to their genders, even within the same activist group. The scant literature that has focused on female participants in the Japanese conservative movement reports that female participants tend to be viewed as a sexual presence both by male participants and by men from outside the movement. Sanami Yuko, who appears on the conservative cable

---

3 Here, 'Nadeshiko' does not refer to the aforementioned organization, but rather to 'good old Japanese women.' Japanese conservative women regard Nadeshiko (dianthus flowers) as a symbol of the ideal Japanese women.

television program 'Channel Sakura,' alluded to the fact that women who participated in demonstrations had been stalked by male participants, and declared that it is 'crucial to create an environment in which it is easier for women to take part' (Sanami 2013: 206). A report by Kitahara Minori and Pak Suni targeting women's groups in the action conservative movement records female participants saying: 'We could not bear being seen by our counterparts as sexual objects' (Kitahara and Pak 2014: 148). The conservative movement is assumed to have an androcentric culture, but a comfortable space for male participants to confirm their identity as 'Japanese' is not necessarily a space where female participants can enjoy the same feeling. Furthermore, I surmise that there are many situations in which female participants are oppressed within the movement.

Second, while the conservative movement is typically an anti-feminist movement, there is need for more detailed investigations into women's opposition to feminism. The Japanese second-wave feminist movement which began in the 1970s indicted latent sexism and women's oppression while aspiring for women's liberation. Moreover, by collaborating with the United Nations, NGOs, and activist groups outside Japan, it promoted domestic laws to eliminate sexual discrimination and rectify the gender gap. Under these circumstances, I propose that women's and men's opposition to feminism have different connotations.

Although some domestic studies have tried to explain from a gender perspective why women participate in the conservative movement, they have done little more than elaborate upon Oguma and Ueno (2003). Ehara Yumiko, for example, presumes that the growing opposition to gender-equality was 'grounded in people's feelings of apprehension and revulsion towards having their gender identity injured' (Ehara 2007: 192), positing that women who oppose gender equality had 'lost self-confidence in being full-time housewives and become anxious due to most married women having begun to work' outside the home (Ehara 2007: 190). Similarly, Ida Hiroyuki proposes that a woman who opposes gender equality:

> feels that "the elite" and "state power" have foisted "the liberated image of the ideal woman" and social change upon her, and this denies and derides the "ordinary me, a housewife" and strips her of her vested rights, and so that vexes her, and she wants to resist. (Ida 2006: 185)

Introduction

This suggestion that some women oppose gender equality because of anxiety about their identity as a 'homemaker' sounds plausible in a context in which women's life-choices have diversified and full-time housewives have become less common. However, this hypothesis is neither supported by empirical evidence, nor does it explain why some women align with the conservative movement.

Indeed, since the formation of women's groups in the action conservative movement, a different explanation has been proposed in terms of mothers who participate in the conservative movement to protect their children and families. The liberal weekly magazine *AERA* published a special feature in December 2012 entitled '*Nippon ga katamuku*' (Japan is leaning) discussing trends in the conservative movement, including the action conservative movement. It included an article focusing on female activists, entitled '"Protect the country" out of apprehension towards the future and motherhood: The "justice" of women who drift to the right,' which argues that women who participate in the action conservative movement are motivated by a 'maternal' desire to 'protect their children,' and 'that "maternity" leads to patriotism, developing into the idea of a "strong Japan" for the sake of their children' (Kinjo 2012: 12).

This seems to be a more plausible explanation of the 'Yasukuni mothers' whose children died as soldiers during the Second World War, and who believe that their spirits are enshrined as 'heroic spirits' at Yasukuni Shrine. In Japan, it seems easy to accept that motherhood would motivate women to participate in the conservative movement. However, while there are certainly some women for whom this applies, I suggest it would only explain a small proportion of the conservative movement.

As such, there is no ready framework for comprehending the women's conservative movement in Japan, and more importantly, it is unclear why the movement has grown in both size and activities since the 2000s.

In contrast, much research has been conducted on conservative movements from a gender perspective in other countries.[4] Indeed, in the

---

4 Bacchetta and Power (2002) includes papers about rightist women in a variety of countries, including the U.S., France, Australia, Greece, and Mexico. Köttig et al. (2017) is a study of the rightist movement in European countries from a gender perspective. There are also historical studies, such as Guido (2010), which examines the anti-feminist movement in Germany in the 1910s, and Power (2002), which explores the rightist movement in Chile in the 1960s and '70s.

8

United States such studies have been conducted since the 1980s, and much excellent research has amassed. Thus, to compensate for the lack of research into the conservative movement in Japan from a gender perspective, I will rely heavily on the accumulated research from the United States in my analysis and investigation.

Moreover, as the connotations and naming of 'conservative movements' differ according to country, region, time, and proponent, following Blee and Creasap in the United States, I will use the three terms 'conservative,' 'right-wing,' and 'rightist,' which they define as follows:

> conservative for movements that support patriotism, free enterprise capitalism, and/or a traditional moral order and for which violence is not a frequent tactic or goal... right-wing for movements that focus specifically on race/ethnicity and/or that promote violence as a primary tactic or goal... [and] rightist as a generic category. (Blee and Creasap 2010: 270–1)[5]

Andrea Dworkin's *Right-wing Women* (1983) is an early study of right-wing women, focusing on the STOP ERA campaign in which Phyllis Schlafly organized grassroots women throughout the U.S.[6] Dworkin criticized women's participation in this movement as 'committing suicide' (Dworkin 1983: 5) setting a precedent, which I will elaborate later, of viewing right-wing women as 'passive' and 'victims.' Although this portrayal was widely criticized, such criticism tended to distract from Dworkin's underlying argument, which was a blistering critique of the social structures that instilled fear in women by making them subordinate and submissive to men. Dworkin contends that what she calls the 'sex-class system' (Dworkin 1983: 221) employs means such as rape and battery to prevent women from escaping the system, and to keep them under the control of men. Dworkin concludes that some women join hands with right-wing men, fully cognizant of this system, in their attempt to defend themselves.

---

5   Blee and Creasap (2010) note that it is difficult to strictly apply this classification to actual groups. For example, the pro-life movement attacks abortion clinics, but does not focus much on issues of race or ethnicity. On the pro-life movement, see Luker (1984), Munson (2008), and Cohen and Connon (2016).

6   On opposition to the ERA, see Mansbridge (1986).

Introduction

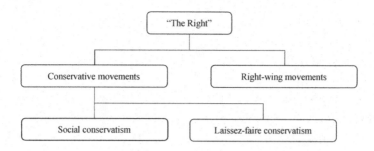

Figure 0.1 Types of U.S. right-wing movements
Based on Blee & Creasap (2010) and Klatch (1987)

Subsequent empirical studies of right-wing women in the U.S. include, Rebecca Klatch's *Women of the New Right* (1987), which criticizes previous research on this topic, including Dworkin, for portraying right-wing women as victims. Through an empirical study of right-wing women's worldviews, Klatch identified different types of conservatives in the U.S. She separates the conservative movement of the day, called the New Right, into two categories: social conservatives, centered on Christian evangelicals, and laissez-faire conservatives who reject government intervention in the market. The latter includes many career-oriented women. These classifications came to be widely referenced. Interweaving Klatch's classification with the Blee and Creasap (2010) definition presented above yields something like Figure I.1. Social conservatives and laissez-faire conservatives have different worldviews, but cooperate to combat what they perceive as common enemies, namely communism, big government, and feminism.

Research on right-wing female activists continued into the 1990s. Referring to Klatch (1987) and others, Kathleen Blee pointed out that women had played a vital role in U.S. conservative movement, but also criticized the fact that research focused excessively on male activists (Blee 1996). Blee conducted life-history interviews with right-wing female activists. What Blee found was that rather than pre-existing racist views drawing them to the movement, they had started to take part in the movement through incidental contact with activists and the like, and then through participation in such groups they learned right-wing ideas and behaviors, and *became activists* (Blee 2002). Additionally, Blee points out that these women's narratives were generally negative, and it was common for incidents such as physical assault, undermining, interference or trauma to mark turning points in their life-narrative (Blee

10

The new conservative movement and gender

1996; 2017).[7] Blee posits that this tendency may be the result of women having constructed themselves as activists in a right-wing movement that highly values a kind of whiteness that was strongly associated with a kind of masculinity.

In the late 2000s, a more incisive debate that positions right-wing women activists as a type of women's movement was developed by scholars such as Ronne Schreiber (2008) and Jean Hardisty (1999).[8] Schreiber identifies Concerned Women for America (CWA) as an example of social conservatives, and the Independent Women's Forum (IWF) as one of laissez-faire conservatives; and argues that though both are conservative organizations, they have won the support of a greater number of women by claiming the right to speak 'on behalf of' women.

Hardisty uses the term 'equality feminists' to refer to laissez-faire conservative women who, while supporting women's access to the public domain, reject government interventions in politics or the economy such as affirmative action or equal pay (Hardisty 1999: 87). In a similar vein, Mary Ziegler calls Sarah Palin, a leader of the Tea Party movement, a 'pro-life feminist' because Palin described herself as both a feminist and as pro-life (Ziegler 2013: 258).

As we can see, then, in U.S. studies since the 1980s, researchers' interpretations of right-wing women have changed significantly. Whereas Dworkin portrayed right-wing women as victims, scholars like Klatch and Blee present them as protagonists who actively participate in the movement. More recent studies have sought to identify 'feminists' amid right-wing political and social movements. Following these developments, in my analysis of Japanese examples, I will consider the implications of each respective position: 'victims,' 'active agents,' and 'feminists.'

First, studies such as Dworkin's that depict right-wing women as 'victims' highlight a need to examine the social structures that disadvantage women. As mentioned, Dworkin has been widely criticized

---

7   Blee emphasizes that these were, without exception, turning points in the life-narratives, not direct triggers for becoming right-wing. It is also worth noting that the narratives were recollections of their journey to becoming right-wing activists *from their current perspective*.

8   However, not all research by feminists on rightist women takes this position. Like Burack and Josephson (2003) which criticizes social conservatives, criticism of the rightist movement from a feminist perspective continues today.

Introduction

for overlooking women's agency. Nevertheless, to investigate Japanese examples, it is necessary to look beyond the individual self-explanations of right-wing women activists, and examine the social structures and social norms in which they operate, and how these things have changed.

Second, from the perspective of right-wing women as 'active agents,' it is necessary to focus on women's relationships with male activists and male-centered groups. Empirical studies have shed light on the difficulties, conflicts, and contradictions that women experience within the movement, and women's strategies to address these. Moreover, there is also a need to investigate how the inherent tension in the women's conservative movement – that is, being both conservative and activist women – influences its participants.

And third, studies that perceive right-wing women as 'feminists' open the possibility to see the women's conservative movement as a women's movement. Naturally, social conditions surrounding women and the women's movement differ from country to country, and it will be necessary to consider whether we can legitimately call women who participate in the Japanese conservative movement 'feminists.' But even if we do not go so far as to call them 'feminists,' understanding female activists in the conservative movement as 'women' is an important perspective for thinking about the Japanese case.

In contrast to this rich U.S. typology, Japanese research lacks the terminology and cognitive framework for understanding right-wing women in terms other than as participants 'who take part in the conservative movement in order to protect their children and their family from the standpoint of mothers, wives, or homemakers.'

Japanese feminist studies have assumed that the direction of social movements will differ according to whether activists take the position of 'mothers' or 'women.' Women's lib (*Uman ribu*), which arose in the 1970s and became the Japanese second-wave feminist movement, was a movement of women who 'refused to consign themselves to hallowed "mothers" and sought self-liberation as women of living flesh' (Kano 2012: 21). However, in Japan today, with its rampant neo-liberal mindset, there is a strong trend towards women's higher education and workforce participation, and motherhood can no longer be seen as the 'normal' life-course for women; it is now merely one of the options for individuals to choose. Under these conditions, differentiating between mothers and women appears to be less important to feminist scholars than at any point since the 1970s, when Japanese women's lib reappeared.[9]

Bearing this in mind, I will nevertheless differentiate the standpoints of mothers and women in these investigations. As mentioned, while the discourse of women who have embraced a spirit of patriotism as mothers to protect their children and their country is easy to understand on the one hand, there are many women in the Japanese conservative movement who do not attribute their activities to having children. In those cases, elucidating how patriotism became important to these women may help to shed light on the major characteristics of the women's conservative movement in Japan today.

Aims, methodology, and structure

Through an empirical investigation of the conditions of the women's conservative movement in contemporary Japan, this book aims to identify the various factors shaping the movement, while focusing on the gendered structure within the movement as well as external social structures.

This book focuses on two trends in contemporary Japanese conservative movements: opposition to gender equality from the perspective of 'mothers;' and 'comfort-women bashing' by various groups in the action conservative movement as examples of conservative movements acting from the standpoint of women. These two topics stand out among the numerous contentious issues that have mobilized the conservative movement in Japan since 2000. Both have been extensively discussed in Japan, but seldom have they been discussed in relation to one another. Examining two quite different types of conservative women's groups will, I think, help to highlight the characteristics of contemporary women's conservative movements in Japan. Furthermore, by investigating why conservative women are so agitated by gender equality and comfort

---

9   In a 2012 Women's Studies Association of Japan symposium 'Reconsideration [of] feminism and 'mothers': Heterosexism and the fragmentation of women,' the limitations of the one-dimensional treatment of the mothers' movement in gender studies was problematized with case studies of mothers in the anti-nuclear power movement and those who have measured radiation levels in the Tokyo area since the Tohoku earthquake in 2011 (Araki et al. 2012).

Introduction

women, the unique positioning of women and women's groups in the conservative movement should become clear.

I employ qualitative surveys as my research method. In addition to data obtained from fieldwork and interviews of two female-centered conservative groups, I also examine articles published in conservative opinion magazines and organs published by male-centered groups, as well as videos of their activities posted on the Internet. Using different types of data and materials should help compensate for analytical limitations inherent in the respective data. For example, in interviews, difficulties often arose when the researcher did not wholly agree with the claims of the informants, and although respondents were guaranteed anonymity, some feared their information would be made public. This study benefitted from the cooperation of many people, including representatives from the groups being surveyed, but it was often not possible to get responses about the personal background of participants. Besides the limitations of the survey, solely targeting discrete activist groups increases the risk of losing sight of their relationship with the general conservative movement of which they are a part. Thus, I decided on a multilateral inquiry through the wide-ranging collection and analysis of available data. Furthermore, I conducted qualitative rather than quantitative analysis of magazine articles in order to include illustrations, photographs and so on in the data set, and to prioritize the identification of differences in narratives about specific topics.

The structure of this book is as follows. In Part I 'A history of the Japanese conservative movement,' I consider how the women's conservative movement is positioned within the history of Japan's conservative movement. Chapter One 'Conservatism, conservative movements, and the right-wing,' sorts out terms which tend to be confused and clarifies what the expression 'conservative movement' is trying to indicate in the Japanese context. Chapter Two: 'The lineage of the conservative movement in postwar Japan,' traces the history of the conservative movement from immediately after World War II to the present, focusing on the Japan War-Bereaved Families Association (Nippon izokukai), to outline the historical context in which women's conservatism arose.

The remainder of the book is dedicated to analyzing data from fieldwork conducted with activist groups, as well as data from group bulletins, newsletters (*minikomi*), magazine articles and so forth, to describe the conditions of the women's conservative movement in contemporary

Japan. In Part II, 'The conservative movement and the family,' I examine the opposition to gender equality, a movement in which family values are posited in opposition to women's human rights, and consider the differences between female activists speaking from positions as 'mothers,' 'wives,' or 'homemakers.' Chapter Three: 'Changes in the family discourse: Image of the "suffering mother,"' analyzes articles in bulletins from Japan War-Bereaved Families Association to investigate how the family image of a husband as breadwinner, wife as full-time homemaker, and their children came to prominence in the conservative movement. Building upon that analysis, Chapter Four: 'The politics of "family values",' analyzes the 'family values' discourse in today's conservative movement, focusing on the gender of the speakers. Between 2000 and 2006, articles with the term 'housewives' in the title that criticized gender equality appeared here and there in conservative opinion magazines and other media. In Chapter Four, through a comparative analysis of articles written from the perspective of 'housewives' and those from a different perspective, I analyze ways in which the housewives' critiques of gender equality intersect with the feminist theory of care. Chapter Five: 'The women's movement against gender equality,' is based upon fieldwork and interviews I conducted with a grassroots civic group opposed to gender equality to develop an understanding of the conditions of the movement opposed to gender equality in a regional area from the perspective of the female activists. As in Chapter Four, I will elucidate the points at which these informants' claims intersect with, and diverge from, a feminist ethic of care.

In Part III: 'The conservative movement and women's life and sexuality,' I deal with women's groups in the action conservative movement. Chapter Six: 'The contentious comfort women issue,' presents a content analysis of videos uploaded to the Internet of activities by women's groups in the action conservative movement to illustrate how these groups concentrate their action upon the comfort women issue and the complexity of their perspectives on that issue. In Chapter Seven: 'Women who cannot sneer at the comfort women issue,' based on fieldwork conducted at another woman-centered group that belongs to the action conservative movement, I describe the interaction among participants at non-demonstration activities. Focusing on the jokes the participants tell, I offer a suggestion as to what the comfort women issue means for them.

Introduction

Finally, the Conclusion, 'The women's conservative movement in Japan: Its difficulties and outlook,' reviews the debates in Parts I to III before offering a reinterpretation of the women's conservative movement as a women's movement. Through this endeavor, I will attempt to explain why the women's conservative movement has grown steadily since the 2000s, and why gender equality and the comfort women issue have been such central topics in the women's conservative movement.

To assist interested readers to keep track of the myriad organization discussed in this work, the Appendix lists the original Japanese name against the translation I have adopted.

PART I

A History of The Japanese Conservative Movement

Chapter 1

Conservatism, the conservative movement, and the right-wing

Conservatism and reactionism

In this chapter, I aim to clarify the definition of the term 'conservative movement' as used in this book. Even within Japan, different nomenclature is used for the groups that I discuss in this volume, including 'right faction' (*uha*), 'rightward drift' (*ukeika*),[1] 'right-wing' (*uyoku*), 'chauvinism/xenophobia' (*haigai shugi*), and 'racism' (*reishizumu*). Furthermore, the phenomena that these expressions point to differ depending on the country or region in question. This book employs the term 'conservative movement,' but I take conservatism as the ideology of the movement to be something different again. Karl Mannheim (1927) posits that there has been conflation of two ways of thought in what has generally been called 'conservatism,' and makes a clear distinction between them. One represents the apprehension and confusion that people feel when they are confronted with the unknown and the novel; this is a universal human attribute that transcends differences in epoch and location. Mannheim calls this 'traditionalist.' The other is a way of thinking that has taken shape under specific historical conditions – to cite a concrete example, the modern mode of thinking that arose in opposition to the progressivism formed along with the French Revolution. Mannheim calls this type 'modern conservatism.'

Mannheim identifies three points as characteristics of the conservative way of thinking. First, conservatism is assumed to avoid abstract theory and systemization, focusing instead on tangible things; second is the view that things which exist here and now are the result of having

---

1   Tsukada, ed. (2017) is one treatment of the general 'rightward drift' in Japan. On the 'rightward drift' in party politics, see Nakano (2015).

Chapter 1

inevitably continued from the past; and third, it emphasizes the significance of organic groups and centrist groups such as families and regional communities (Mannheim 1927).

Edmund Burke is considered to be the 'father of modern conservatism' in the sense that Mannheim describes, and Burke's work, *Reflections on the Revolution in France*, is appraised as having condensed the essence of modern conservatism as it is found in different ages and regions (Hashikawa 1968). Although Burke was a staunch critic of the French Revolution, I want to focus on the logic behind his criticism.

> Is it, then, true that the French government was such as to be incapable or undeserving of reform, so that it was of absolute necessity that the whole fabric should be at once pulled down and the area cleared for the erection of a theoretic, experimental edifice in its place? (Burke 1790: 105)

In this quote, Burke casts doubt on the post-revolution French government, but he is not necessarily criticizing that government *per se*; rather, he is questioning its means, namely, 'revolution.' Burke sharply criticizes the progressivism promoting and supporting the French Revolution, but what he is most troubled by is its removal in one fell swoop of something that had historically existed, and constructing something completely new, based on an abstract which he terms a 'theoretic.'

While Burke opposes the creation of something from scratch, this does not imply that the status quo should be maintained unchanged in remembrance of the past. Burke advocates 'improvement' as a third alternative which consists of neither destruction nor preservation of the present situation. 'Improvement' was what Burke thought politics needed, as evidenced by his words: 'A disposition to preserve and an ability to improve, taken together, would be my standard of a statesman' (Burke 1790: 129). Burke does not disavow change to social systems or political regimes. In fact, he declares: 'A state without the means of some change is without the means of its conservation' (Burke 1790: 18). Thus, his conservatism is not a refusal to transform society, but it is critical of the means that progressivism employs for social transformation, and the speed of that change.

If we take Burke's position as the definition of conservatism as an ideology, then it is clear that the individuals and groups that either

20

self-identify as 'conservative' in Japan today, or are so designated, are far removed from it.[2] This has been pointed out in Japan, both by self-identified conservatives and their critics. The self-proclaimed 'liberal conservative' Nakajima Takeshi states that answers to the question 'What does conservative mean?' are 'nothing but fragments,' such as the 'constitutional amendment of Article Nine' or 'the need for patriotism' (Nakajima 2013: 28). Nakamasa Masaki, in contrast, having outlined how such conservative political thinkers such as Hume, Burke, Tocqueville, Bagehot, Schmitt, and Hayek understood social institutions and traditional practices, identifies a consistent position: 'Institutional conservatism since Hume has focused on institutions that stabilize society, and has made all possible efforts to preserve them' (Nakamasa 2014: 234). Nakamasa further observes that if self-proclaimed 'conservatives' in Japan think they can restore 'proper Japanese-ness' (*Nihon-rashisa*) by parading the cultivation of 'a country-loving spirit' like a slogan, rather than conservative, this would constitute a mindset that strives to remodel society based on their own blueprint (Nakamasa 2014: 234–5).[3]

From an ideological point of view, the contemporary Japanese conservative movement, which endeavors to foster patriotism by changing legal and social institutions through constitutional reform and education, is closer to reactionism than conservatism. Strictly speaking, the terms 'conservative' (*hoshu*) and 'reactionary' (*hando*), which are often employed interchangeably, are quite different concepts. According to Albert Hirschman (1991), reaction originally only meant a response to an action, but, like conservatism, the term 'reactionary' acquired a negative political flavor after the French Revolution.

Unlike conservatism, reactionism is strongly orientated towards a return to a previous political system. Hirschman conducted discourse

---

2   For Japanese domestic research discussing conservative ideology, see Ochiai (1987) and Uno (2016).

3   In contrast to Western conservative thinkers' focus on institutionalism, Japanese conservative thinkers have set 'discussion of the nature of the Japanese spirit' as their primary focus (Nakamasa 2014: 214). On this difference, Nakamasa points out that because Britain and the United States have maintained continuity in their political systems, it is easy to focus on the conventions conducive to social stability, but in the case of Japan, massive interruptions in the political structure due to the Meiji Restoration (1868) and WWII make it difficult to identify the conventions that have continued to the present.

Chapter 1

analysis on the 'rhetoric of reaction,' and hypothesized that it is a discourse that repudiates civil rights, the institution of ordinary elections (i.e., democracy), and the welfare state (Hirschman 1991). Reactionism disavows any progressivist political or social ambitions and seeks to return to a previous condition. In contrast, while conservatism cherishes the functions inherent in practices that have existed for many years, it does not reject everything in the present situation, or seek to return to a political system of the past. Conservatism and reactionism are often used as synonyms, but ideologically they are distinctly different philosophies.

Maruyama Masao (1957) declared that the term 'conservative' had not become established in Japan; but today, more than sixty years later, many groups and individuals have begun to call themselves 'conservative'. Their claims may be diverse, but they share certain demands, such as constitutional amendment, official visits to the Yasukuni Shrine, support for rearmament, and so forth. Ideologically speaking, these probably could be called reactionism rather than conservatism in the sense of assertively changing the political and social institutions established in the postwar period to revert to their previous condition. For that reason, in this book, I treat conservatism (*hoshu shugi*) and conservative movements (*hoshu undo*) as separate things: if a movement group calls itself 'conservative' (*hoshu*), my referring to it as a 'conservative movement' is not conditional upon nor does it imply that its ideology is conservatism.[4]

The dichotomous political consciousness in Japan

In many countries, people's political awareness is depicted in a binary schema. The 'conservative' versus 'liberal' schema is used to designate the key political divide in the U.S., for example, but according to Nakayama

---

4   If we deem conservatism to be an idea discoverable in social movements, the environmental protection movement might qualify as an example. Noda Yasuhisa, ed. (2010), is a collection of papers analyzing the British National Trust and Western political conservatism. In considering the creation of the National Trust in Britain at the end of the nineteenth century, Sano (2010) identifies several conservative elements such as: 1) a backlash against modernization and industrialization; 2) customs and esthetic sense as Britons; 3) nationalism; and 4) backlash against commercialism. However, while Sano makes some interesting points, there seems to be a certain affinity between conservationists and conservatism, although they do not coincide exactly, just as the conservative movement and conservatism differ.

22

Toshihiro, who has studied the formation of the U.S. conservative movement: 'conservative and liberal are positions that surface within a reciprocal relationship, not positions based in an unshakeable ideological system that transcends a temporal axis' (Nakayama 2013: 18). Nakayama therefore does not treat the concepts 'conservative' and 'liberal' as having 'an explanatory function,' but as 'binary opposites that bring together the political enmity that motivates people' (Nakayama 2013: 36). Rather than people forming value judgements of the politico-social situation based in a clear 'conservative' or 'liberal' ideology, diverse views on separate political and social issues are gathered together under the opposing banners of 'conservative' or 'liberal.'[5]

In Japan, an oppositional structure of 'conservative' versus 'progressive' was long used to describe political consciousness. However, it has been pointed out that political consciousness in Japan does not divide along one consistent axis. According to Kabashima Ikuo and Takenaka Yoshihiko (1996), the oppositional axes of political ideology in postwar Japan was first divided over support for or opposition to the prewar regime, and the security guarantee in the Japan–U.S. Security Treaty. The oppositional axes relating to the 'old regime/security' first appeared as a revival of Marxism disavowed the former regime immediately after the war, and the so-called 'reverse course' that subsequently arose as a backlash towards 'leftists.' Conflict between these two camps peaked over the 1960 Treaty of Mutual Cooperation and Security between the United States and Japan and then largely disappeared due to rapid economic growth. However, in the 1970s, the negative effects of capitalist economic growth such as pollution and environmental destruction became social issues, mobilizing progressive forces with such catchwords as 'anti-growth' and 'welfare' (Kabashima and Takenaka 1996: 88). Kabashima and Takenaka point out that these new movements generated a second axis of opposition, with a new axis of welfare, participation, and equality being added to the domestic political oppositional structure (see Figure 1.1).

Kabashima and Takenaka (1996) also point out that, coupled with the collapse of the Cold War system, this particular 'conservative' versus 'progressive' political division weakened from the 1980s as the political

---

5 Haidt (2012) similarly investigates the 'moral foundations' of people's political awareness from a psychological perspective.

Chapter 1

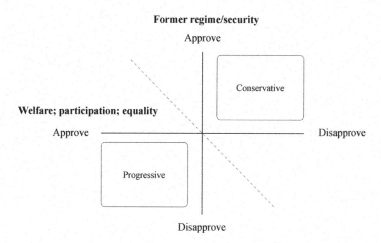

Figure 1.1 Political awareness in postwar Japan
Based on Kabashima and Takenaka (1996)

oppositional structure diversified with the emergence of a new conservatism focused on the principle of market non-interference. However, from the perspective of social movements, rather than individual political consciousness, the schematic representation of political ideology remains valid today. Hence, in this study, I define a 'conservative movement' as one linked with a nationalism that extols 'patriotism,' supports the prewar regime and the Japan–U.S. Security Treaty, and is opposed to enhancing the welfare system and equal political participation. In concrete terms, the groups I have in mind advocate constitutional reform; strengthening the military; a hardline stance towards East Asian nations (especially China, and South and North Korea, which had experience of Japanese colonization in the early twentieth century); defense of the emperor system; support for official visits to the Yasukuni Shrine; and the gendered division of labor and the family unit.

It is not possible to discuss contemporary conservative movements without addressing nationalism. What I call nationalism here follows Ernest Gellner's definition, namely: 'primarily a political principle, which holds that the political and the national unit should be congruent' (Gellner 1983: 1). There is much debate over the definition of nationalism, with some criticism that Gellner's definition is too succinct (Shiokawa 2008). Moreover, nationalism is not necessarily 'conservative,' and in the postwar period, there was a time when progressive intellectuals were fumbling to construct 'a nationalism that defied the state' (Oguma 2002:

826). Nevertheless, with groups calling for the expulsion of resident foreigners dubbing themselves 'action conservatives,' and with conservative critical circles and conservative groups vehemently rejecting criticism from China and South Korea regarding official visits to the Yasukuni Shrine and history textbooks descriptions of World War II (WWII), Gellner's definition is appropriate for our purposes.[6]

The conservative movement and right-wing movement

Finally, I distinguish between conservative movements and right-wing movements, and deal solely with the former. The expressions 'conservative' and 'right-wing' are often used as interchangeable, and there are studies in Japan that treat the groups which I discuss in this book as belonging to the 'right-wing movement.'[7] The term 'right-wing movement,' of course, refers to a range of activity styles, and among the conservative movements addressed in this book, there are groups that overlap with the right-wing movement. In this book, I shall use the term 'conservative movement' to include such groups, but I shall exclude from this study the right-wing movement in a narrow sense, especially those who are the first thing Japanese people imagine when they hear the term 'right-wing movement' in Japan: those who ride in vehicles called 'propaganda trucks' (*gaisensya*), black cars with political propaganda emblazoned on the body and speakers on the roof blaring military songs of the former Japanese army, and who espouse violence as a movement methodology.

---

6   Yamazaki Nozomu (2015) argues that what is seen in Japan today is a 'strange nationalism' that does not fit any of the conventional definitions. There is ample scope to explore the relationship between the conservative movement and nationalism, but my focus in this book is to discuss the conservative movement from the perspective of gender without a more detailed discussion of nationalism.

7   Hori (2000), for example, treats groups such as House of Growth and the National Conference to Protect Japan (Nihon o mamoru kokumin kaigi) as 'right-wing movements.' Of course, the border between a conservative movement and a right-wing movement is vague, but I have defined these groups as 'conservative movement' in this book.

Chapter 1

The Japanese right-wing movement began with the formation in 1878 of Gen'yosha (Black Ocean Society), but after the defeat in WWII and the U.S. occupation of Japan, the right-wing movement was in shambles. Kinoshita Hanji (1951a, 1976) posits four factors for this: 1) right-wing activity was banned by a dissolution order for ultranationalist groups issued in 1946;[8] 2) loss of an ideological basis with the disavowal of the emperor's divinity; 3) loss of an economic basis with the dissolution of the military and the industrial and financial conglomerates known as *zaibatsu*; and 4) economic disruption following land reform and the democratization of agricultural communities. Another factor was the political expulsion of right-wing movement leaders in the 1945 purge of war criminals, which had a huge influence on the decline of the right-wing movement.

In the early 1950s, however, U.S. occupation policy for Japan shifted from democratization to economic revitalization, and the right-wing movement resumed activities. First, prewar right-wing groups whose prohibition was lifted, such as the Cooperative Party (Kyodo-to) and Republican Party (Kyowa-to) were resurrected and began to oppose pacifism while touting rearmament. New groups also started to form; by 1956 there were 272 such groups (Kanto area: 73; Tohoku: 20; Hokkaido: 23; Chubu: 18; Kinki: 26; Chugoku and Shikoku: 50; Kyushu: 62) (Kinoshita 1977).

Kinoshita (1965) refers to postwar right-wing movements as 'new right-wing movements,' classifying them into three types. First is the 'political right-wing,' which carried on the traditions of prewar right-wing movements, including the Greater East Institute (Daito-juku), the Gathering to Study the Eastern Thought of Yasuoka Masahiro (Zenkoku shiyu kyokai), and the Association of National Comrades (Kokumin doshikai), for example. Second is the 'streetside right-wing,' which emphasizes the use of violent force. Greater Japan Patriotic Party (Dai Nippon aikoku-to), Greater Japan Production Party (Dai Nippon seisan-to), Japan Youth League (Nihon seinen renmei) and Greater Japan Nationalist Party (Dai Nippon kokumin-to) correspond to this type. The third is the 'yakuza right-wing,' whose boundaries with organized crime

---

8 More than 210 of the approximately 350 right-wing groups that existed before the war are believed to have disbanded for this reason (Kinoshita 1951b).

are blurry, exemplified by the Party of the Righteous (Gijin-to) and Great Japan Patriotic Society (Dai Nippon kokusui kai).

In the late 1950s, to counter the growth of left-wing movements in response to the Japan–U.S. Security Treaty issue, right-wing groups gathered under three alliances. In 1959, a coalition of the 'political right-wing' formed the Conference of Japanese Nationals (Nihon kokumin kaigi), with Ito Musojiro from League of East Asia Kindred Spirits' Association (Toa renmei doshi kai) as Secretary-General. Other participants included House of Growth (Seicho no ie), Gathering to Study the Eastern Thought of Yasuoka Masahiro , and the Japan Community Friends' League (Nippon goyu renmei, or Goyuren). In the same year, the 'streetside right-wing' organized the All-Japan Council of Patriotic Organizations (Zen Nippon aikokusha dantai kaigi), with Sagoya Yoshiaki of the National Protection Corps (Gokokudan) being installed as president and group representative, with Arakawa Bokusui from Greater Japan Nationalist Party as secretary-general, and Kodama Yoshio, Miura Giichi and Sasakawa Ryoichi as advisors. Another 'streetside right-wing' alliance, the Confederation of Greater Japan Patriotic Organizations: Council for Countermeasures to the Current Situation (Dai Nippon aikokusha dantai rengo: Jikyoku taisaku kyogikai), was formed, centered on Fukuda Soken of The Break Communism News (*Bokyo Shinbun*), with Honda Kido from the Greater Japan Imperial Banner Association (Dai Nippon kinki kai) as its president, and Hase Yukihiro of the Association of Friends of [Free] Speech (Genron doshi kai) as its secretary-general. The Confederation was hostile to the All-Japan Council of Patriotic Organizations. In 1961, the Japanism Federation (Nippon shugi rengo) was formed as an alliance of the 'yakuza right-wing.'

It is difficult to summarize a movement comprising numerous groups with long histories in a few words. Indeed, defining the right-wing movement as the 'avant-garde part of opposition forces that counter the left wing,' (Ino 2005: 11), Ino Kenji identified twenty distinct characteristics:

1. absolute loyalty to the emperor system and the state,
2. opposition and vigilance towards communism, socialism, and aligned forces,
3. emphasis on action over theory,

Chapter 1

4. preservation of ethnic traditions and culture, and vigilance towards foreign ideas and culture,
5. placing importance on duty, order, and authority,
6. an ethnic sense of duty,
7. authoritarianism in the chain of command,
8. paternalistic totalitarianism,
9. a conservative inclination,
10. a 'party of one' tendency (partisanship),
11. elitism,
12. patriarchal human relations,
13. vigilance towards intellectuals – especially journalists and teachers,
14. impetuous direct action (direct appeal, terrorism, coup d'état-oriented),
15. highest prioritization of national interest,
16. orientation towards expansion and strengthening of military force,
17. promotion of patriotic education,
18. total repudiation of the postwar system (abolishing the Yalta and Potsdam regimes),
19. intense vigilance towards bias in mass communications, and
20. emphasis on ceremony (festivals, rituals, etiquette, parties, and so on)

(Ino 2005: 11–12)

Many of these characteristics are shared by the conservative movement, as well, but two points of difference can be cited. First, the 'party of one tendency' (no. 10) has frequently been observed in right-wing movements (Kinoshita 1951, 1965; Hori 2000). Hori Yukio (2000), referring to the 1972 edition of the *Handbook of Right-Wing-Related Groups*, highlights the number of people per group, observing that 85 (36 percent) of the 234 right-wing groups mentioned in the Handbook had ten or fewer members, and among these, 22 groups (about ten percent of the total) were deemed to have only one member. Of the 148 groups comprising the remaining 63 percent of the groups, membership numbered 50 or fewer.[9]

---

9   The right-wing movement's 'party of one' tendency may be a factor in the paucity of theory to support the movement. Kinoshita refers to the 'absence'

Second is 'impetuous direct action' (no. 14) involving direct appeal, terrorism, and coup d'état-orientation. Violence was an important way for the right-wing movement to demonstrate its principles and position to society. Nomura Shusuke, who set fire to the residence of politician Kono Ichiro in 1963, mounted an attack on the Japan Business Federation (Keidanren) in 1975, and committed suicide in 1993 at the offices of the Asahi Shinbun, explained to a roundtable discussion entitled 'What is the right-wing?' that: 'Raising problematic issues by means of body language is the job of the action right-wing' (Ino ed. 2006: 61). What is glossed here as 'body language' was an incident in which a young man claiming to be from a right-wing group broke into the prime minister's official residence in a pickup truck loaded with gasoline in plastic buckets. Protest action accompanied by violence has a huge impact on society, and the right wing appears 'to have lost the support of the general public for that reason' (Hori 2000: 135–6).

Although conservative and right-wing movements overlap to some extent, in this book I have omitted the 'streetside right-wing' and 'yakuza right-wing' from my target of research based on Kinoshita's classification.

At the time of writing, the conservative movement is again growing stronger, both socially and politically. The conservative movement is not a 'party of one' elite movement. Moreover, if its activities were invariably accompanied by violence, it would have been impossible for it to mobilize a lot of people and develop a stable movement. For that reason, this book distinguishes the right-wing movement in a narrow sense from the conservative movement and will not discuss the former. Furthermore, I apply the term 'conservative movement' to right-wing groups that intersect with the orthodox conservative movement.

---

of theory in the right-wing movement as 'negative left-wing emulation' (Kinoshita 1965: 13). Certainly, ideological orientations towards imperialism and anti-communism can be found in the right-wing movements, but there is no theory to integrate or systematize them. Hence, what most ignited the right-wing movement was resentment of the left-wing movement. At the same time, the right-wing movement has 'advanced the movement with [key] persons as its center' (Hori 2000: 193–6). In fact, there is no dearth of research relating to the right-wing movement focusing on the careers and thinking of its leaders as individuals.

Chapter 2

Lineage of the conservative movement in postwar Japan

Fetal stirrings of the conservative movement: The Japan War-Bereaved Families Association

2.1.1 Tracing the lineage of the conservative movement

This chapter outlines trends in the conservative movement from the end of World War II to the present to shed light on the historical background in which the women's conservative movement emerged. There has been some research that discusses the development of various conservative groups in postwar Japanese society, albeit in a fragmentary form. As the groups which have spawned the conservative movement are extremely diverse, which group lies at the core of those trends differs according to their respective proponents. In unpacking the currents in the era-name legislation (*gengo hoseika*) movement (which I will discuss later), which expanded from the late 1960s into the 1970s, Hori Yukio (2000) and Kenneth Ruoff (2001) situate the House of Growth and Association of Shinto Shrines (Jinja honcho), respectively, at the center of the movement. More recently, Japan Conference (Nippon kaigi) has attracted the attention of journalists. Reports on Japan Conference and its beginnings were published by Sugano Tamotsu, Aoki Osamu, and Yamazaki Masahiro in 2016, and by Fujiu Akira in 2017. The successive publication of these books was dubbed the 'Japan Conference books boom,' and brought the organization wide-recognition. One reason for Japan Conference attracting wide public interest was the depth of its political connections, with its subordinate Colloquium of Diet Members reportedly including thirteen of the twenty cabinet ministers in the third Abe cabinet (2015).

Chapter 2

The authors who reported on Japan Conference focused on the sequence of events leading to the creation of the largest conservative organization in Japan and the extent of its political influence. The formation of Japan Conference was depicted as follows.

Its origins date to the 1960s, when a right-wing student movement was organized at some universities by devotees of the House of Growth religion to counter the left-wing student movement. The All-Campus Joint Struggle Committee (Zenkyoto) is a prominent example. The male students who comprised its core later formed the Japan Youth Council (Nihon seinen kyogikai) and Japan Council (Nippon kyogikai), which became the nucleus or 'operational unit' (*jitsudo butai*) of the present-day Japan Conference.

Although describing the history of a movement by tracing the progress of specific individuals, such as powerful leaders, is clear and easy to understand, it is not adequate. Social movements do not survive merely on the presence of one charismatic leader; they require many people to engage in various ways, such as publicizing the group's agenda in speeches and writings, handling practical matters and odd jobs behind the scenes, people who join and support the group even when not substantially involved in action, people who support a group's activity without becoming members, people who can forge relationships with other groups, and people who can present contentious issues to appeal for broader support.

Moreover, focusing solely on the leadership of activist groups can obstruct understanding social movements from a gender perspective. In androcentric societies, men tend to fill the top positions and key roles in organizations and groups, and women's participation is not always apparent. Furthermore, even when members of a group energetically seek to raise contentious gender issues, these issues are often perceived as trivial by male leaders. What is more, leaders' acknowledgement of the importance of such issues does not necessarily match that of the multitude of other participants.

In this chapter, I aim to sketch the lineage of the conservative movement in postwar Japanese society, focusing on the Japan War-Bereaved Families Association which formed immediately after WWII, predating the 1960s student movement. I will then position the women's conservative movement within it.[1] The association was formed by the bereaved families of soldiers and civilian army employees who perished in the war, and is reputedly the Liberal Democratic Party (LDP)'s largest base of support. It has been active since immediately after the war, with the aim of improving the economic and spiritual treatment of bereaved families after the loss of their husbands and fathers who had been the household breadwinners. In its earliest iteration, it was an interest group demanding economic support from the state for the bereaved families of fallen soldiers and civilian army employees. Later, it turned its attention to restoring state maintenance of the Yasukuni Shrine – which became a non-government religious corporation after the war – and attracting support from other conservative groups. Taking up the controversial cause of state maintenance of the Yasukuni Shrine led to further changes in the association's political positioning. Focusing on that association will reveal the features of the pre-1980s conservative movement, laying the groundwork for elucidating the characteristics of the conservative movement that has grown since the 1990s through small grassroots groups. Having achieved that, I aim to position women within the history of conservative movements.

Launch of the Japan War-Bereaved Families Association

The indicator long used in postwar Japan to gauge people's political alignment was the binary schema of 'conservative' versus 'progressive.' The basis of the postwar Japanese political system began with the birth in October 1955 of the Japan Socialist Party (now the Social Democratic Party of Japan, SDPJ) through the amalgamation of the left and right wings of the Socialist Party, and the formation of the LDP from the merger of the Liberal and Democratic Parties the following November. The ideological conflict structure composed of 'conservative' versus 'progressive' also

---

1   Many in the conservative movement work closely with conservative media such as *Seiron* (Sound Argument), and occasionally they are referred to collectively as the 'conservative movement'. As I am focused on the formation of conservative movement groups in this chapter, I do not pay much attention to the conservative media. For research on *Seiron* and *Shokun!* magazines, which have long driven conservative commentary, see Jomaru (2011). For research on the media's role in historical revisionism since the 1990s, see Kurahashi (2018).

Chapter 2

took shape in this rivalry between the LDP and the Socialist Party over political points at issue such as security and rearmament (Otake 2005; Aiba 2000).[2]

The Bereaved Families Association became a support base for the 'conservative' LDP, but the bereaved families' movement was initially constituted by war widows. The cessation of soldiers' pensions and survivors' benefits after the war and the Yasukuni Shrine's incorporation as a religious juridical person were perceived by the bereaved families as an 'indignity' (Imai 2002: 83). The war widows who had lost their breadwinner husbands, in particular, suffered severe impoverishment, and formed the Alliance of Families of War Victims (Senso giseisha izoku domei) based on a 'philosophy of anti-militarism and peace' and 'feelings of privation in their practical lives' (Imai 2002: 93–4).

The Japan Bereaved Family-Welfare Federation (Nippon izoku kosei renmei), the forerunner of the Bereaved Families Association, formed as a break-away from the Alliance of Families of War Victims. In 1947, at a meeting of regional representatives of the Alliance, conflict arose between bereaved male family members seeking to celebrate the heroic spirits of the war dead, and war widows who sought economic assistance (Kitagawa 2000, 2005; Obinata 2009).[3] The bereaved men broke away from the Alliance of Families of War Victims and, in November the same year, formed the Japan Bereaved Family-Welfare Federation, which was reorganized in 1953 as the Japan War-Bereaved Families Association, Incorporated.[4] Hereafter, reference to the Japan

---

2   The problem of perceiving the 1955 system as 'fixed' has also been pointed out. It was only around the system's initial period that the conservative-versus-progressive ideological conflict was brought to the fore, and the 1955 system itself also changed over time, 'transforming into a system with a style that aimed for social integration by undertaking such benefit-sharing as government spending' (Aiba 2000: 15) in the ensuing period of rapid economic growth.

3   At a meeting of regional representatives at this time, a strong call by Communist Party assembly members for abolition of the emperor system reportedly triggered a walkout by men who were angered by it and who subsequently held a separate meeting in the open air (Imai 2002).

4   Obtaining the necessary qualifications to take control of Kudan kaikan (Kudan hall, previously the Gunjin kaikan, Ex-soldiers' Hall) upon government disposal of this former national property is understood to have been the primary motivation for the Bereaved Families Association's acquisition of incorporated foundation status. See Tanaka (1995) for details.

War-Bereaved Families Association includes its predecessor, the Family-Welfare Federation.

The association is composed mainly of the parents, siblings, wives and children of soldiers and civilian army employees who perished in WWII. However, according to a survey conducted by Tanaka Nobumasa, as of 1978 only 56 percent of war-bereaved families were members of the group (Tanaka 1995).[5] Nevertheless, it has become the largest organization in Japan for the bereaved families of WWII.

The association's activities stand on two pillars: 1) Improving the economic well-being of war-bereaved families; and 2) State maintenance of the Yasukuni Shrine. Its aims were set out in the Family-Welfare Federation's inaugural bulletin (Nippon izoku kosei renmei 1949):

> Along with opening the way for mutual aid, consolation payments and relief for bereaved families; striving for the raising of morality and the cultivation of character; and pushing forward for the building of a peaceful Japan, to contribute to the welfare of all humankind by preventing war, and, by extension, to hope for the establishment of lasting world peace.

The association represents bereaved families who seek to honor the 'heroic spirits' of the war dead, but at the time of its inauguration, its advocacy for state maintenance of the Yasukuni Shrine conflicted with GHQ's occupation policy. Its first initiative, therefore, was to improve the economic situation of war-bereaved families – especially war widows – who were living in poverty.

To this end, it lobbied politicians and authorities for the resurrection of soldiers' pensions and survivors' benefits. In November 1947, it petitioned the GHQ Welfare Division, the Prime Minister's official residence, the Chair and President of the respective Houses of Parliament, and the Ministry of Health and Welfare, and in November the following year the association's representatives in each prefecture lobbied the government and Diet. Its women's representatives also appealed to the Chief of the GHQ Welfare Division, Colonel Nelson B. Neff (Nippon izokukai ed. 1987). As a result, in 1949, two years after the association's

---

5   Precise statistics on the association's membership numbers have not been published; Tanaka's 1978 figures (1995) appear to be the only available data.

Chapter 2

formation, a 'Resolution relating to the support of bereaved families' and 'Resolution relating to the welfare of widows and war-bereaved families' were passed by the Diet. These resolutions recognized the association's claims that soldiers and civilian army employees had lost their lives in the course of their public duties, and 'marked the first step in the positive reappraisal' of soldiers and civilian army employees who had died in the war (Imai 2003: 129).

Following these resolutions, a succession of the association's demands were implemented in the 1950s. In 1952, the 'Law for Relief of War Victims and Survivors' was enacted, and in 1953 the pensions law was amended, resurrecting pensions for bereaved families and survivors' benefits. Nevertheless, the organization continued to demand increasing the monetary amount of survivors' benefits and expanding eligibility for bereaved families' pensions. The 'All-Japan war-bereaved families rally' held each year passed resolutions to make demands on the state, and from 1957 to 1958, resolutions were passed to demand rectifying the imbalance between survivors' benefits and those of civil officials, as well as for improved treatment of civilian quasi-employees of the military such as students mobilized to work in factories (Nippon izokukai, ed. 1987).

The association's approach focused on appeals to politicians. Most notable, in addition to petitions and face-to-face meetings with politicians and bureaucrats, is its collaboration with politicians. After the first postwar national elections on 23 January 1949, the association's representatives visited both the House of Representatives and House of Councillors in the Diet on 25 March the same year to lobby for better treatment of war-bereaved families. According to Joshita Ken'ichi, the Diet members who were lobbied belonged to a wide range of political parties, not only the ruling party at the time, Democratic Liberal Party (Minji-to); and they typically had not been elected many times (Joshita 2012). The association specifically targeted parliamentarians who, due to being relatively newly elected, 'had not solidified [their electoral base], and so they desired a mutually-collaborative relationship with the Bereaved Family-Welfare Federation' (Joshita 2012: 110–11).

In this manner, the association deepened its connections with the LDP, becoming an important part of its support base. Since Kaya Okinori became its president in 1969, a succession of LDP Members of the House of Councillors have served in that role.[6] Moreover, there is a group within the association permitted under the Public Offices Election Act called the Japan Bereaved Families Political League (Nihon izoku seiji renmei), which, as of 1997, had endorsed 280 parliamentarians (Tanaka 1997). At the same time, within the LDP, a group was formed with deep links to the association called the Bereaved Families' Council of Diet Members (Ikazoku giin kyogikai), which has been described as a 'mechanism by which votes in elections from bereaved families were assured as a reward for political action towards the implementation of the association's demands' (Tanaka 1997: 69). Thus, the association came to be a 'dominant interest group' for the LDP (Oku 2009: 69).

Failure of the Yasukuni Shrine Bill

After its efforts to improve the economic treatment of war-bereaved families had achieved a measure of success, the association began to advocate for the state to maintain the Yasukuni Shrine. At its eighteenth national rally in 1963, this issue was elevated to the top of the list of demands for the year, and the following year, a petition to this effect was presented with 6,428,088 signatures (Nippon izokukai ed. 1987).

Through this initiative, the association began to collaborate with a variety of activist groups. In 1966, it hosted a social gathering with numerous veterans' and allied support groups.[7] In 1969, a national rally demanding state maintenance of the Yasukuni Shrine was joined by thirty-one groups, including those listed in note 7. The rally's executive committee later developed into the National Convention for Realizing State Support for Yasukuni Shrine (Yasukuni-jinja kokka goji kantetsu kokumin kyogikai) (hereafter, 'National Convention for Yasukuni') (Nippon izokukai ed. 1987).

---

6 Only Nakai Sumiko, who served as president from 1996 to 2001, assumed the presidency upon endorsement from within the organization.

7 These included, among others, the Japan Community Friends' League (Nippon goyu renmei), the Military Pensioners' Association (Gun'on renmei), the Japan Wounded Soldiers' Association (Nippon shoi gunjinkai), the War Victims' Relief Association (Senso giseisha engokai), the Military Club (Kaikosha), the Association of Former Naval Officers (Suikokai), and the Japan Heroic Spirits' Support Association (Nippon eirei hosankai).

Chapter 2

Moves to provide state support for the shrine accelerated around 1970. A private member's bill (the Yasukuni Shrine Bill) was tabled in the Diet seven times from 1969 to 1974. The Bereaved Families Association energetically agitated for the enactment of the bill, both independently and through the National Convention for Yasukuni. In 1970, representatives from each regional branch lobbied their locally-elected parliamentarians to sign a statement of intention to commit to 'making efforts in anticipation of the enactment of the Yasukuni Shrine Bill in this Diet session,' and 263 members from the House of Representatives and 103 from the House of Councillors complied (Nippon izokukai ed. 1987: 82). Then, in 1973, the Bereaved Families Association's youth division held a street parade in conjunction with 500 members of the National Convention for Yasukuni youth division, carrying photographs of the remains of the war dead (Nippon izokukai, ed. 1987: 97). The women's division of the Bereaved Families Association also held a rally for the 'necessary achievement of the Yasukuni Shrine bill' in 1974. After the rally, 250 participants staged a sit-in outside the main gate of the Prime Minister's official residence demanding a face-to-face meeting with him (Nippon izokukai ed. 1987: 101). However, the bill tabled in the Diet was rejected all seven times on the grounds that it violated the constitutional separation of church and state (Hatano 2011).

The failure of the Yasukuni Shrine Bill triggered a shift in the movement's approach. Until then, through direct negotiation in face-to-face meetings, petitions of politicians and bureaucrats, and electoral cooperation with politicians, the Bereaved Families Association succeeded in its efforts for improvements in the economic treatment of bereaved families who were left destitute by the death of their husbands and fathers. However, the group was faced with the need to change the constitutional separation of church and state and it became clear that their approach to realizing their objectives through collaboration with parliamentarians was not sufficient to this end.

The organization of the conservative movement

The Society for Honoring the Glorious War Dead

The various groups that pushed for state maintenance of the Yasukuni Shrine began a broad shift in movement strategy in the late 1970s, emphasizing a wide appeal to national public opinion rather than directly pressuring politicians and bureaucrats. This change in strategy fundamentally changed the nature of the movement. A forerunner to this shift was a public opinion poll conducted in April 1976 by the Japan Religious Broadcasting Corporation. This survey of ten thousand adult men and women recruited by stratified random sampling from across Japan, used interviews to investigate the pros and cons of the state managing and operating the Yasukuni Shrine, ways of consoling the spirits of the dead, and so forth. The survey methodology was problematic, asking leading questions, such as: 'There is a view that "it is natural for the state to undertake memorial events for people who died in wars and suchlike for their country?" but what do you think? Do you/Don't you think it would be better for that to happen?'[8] Despite these problems, the survey clearly marks the beginning of a shift in the tactics of the conservative movement from direct politics to public opinion.

The groups that formed the National Convention for Yasukuni began to establish a new body to agitate for official visits by the emperor and prime minister to the Yasukuni Shrine through shifting national public opinion. In January 1976, a sponsors' group was established to form the new organization, and in April that year, the sponsors' group established three committees: general affairs; organization; and public relations. In May, an instigators' meeting inaugurated committees for determination of all original bills and rally execution.

Through this process, the Society for Honoring the Glorious War Dead (Eirei ni kotaeru kai) was created on June 22, 1976.[9] Former Supreme Court President Ishida Kazuto assumed office as president, with Ogiya Shozo (journalist), Uno Seiichi (Emeritus Professor, University of Tokyo), Ishii Yoshiko (musician), Arisue Seizo (President of the Japan Community Friends' League), Koro Mitsu (President of the Federation of Women's Groups [Kakushu josei dantai rengokai]), and Sato Shin (Managing Director of the Bereaved Families Association)

---

8   The entire set of questions and their responses are published in Fujisawa (1977).

9   With the establishment of the Society for Honoring the Glorious War Dead, the National Convention for Yasukuni disbanded and its residual funds of more than 2.24 million yen were donated to the new organization (*Tsushin*, no. 306, July 15, 1976).

Chapter 2

as vice-presidents.[10] Sixty-three individuals, including Ikeda Yasaburo, Kurokawa Kisho, and Kayama Ken'ichi were installed as advisors. There were forty-five participant groups, headed by the Bereaved Families Association,[11] and others also took part.

Its statement of purpose declares:

> Upon the acknowledgment that "it is wholly reasonable to pay the most appropriate courtesy to the heroic spirits of Yasukuni in the name of the country"… the establishment of a national basic stance towards our heroic spirits by the country and its nationals is precisely the urgent task of today, and to that end each and every member of the nation must courageously initiate action, no longer entrusting it to the political arena. (Eirei ni kotaeru kai, 1977: 2)

In addition to the stated purpose of shaping public opinion its objectives included: 1) enlightenment and propaganda activities to honor the heroic spirits of the war dead; 2) events at Yasukuni Shrine to honor and console the spirits of the war dead; 3) realization of official visits to Yasukuni Shrine; 4) accomplish the collection of the remains of the war dead; and 5) a movement to establish a day for consolation of the spirits of the war dead. The creation of the Society for Honoring the Glorious War

---

10 Hereafter, titles reflect those then current.

11 The most prominent of these groups included: the SDF Friendship Association (Taiyukai), the Japan Community Friends' League, the Military Pensioners' Association, the Military club, the Association of Former Naval Officers, the Nationwide War Comrades' Association (Zenkoku sen'yukai), the Association of Shinto Shrines, the Buddhist Prayer Society (Bussho gonenkai kyodan), the Pillar of the Nation Society (Kokuchukai), the Council for a New Japan (Shin Nippon kyogikai), the Association for Self-Cultivation Youth Division (Shuyodan seinenbu), Regimen Society (Yojokai), Gathering to Study the Eastern Thought of Yasuoka Masahiro, the Church of World Messianity (Sekai kyusei kyo), Japan Religious Broadcasting Corporation, Japan Sumo Association, and later, the Central Division of the House of Growth's Political Alliance, Central Nogi Association (Chuo Nogi kai), the Tokyo Japan–Korea Friendship Association (Tokyo Nik–kan shinzen kyokai), and the Japan Youth Council.
  See Fujiu (2018) on the Association of Shinto Shrines. See Tsukada (2015) on postwar Japanese religious organizations and conservative political parties.

Dead marked a new stage for the movement (Iguchi 1981; Miyachi 1981; Hata 2002).

Miyachi Masato, focusing on the organizational form of the society, cites its 'creation of proactive regional headquarters based on prefectures and regional branches based on municipalities as strongholds for a "national movement"' (Miyachi 1981: 95). The society's regional moves began with its Yamaguchi prefectural headquarters, established 15 December 1976; with Nishikawa Sadaichi (President of *Ube Jiho* [Ube Times)) taking office as president; and Yoshitomi Kosuke (President of the Yamaguchi Prefecture Association of Bereaved Families) and Kurokami Naohisa (Yamaguchi Prefecture Association of Shinto Shrines) as vice-presidents. The following year, headquarters were established in Yamanashi Prefecture in February, in Tokushima Prefecture in March, and by the end of October 1978, headquarters had been set up in all prefectures. In this way, the society rapidly established regional headquarters and branches, but its procedures for formation of regional headquarters and branches were determined by:

> making the Bereaved Families Association, the Japan Community Friends' League, the All-Japan Federation of Military Pensioners' Associations (Gun'on renmei zenkoku rengokai), the Military Club, the Association of Shinto Shrines, and the Japan Wounded Soldiers' Association into the executive group, and the Bereaved Families Association [branches] in each prefecture into the leading advocates; the executive group will hold preparatory meetings focusing on each branch, and each group in their successive location will call upon others and complete the establishment. (Eirei ni kotaeru kai 1977)[12]

This stipulation demonstrates that the Society for Honoring the Glorious War Dead organized regional headquarters and branches by exploiting existing national-level groups, centering on the Bereaved Families Association.

Article 5 of the society's constitution set out three types of membership: 'individual membership,' 'group membership,' and 'supporting member-ship.' Individual members were taken to be 'individuals who concur with

---

12 Gun'yukai also joined this executive group.

Figure 2.1 Signature-collecting for formalization of Yasukuni Shrine visits (1977)
Source: Nippon izokukai (1977)

the aims of the society.'[13] Groups that until then had advocated for state maintenance of the Yasukuni Shrine were typically connected with former soldiers, religious bodies, people in similar circumstances, or who shared similar doctrines or beliefs. By contrast, anyone who agreed with the intent of the society could join; and, furthermore, the fact that 'individual members' were listed first in the membership system might indicate an intention to expand the movement participants' cohort. This effort seems to have been successful, as individual membership reportedly reached 667,160 as of 1980 (Miyachi 1981).

The society's activities can be broadly divided into two types, the first being gathering signatures on petitions for official visits to Yasukuni Shrine. This campaign, with its target of ten million signatures, began in 1977 (Figure 2.1), and by April 1978, two years after the society was founded, it had amassed 4.44 million signatures in its first batch, and in August the same year it presented an additional 1.77 million signatures to

---

13 *Tsushin*, no. 306, 15 July 1976.

the Prime Minister's Office. According to Miyachi (1981), this petitioning activity had garnered an astonishing 8.74 million signatures by April 1980. The second type of activity was a campaign to table resolutions for official visits to Yasukuni Shrine at regional assemblies. A petition presented to the Mie Prefectural Assembly on 15 December 1978 by the society's Mie Prefectural headquarters was passed with 29 for and 15 against, setting a national precedent. In 1979, 16 prefectures, and in 1980 a further ten prefectures passed resolutions demanding official visits to Yasukuni Shrine.

The era-name legislation movement

While the society was expanding its activity, another movement was advancing through a similar approach. This movement was seeking the legalization of Japanese imperial era names (*gengo*). The use of one era name per imperial reign was first prescribed by a government edict in 1868, and a stipulation was later added to the former Imperial House Law. However, no stipulation as to era names was made in the postwar Imperial House Law, and the movement to legislate use of era names (*gengo hoseika*) aimed to resurrect the old stipulation. In Japan, there are two ways of marking the year; the Western calendar and this imperial era name. As previously mentioned, the use of imperial era names was legislated before World War II, but this provision was abolished after the war during the U.S. occupation. The reason was that the use of the imperial era names meant that people considered time as centered on the emperor. However, since then, the imperial era has been used as a matter of convention in official documents prepared by Japanese government agencies. The struggle for the legalization of the imperial era names sought to resolve this problem.

The alliance was called the Society for the Protection of Japan (Nihon o mamoru kai), a group with Shinto and Buddhist affiliations that substantially steered the era-name legislation movement. Established in April 1974, this body sought to deal 'with chaotic social conditions, returning to the origin of Japanese traditional spirit, inspiring patriotism, and bringing about an ethical state.' Its inaugural representative committee consisted of Asahina Sogen (Chief Abbot of the Rinzai Sect); Ogura Reigen (Founder of Buddist organization of Nenpo shinkyo); Shinoda Yasuo (Secretary-General of the Association of Shinto Shrines);

Chapter 2

Sekiguchi Tomino (President of the Buddhist Prayer Society); Taniguchi Masaharu (President of the House of Growth); Hanawa Mizuhiko (Chief Priest of Kasama Inari Shrine); Yasuoka Masahiro (President of the Gathering to Study the Eastern Thought of Yasuoka Masahiro); Iwamoto Shoshun (Chief Abbot of the Soto Sect of Zen Buddhism and Chief Priest, Daihonzan Sojiji Temple); Kaneko Nichii (Chief Abbot of Nichiren Sect and Chief Priest of Daihonzan Ikegami Honmonji); Shimizudani Kyojun (Chief Abbot of Seikannon Sect's Sensoji); Date Tatsumi (Chief Priest of Meiji Shrine), Asanuma Monzo (leader of the Association for Self-Cultivation and Sincerity [Shuyodan]); Hiroike Sentaro (Director of the Institute of Moralogy [Moraroji kenkyujo]); Yamaoka Sohachi (President of the Japan Association [Nippon kai]), and was described as a 'mighty alliance of religious organizations centering on right-wing religious bodies that support today's LDP in elections' (Nakajima 1981a: 155).

The Society for the Protection of Japan's published policy was:

> 1) To inspire a patriotic mindset in accordance with our country's traditional spirit, and to anticipate the attainment of an ethical state; 2) To protect righteous democracy and build a cheerful welfare society; 3) To eliminate biased education, and promote educational normalization; 4) To demand impartiality in speech and reporting, and eliminate materialistic ideology and authoritarian reformism; and 5) To carry through the protection of Japan, our ancestral land, while seeking all paths to world peace amid international collaboration. (Nakajima 1981a: 155)

This policy was criticized for 'its objectives of backlash and rightward swing that centered on its current ideology having been hammered in along with all its tenets' (Nakajima 1981a: 155). However, while from a contemporary perspective, these references to traditional spirit, patriotism, biased education, and 'impartiality of speech and reporting' can be seen as laying the groundwork for the contemporary conservative movement, the aspirations for a 'welfare society' are notable.

Action by the Society for the Protection of Japan began in the late 1970s. In January 1977, in an interview with then Prime Minister, Fukuda Takeo, it presented a 'written request regarding the propagation of a national spirit of solidarity' which incorporated demands for the legislation of era names, the national flag and national anthem,

44

and an official National Foundation Day (Kenkoku kinen no hi) to be organized by the government. On 11 February that year, Foundation Day celebrations were held at more than twenty locations around the country, and resolutions calling for the legalization of imperial era names were raised. Moreover, on 3 May, a 'central national rally to demand legislation of imperial era names' was held by the Association of Shinto Shrines, the House of Growth, the Japan Community Friends' League, the Society for the Protection of Japan, and the National Congress for the Establishment of an Autonomous Constitution (Jishu kenpo seitei kokumin kaigi),[14] attended by 1500 people (including five Diet members) from fifty groups (Ruoff 2001). Through this rally 'the movement which each of the civic groups hitherto had [separately] pressed forward was unified for the first time' (Nakajima 1981a: 168–9).

Subsequently, the era-name movement swiftly petitioned the regional assemblies, just as the Society for Honoring the Glorious War Dead had done. In August 1977, the Japan Youth Council[15] took the lead in assembling a caravan in conjunction with the Association of Shinto Shrines and the National Congress for the Establishment of an Autonomous Constitution, visiting all the cities of western Japan. This caravan held 'talk and film evenings' in 20 cities and delivered streetside speeches in 50 cities. Partly as a result, on 22 September 1977, a resolution seeking legislation to reintroduce imperial era names was adopted for the first time anywhere in Japan in Imari City, Saga Prefecture. The regional assemblies of another five prefectures and four cities passed resolutions on the petition that month, and in the eight months following its adoption in Imari City, petitions seeking the legislation of imperial era names were adopted by 36 prefectural assemblies and 342 municipal councils in turn.

---

14 This group was set up in 1969 with the aim of Constitutional revision, joined by the House of Growth, Association of Shinto Shrines, the Bereaved Families Association, the Military Pensioners Association and the Japan Community Friends' League.

15 This group was formed by university students from ethnic factions in the 1970s with the aim of countering the left-wing student movement (Ruoff 2001). Because of its opposition to the left-wing student movement, this group can be categorized as a right-wing student movement. However, in Japan, people associated the term 'right-wing' with gangs. Therefore, students who participated in the right-wing student movement called themselves 'ethnic factions' to distinguish themselves from the gangs. In short, the student movement's ethnic factions were not necessarily ethno-nationalists.

Chapter 2

The movement in each area was vitalized by caravans dispatched from the center, and the presentation of petitions to assemblies and their adoption were responding to that momentum (Nakajima 1981a). In the winter of that year, caravans were dispatched to Eastern Japan. In December 1977, resolutions seeking legalization of imperial era names were adopted by twenty prefectural assemblies, and by the end of March 1978, resolutions were passed in thirty-six prefectures.

Moves in the regions also influenced the political arena, and on 14 June 1978, the Alliance of Diet Members for Promotion of Imperial Era-name Legislation (Gengo hoseika sokushin kokkai giin renmei) was launched. This was a large alliance, with a total of 411 Diet members participating: 346 from the LDP, 39 from the Democratic Socialist Party (Minsha-to), 22 from the New Liberal Club (Shin jiyu kurabu), and four from other political parties. This alliance was viewed as 'supra-partisan,' meaning that the implementation of anti-socialism/communism and anti-progressivism was seen as its distinctive feature (Nakajima 1981a: 170).[16]

With this tremendous growth in the era-name legislation movement, people connected with the Society for Honoring the Glorious War Dead began to join that current. On 18 July 1978, the National Council for Achievement of Legalization of Imperial Era Names (Gengo hoseika jitsugen kokumin kaigi) was launched. There were ten proposers: Tokugawa Muneyoshi (administrator, Association of Shinto Shrines); Ishida Kazuto (former Chief Justice of the Supreme Court of Japan); Uno Seiichi (emeritus professor at University of Tokyo); Amaike Seiji (Alliance president); Mayuzumi Toshiro (composer); Yamaoka Sohachi (writer); Hosokawa Takachika (political commentator); Nagano Shigeo (president, Japan Chamber of Commerce and Industry); Kasugano Kiyotaka (chair, Japan Sumo Association); and Ohama Hideko (former chair, Central Election Management Council). Ishida Kazuto became President, with Suetsugu Ichiro (Young Men's Association for Japanese Reconstruction [Nippon kenseikai]) as steering committee chair, and Soejima Hiroyuki (Society for the Protection of Japan) as secretary-general. On 3 October 1979, an 'all-out national rally for achievement of legalization of imperial era names' was held with 19,000 participants. The National Council for Achievement of Legalization of Imperial Era

---

16 The Democratic Socialist Party was considered as a right-wing socialist party due to its opposition to communism.

46

Names proceeded to create regional organizations, but these typically overlapped with bodies affiliated with the Society for Honoring the Glorious War Dead (Miyachi 1981).

Through regional resolutions and vigorous expansion of a variety of groups, on 6 June 1979, the Era Name Law (Gengo-ho) was finally enacted by the Diet. The Era Name Law is an extremely brief law composed of only two articles: Article One, 'Era names will be set by government ordinance,' and Article Two, 'An era name will only be changed upon succession to the imperial throne [of a new emperor],' with a supplementary provision declaring that the Showa era name would be deemed to have been determined in accordance with Article One, since it was already the Showa era at that time. By October 1979, resolutions calling for the legislation of imperial era names had been made in 45 prefectures (excluding Okinawa and Hokkaido) and 800 municipalities. The era-name legislation movement had achieved its objective.

The birth of Japan Conference

The various groups that led the era-name legislation movement launched new action as soon as the law was enacted. In October 1981, two years after the law's enactment, the National Council for Achievement of Legalization of Imperial Era Names was reorganized into the National Conference to Protect Japan. Kase Toshikazu (former Ambassador to the United Nations) became president, and Mayuzumi Toshiro (composer) and Soejima Hiroyuki (Society for the Protection of Japan) became steering committee chair and secretary-general, respectively. The group was joined by leading cultural figures such Eto Jun, Shimizu Ikutaro, Uno Seiichi and Miyoshi Osamu, former Self-Defense Force (SDF) bureaucrats like Kurisu Hiroomi (former Chair of the Joint Staff Council), Takeda Goro (former Chair of the Joint Staff Council) and Nagano Shigeto (former Chief of Staff of the Japanese Ground Self-Defense Force), as well as numerous LDP Diet members and business leaders (Narita 1982). However, individual members 'needed either to belong to or have a letter of introduction from an office-bearer from a related body' to join (Aoki 1986: 50–1).

In contrast to the organizations discussed above, which began with a central organizing body, and then established regional bodies by

Chapter 2

a touring caravan, the National Conference to Protect Japan was preceded by regional bodies. On 5 September 1981, the Prefectural Residents' Council (Fumin kaigi) was launched in Osaka, followed by the 7 September establishment of the Hiroshima Prefectural Residents' Council for Protecting Japan (Nihon o mamoru Hiroshima kenmin kaigi), and the Aichi Prefectural Residents' Council (Aichi kenmin kaigi) on 8 September; and in October that same year, the National Conference to Protect Japan was formed in Tokyo as a central organization of the regional bodies. After the creation of the central body, branches were systematically established at prefectural and municipal levels, but 'most offices and contact locations were regional branches of the House of Growth or Association of Shinto Shrines and branch policies were largely 'the same as the central organization, with hardly any individuality' (Sato 1982: 230–1). The primary objective of the National Conference to Protect Japan was constitutional reform. As Sato Tatsuya points out, the National Conference was an 'all-out mobilization by the constitutional amendment faction,' and a 'constitutional amendment movement from the "grassroots"' (Sato 1982: 227) with a distinct vision of constitutional reform. Its tactic of arousing public opinion had been shared by groups since the Society for Honoring the Glorious War Dead, but the National Conference agitated for vague constitutional amendments, instead homing in on convincing people of the necessity for constitutional reform by enumerating specific problematic issues of defense and education.

The most controversial action undertaken by the National Conference in education was the compilation and publication of *New Edition Japanese History* (Shinpen Nihon shi). This publication was approved by the Ministry of Education in 1986 for use as a senior high school textbook, but it was strongly criticized, mainly by historians. Kitajima Manji argued it was 'non-scientific' and ignored the findings of historical research, noting that it was based on an emperor-centric historiography comprising a 'historical view that saw [Japan's] history as pivoting on the emperor and the national polity' (Kitajima 1987: 12). After it passed the government screening process, the campaign for its adoption was invigorated, and 32 schools chose the *New Edition* for the 1987 fiscal year. In total, 8,321 copies were distributed, an adoption ratio of 0.7 percent of senior high school textbooks that year (Momota 1987).

After the Era Name Law passed and the textbook was compiled, both the Society and the National Conference turned their attention to various

48

new activities. These included a movement to mark the 60th anniversary of Emperor Hirohito's ascension to the throne; celebrations of Emperor Akihito's coronation; a commemoration of the war dead on the 50th anniversary of the end of the war; and advocating for a new constitution.

At a hundred-member committee meeting of the Society for the Protection of Japan on 19 March 1997, the decision was made to merge with the National Conference to Protect Japan and set up a new organization. The following day, the 14th general meeting of the National Conference also decided to form a new organization, and the Japan Conference was established on 30 May 1977. It is reportedly the largest conservative group in Japan today.

After the amalgamation of the two groups, Breath of Japan (*Nihon no ibuki*), originally published by the National Conference and continued by the Japan Conference, expressed 'apprehension' that 'national fighting spirit as an independent state has faded,' 'the rampancy of the historical view of the Tokyo [war crimes] trials' had resulted in 'abject apology diplomacy vis-à-vis other countries,' and had 'given rise to such serious social problems as the breakdown of the family and education' in contemporary Japanese society.[17] Furthermore, it describes the new organization as having been founded with the aims of 'breaking the deadlock of our country's worsening crisis situation, looking to the future of the state and members of the nation that live in the new century, and [aspiring] for formation of a national movement aimed at building a new country and human resource development.'

The primary objective of Japan Conference was constitutional reform. In his inaugural address as its president, the Chair of Wacoal Corporation Tsukamoto Koichi, remarked: 'The democracy granted [to us] in the postwar at first glance sounds pretty, but now all kinds of ill effects have emerged,' and therefore, 'first, above all, [we] must change the Constitution. If that is rotten at the core, this country will be unable to regain its feet.'[18] The article proceeded to outline the new organization's vision:

Japan Conference raised the following six points: 1) prompt approaches to current issues; 2) collaboration with the Colloquium of Diet Mem-

---

17 *Nippon no ibuki* (Breath of Japan), 1997, January issue.
18 *Nippon no ibuki*, 1997, July issue.

Chapter 2

bers formed in response to the establishment of Japan Conference; 3) expansion of a "grassroots movement of people who love their country"; 4) initiatives for a women's movement and education movement; 5) construction of a nationwide information network; and 6) cultural projects for "conveying the beautiful Japanese spirit."[19]

Its pursuit of Constitutional reform, its collaboration with Diet members and the expansion of a 'national movement,' are shared with groups from the Society for Honoring the Glorious War Dead onwards, but its approach to current issues, its development of a women's movement, construction of an information network, and so forth were unique responses to the times.

The characteristics of organized conservative movements

The Japan Conference expanded in the late 1970s, assuming responsibility for the campaigns for official visits to Yasukuni Shrine and the legislation of imperial era-names. As we have seen, they were successful in their campaign for the era-name legislation, but the campaign to legislate official visits to Yasukuni Shrine was not as clearcut. Although they failed to achieve the legislated result they sought, they arguably achieved a measure of success in the sense that the prime minister, some cabinet ministers, and others began to formally visit and pay their respects at the shrine.

Two distinct characteristics are notable about the two campaigns that launched in the late 1970s. First, regarding their organizational formation, as we have seen, they initially created a central body in Tokyo, and then established regional headquarters and branches. Thus, the conservative movement was advanced by strengthening horizontal ties among conservative movement groups and the creation of regional organizations 'from the top down.'

Second, regional assemblies were exploited to realize the movement's goals. Both the campaign for official visits to Yasukuni Shrine and for era-name legislation employed a strategy of regional bodies petitioning local regional assemblies to pass resolutions. The regional assemblies' passage of corresponding resolutions subsequently gave impetus to the

---

19 *Nippon no ibuki*, 1997, July issue.

50

center. Both of these movements involved numerous collaborating groups and individuals across Japan, who assertively promoted the movements through their regional assemblies.

Having applied the term 'organized conservative movements' to nationwide activist groups whose organizational structure comprised a central organization and regional bodies, in the next section I will examine new tendencies in the conservative movement from the 1990s which differ from these 'organized conservative movements.'

The grassroots turn of the conservative movement

Japanese Society for History Textbook Reform

At the same time as the Japan Conference was forming, a movement appeared that focused on a different history textbook issue than the conventional conservative movement, triggered by a series of articles by University of Tokyo Professor Fujioka Nobukatsu in the journal *Shakaika kyoiku* (Social studies education), starting from April 1994, entitled 'How to remodel modern history lessons.' Fujioka criticized the history education of the time as having a 'masochistic historical view' and a 'historical view [reflecting] the Tokyo [war-crimes] trials.' These articles advocated history education based on a 'liberal historical view.'

Fujioka posited four characteristics of this 'liberal historical view': 1) a healthy nationalism; 2) realism; 3) distrust of ideology; and 4) criticism of bureaucracy (Fujioka 1996). Historians and educators fiercely criticized Fujioka's 'liberal historical view,' with Moriwaki Takeo identifying three significant problems with Fujioka's proposals, namely: 1) 'dubious submissions vis-à-vis the fruits of past history studies' such as the number of victims of the Nanking massacre and military comfort women; 2) the 'institution of upheaval in history education;' and 3) Fujioka's problematization of what he calls the 'one-country pacifism' and 'postwar democracy' constituting the 'prevailing thought of the postwar' (Moriwaki 1997: 40). History scholars continue to vehemently criticize that first dimension which, as Moriwaki pointed out, ignores the accomplishments and accumulation of history studies, but at a symposium on this 'Fujioka issue' held by the Nara Prefecture History Research Group (Nara-ken rekishi kenkyukai), there was no shortage of scholars and teachers who sincerely accepted points 2) and

Chapter 2

3) which, Moriwaki pointed out, were about the current state of history education, and expressed a desire to ponder them together (Nara-ken rekishi kenkyukai ed. 1997). At first, the 'Fujioka issue' was potentially an opportunity to reconsider what kind of historical view children's education should be based upon, but that was not fulfilled.

In 1995, in the January issue of *Social Studies Education*, Fujioka announced the launch of a new magazine to implement history education based on a 'liberal view of history.' Moreover, a Liberal Historical View Study Group (Jiyu-shugi shikan kenkyukai) was organized to solicit contributors for this new magazine, named *Reforms in Modern History Teaching* (Kingendai shi no jugyo kaikaku). Its first issue was published in September, and the second in November 1995. Sales were reportedly more than 10,000 copies each (Murai 1997).

Initially, there was potential for positive discussion of history education at the Liberal Historical View Study Group. However, the intention to readdress history education pedagogy soon receded into the background, displaced by advocates of historical revisionism. In January 1996, the *Sankei Shinbun* began to search for writers based on 'teaching materials based on [historical] figures' carried in *Reforms in Modern History Teaching*, and launched a series of articles entitled: 'The history that textbooks do not teach.' At the same time, Fujioka published a string of commentaries in *Shokun!*, *Bungei Shunju*, *Seiron*, and similar magazines. Moreover, in July, an incident occurred that completely changed the study group's direction. The Liberal Historical View Study Group put out a statement demanding the deletion from textbooks of descriptions relating to military comfort women. One consequence of this was that field-oriented teachers who had joined the group to explore new pedagogy for history and social studies left the study group. In their place, non-teachers interested in historical, political, and diplomatic issues began to join (Murai 1997).[20]

In 1997, when Japan Conference was formed, the Textbook Society was instigated by nine prominent figures, including Fujioka, Agawa

---

20 Murai interviewed teachers who had been members of the Liberal Historical View Study Group, many of whom reported leaving the group because of its statement on military comfort women. Teachers who left had agreed with the group's 'intent to develop classes that departed from the conventional view, and to that end, aimed to promote exchange of diverse ways of thinking,' and had anticipated the group to be a place for exploring new lesson development (Murai 1997: 200).

Sawako, Kobayashi Yoshinori, Hayashi Mariko, and Fukada Yusuke. The society produced the *New History Textbook* (Atarashii rekishi kyokasho) and *New Civics Textbook* (Atarashii komin kyokasho) to promote teaching a revisionist history that denied the Nanking massacre and the existence of military comfort women, and then campaigned for these books to be widely adopted. In the *New History Textbook*, its guiding principle is described as: 'To learn history is to learn how people of the past thought, what they worried about, and how they overcame problems amid what happened in the past – in other words, to learn how people of the past lived' (Fujioka et al. 2005: 6). There is extremely little discussion of the invasion of China and the Korean Peninsula in relation to the Asia-Pacific War, and the Japanese military invasion of South-East Asia is depicted in a positive light, with the 'victory' of the attack on Pearl Harbor being portrayed as having 'nurtured the dream of independence and bolstered the courage of the peoples of South-East Asia and India. The sweeping advance of the Japanese military in South-East Asia was made possible for the very reason of the local inhabitants' cooperation' (Fujioka et al. 2005: 206). The adoption rate of the *New History Textbook* was 0.039 percent in 2001–02, 0.4 percent in 2005–06, (Ku 2009), and 1.6 percent in 2009–10,[21] slightly increasing year by year.[22]

However, from the beginning there was enmity within the Textbook Society's directorate (Ku 2009), and in 2006 some directors left and established a new Society for the Revival of Japanese Education (Nippon kyoiku saisei kiko). Upon this impetus, the Textbook Society and the Society for the Revival of Japanese Education created separate junior high school history textbooks, each from the standpoint of historical revisionism. The former began publishing textbooks through Jiyusha, and the latter through Ikuhosha, a subsidiary of Fusosha, and the two groups expanded their campaigns to get the texts adopted (Tawara 2008).

---

21 Atarashii rekishi kyokasho o Tsukuru kai (2009), 'Tsukuru kai publishes statement on adoption result. "Tsukuru kai's history textbooks" smash 20,000 copy mark! Copyright suit "will not appeal" from a broader perspective,' *Tsukuru kai Web News*, no. 264. (http://www.tsukurukai.com/01_top_news/file_news/news_264.html. Accessed September 26, 2012).

22 Various school history textbook battles had been fought before the conservative group intervened, as in the 'Ienaga lawsuits.' Nozaki (2008) discusses the *New Edition Japanese History* and the *New History Textbook*, situating them in debates about history education in postwar Japan.

Chapter 2

The Textbook Society had been formed by people who had no prior connection with the conservative movement, and it had different characteristics than the 'organized conservative movement.'

The first difference was that the Textbook Society's regional branches arose spontaneously, led by local citizens, in contrast to the 'top-down' creation of regional offices by the organized conservative movement. Ueno Yoko conducted a survey on the Kanagawa Prefecture branch of Textbook Society called History Circle (Oguma and Ueno 2003). While the History Circle was supposed to be a regional body comprising interested parties from the Textbook Society, it had originally formed as a study group of people who had established rapport at separate prefectural gatherings following a symposium held by the Textbook Society in 1998. Events unfolded as follows: the History Circle was established in October 1998, and in February the following year, after the launch of the Kanagawa Prefecture branch of the Textbook Society, the 'group of interested parties' was positioned as part of the branch's activity amid negotiations with the branch president (Oguma and Ueno 2003).

In response to Ueno's survey of the History Circle, Oguma Eiji discusses the novelty of its configuration, identifying five characteristics never before seen in the conservative movement: 1) its emphasis on voluntary participation; 2) its being a 'loosely-connected composite body' without fixed office-bearers or hierarchical relationships; 3) its taking a 'semi-independent' posture vis-à-vis the upper echelon; 4) its utilization of communication technology such as the Internet; and 5) its self-reference as a movement by 'ordinary citizens' who distance themselves from existing political parties (Oguma and Ueno 2003: 189).

The second trait refers to its participants' mindset. According to Ueno's survey, there were some elderly men with experience of the war in the History Circle, but they were a minority. In practical terms, the people in charge of the movement had sparse consciousness of the emperor or imperial house, and differed in other ways from those who had so far led the conservative movement. History Circle participants had shared hostility towards the 'left wing,' the Asahi newspaper, and bureaucrats, but they apparently felt 'anxiety at not having a term that positively defined themselves' (Oguma and Ueno 2003: 197), and were 'trying to secure a stable identity' by mutually confirming that they shared the same values (Oguma and Ueno 2003: 203)

54

Collaboration in the conservative movement: Opposition to gender-equality

Although the organized conservative movement that formed in the 1970s and 1980s had a different shape and different participants than the new conservative movements arising from the 1990s onwards, they shared common objectives. The opposition to gender equality that emerged in the early 2000s was advanced through the collaboration of new and old conservative groups. The preamble in the Basic Law for a Gender-Equal Society enacted in 1999 states: '[I]t has become a matter of urgent importance to realize a gender-equal society in which men and women respect the other's human rights and share their responsibilities, and every citizen is able to fully exercise their individuality and abilities regardless of gender.' From around 2000, feminism, which was deemed to have influenced this Basic Law, began to be intensely criticized, and the term 'gender-free' was the central point of contention.[23] Arguments that gender equality and the idea of 'gender-free' would 'erase' gender differences between males and females,' deny 'orthodox masculinity (*otokorashisa*) and femininity (*onnarashisa*),' and were 'plotting to destroy the family and cause household breakdown, and repudiate traditional culture like the Dolls' Festival (celebrated by girls) and carp streamers (flown to celebrate Boy's Day)' began to appear regularly in conservative media such as the *Sankei Shinbun*, *Seiron* and *Shokun!*

In the women's movement and feminist studies, this phenomenon is called 'backlash.' U.S. journalist Susan Faludi (1991) coined the term meaning a 'recoil' or 'rebound' against the advance of the women's movement and gender equality policies. Faludi was responding to the promotion of 'family-values' policies that began in the 1980s during the Reagan administration, which pushed back against the progress of second-wave feminism. She especially noted the subtle ways this backlash was expressed, as in the growing tendency to negatively portray women who had entered the workforce in media such as films, novels, and advertisements. These same tendencies started to appear in the 2000s in Japan.[24]

---

23 'Gender-free' is an expression coined by teachers at the chalk face who were engaged in the practice of gender-equality education and at women's centers, with the sense of 'developing gender sensitivity.'

24 In this book, I will employ the term 'movement against gender equality' rather than 'backlash' when focusing particularly on movement groups

Chapter 2

The target at this time was not solely the Basic Law for a Gender-Equal Society. The practices undertaken since about 2002 by teachers who aimed for gender equality at schools through the provision of a 'gender-free education,' and the introduction of mixed rolls of male and female students' names, were also targets of the backlash (Kimura 2005). Criticism of sex education intensified, as well. This was taken up in the Diet by House of Councillors Member Yamatani Eriko, who questioned the inclusion of information on the pill and abortion in a pamphlet for junior high school students entitled *Love and Body Book for Puberty* (Shishunki no tame no rabu & bodi BOOK) produced by an auxiliary organization of the Ministry of Health, Labor and Welfare. A lament that 'extreme sex education' was being conducted in school settings began to be widely echoed in the conservative media and conservative movement groups, including claims that teaching the names for genitalia and contraceptive methods was 'imposing sex on children.'[25]

Conservative groups were the driving force for the 'backlash,' but they found ample support in the conservative media, conservative Diet members and members of regional assemblies. In addition to Japan Conference and Textbook Society, the leading groups included the Shinto Political Alliance (Shinto seiji renmei), Japan Council, and Japan Youth Council, which also led the movement opposed to gender equality along with the Association of 100 Regional Assembly Members and Citizens for Educational Rebirth (Kyoiku saisei chiho giin hyakunin to shimin no kai) (Ida 2006). Following the enactment of the Basic Law, gender equality ordinances were adopted by local government bodies around the nation,

---

because 'backlash' refers to a broader 'phenomenon' than social movements, including political and cultural changes, while this book focuses on social movements.

25 Amidst these debates, the 'Nanao Special Needs School Incident' erupted in 2003 when teaching material called 'The body song (*Karada uta*)' was being used to promote understanding by children with intellectual disabilities of the makeup of their own and other people's bodies. The song's inclusion of the names for genitalia was raised at the Tokyo Metropolitan Assembly, and three Assembly members and representatives from the Tokyo Metropolitan Board of Education conducted an inspection of the school and confiscated the teaching material. The school principal was penalized. The principal mounted a court case against Tokyo Metropolis and the Tokyo Metropolitan Assembly members involved, citing unjustifiable interference in education, and seeking reversal of the penalty. A Tokyo High Court judgement found in favor of the principal in 2003. See Kodama (2009) for details.

56

with Chiba Prefecture being the only prefecture in Japan without a gender equality ordinance due to the strong objections of these conservative groups. An opposition movement led by Japan Conference and Textbook Society grew in Chiba Prefecture, according to Funabashi Kuniko, who, as a member of Chiba Prefecture Gender Equality Ordinance Network (Chiba-ken danjo byodo jorei nettowaku), was an eye-witness to the tug-of-war over the Chiba Prefecture ordinance.

Funabashi posits that in the 'backlash,' a movement involving Japan Conference, its parliamentarian alliance, the Textbook Society, and media including the *Sankei Shinbun* 'formed laterally in an extremely systematic manner, based on their view of the state,' and 'established lateral ties as a grassroots conservative faction at the juncture of 2000' (Funabashi 2007: 25–6). The growth, jointly and severally, of the Textbook Society, a conservative group with a new style of activism, and Japan Conference, an older type of conservative organization, is characteristic of the movement opposed to gender equality.

A further characteristic of the movement against gender equality was arguably the conspicuous action by local grassroots groups. When local government bodies moved to create gender equality ordinances, an opposition movement began to spread, driven by local people. While on the one hand, Japan Conference and Textbook Society have been credited for playing a core role in the anti-gender-equality movement, Yamaguchi Tomomi, Saito Masami and Ogiue Chiki (2012), focus on groups that led the movement in the regions, such as Yamaguchi and Chiba Prefectures. They point out that Nippon Jiji Hyoronsha, a publishing company based in Yamaguchi Prefecture, began printing articles expressing opposition to gender equality in its newspaper, *Japan Current Review* (Nippon jiji hyoron) quite early, and had taken the lead in the anti-gender-equality movement. Other groups that objected to gender equality were formed, including Kyoto Citizens' Group to Ponder a Society Jointly Created by Men and Women (Danjo kyoso shakai o kangaeru Kyoto shimin no kai) in Kyoto City, Association Aiming for a Wholesome Gender-equal Society (Kenzen na danjo kyodo sankaku shakai o mezasu kai)' in Ehime Prefecture, and Prefectural Citizens' Network for Human Development (Hitozukuri kenmin nettowaku)' in Niigata City. These groups petitioned regional assemblies to limit the effects of gender equality ordinances, or campaigned to prevent the enactment of ordinances.

Chapter 2

The action conservative movement and movement radicalization

In the late 2000s, many groups with differing approaches began to emerge, many at the grassroots-level. These were collectively dubbed the 'action conservative movement.' Their rise coincided with a period in which public opinion towards South Korea declined. Figure 2.2 shows changes in the responses to a question in a 'Public opinion poll on diplomacy' implemented by the Cabinet Office that asked: 'Do you feel any affinity towards South Korea?' Initially, the majority of responses were negative, but in the early 2000s, partly due to the influence of the so-called Korean wave, responses became more positive. However, in the late 2000s, the trend rapidly turned negative again, and remain so today. Several factors may contribute to these negative attitudes towards South Korea, including diplomatic tensions over territorial rights to an island called Takeshima in Japanese, or Dokdo in Korean, and major events such as the World Cup which was jointly held by Japan and South Korea in 2002. The role of the Internet which spread rapidly in this period cannot be overlooked. According to the Ministry of Internal Affairs and Communications, in the '2009 Survey on communications usage trends' (Somusho 2009), the Internet dissemination rate, which had been 37.1 percent in 2000, had grown to 78.0 percent in 2011. Blatant expressions of animosity towards South Korea began to appear frequently on the Internet, and conservative groups that spread that discourse on the Internet extended their activities in the offline world (Okamoto 2013).[26]

Yasuda Koichi's nonfiction work, *The Internet and Patriotism* (2012), widely publicized the 'action conservative movement.' Among the various groups associated with this movement, the Association of Citizens is the largest organization advocating racism/ethnocentrism, hatred of foreigners, and their expulsion. Since its establishment in 2007, it has repeatedly held political rallies, demonstration marches and so forth on the fringes of areas with dense populations of Korean residents. Its membership was estimated at 15,000 as of May 2015.[27] Discrimination against ethnic minorities, especially resident-Koreans,

---

26 Taka (2015) analyzes the animosity and hate speech towards Japan-residing Koreans on the Internet.

27 However, as many writers have indicated, strictly speaking this should be the 'number of registrants,' because anyone who registered their email address could become a member of the association (Yasuda 2012, Higuchi 2014).

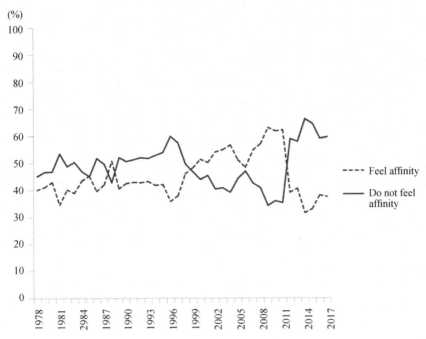

Figure 2.2 Changes in feelings of affinity towards South Korea
Created by the author based on Naikakufu (multiple years), *Gaikō ni kansuru yoron chōsa* (Opinion poll on diplomacy), https://survey.gov-online.go.jp/index-gai.html.

has long been widespread, but the Association of Citizens is recognized as the first movement to brazenly demonstrate its discriminatory views in public (Higuchi 2014). As the group attracted more attention, the term 'hate speech' received greater social recognition, as well.[28]

Soon, the so-called 'counterculture' movement began protesting against activities by these so-called action conservatives which blatantly expressed discriminatory sentiments, objecting to racial and ethnic bias. These counter protests have contributed to a gradual decline in the number of participants in the activities of the various action conservative groups. Today, the Association of Citizens is less vigorous. The effectiveness of the counter protests was enhanced by the June 2016 Act on the Promotion of Efforts to Eliminate Unfair Discriminatory Speech and Behaviour against Persons Originating from Outside Japan (known as the Hate Speech Elimination Act, or HSEA), and the 2014 resignation of Sakurai Makoto, the founder of the Association of Citizens, who then established

---

28 See Yasuda (2015) on the Association of Citizens.

Chapter 2

the Japan First Party (Nippon Dai-ichi-to) in 2016, and committed to its activities.

The Association of Citizens is often discussed in the context of chauvinistic movements (Higuchi 2014), and is also associated with the action conservative movement. However, few previous studies in Japan have examined it from the perspective of a conservative movement. According to Yasuda, the 'action conservative movement' refers to 'conservatives who leapt out into the streets' (Yasuda 2012: 152). The conventional conservative movement, from organized groups such as Japan Conference to the grassroots conservative groups from Textbook Society onwards, made lectures and study groups their main activities. By contrast, the groups called the 'action conservative movement' exhibit a tendency towards more direct actions such as streetside speeches, demonstration marches, and protest action.

The action conservative movement comprises a variety of groups. Yasuda (2012) identifies five alongside the Association of Citizens: the Society to Seek Restoration of Sovereignty (Shuken kaifuku o mezasu kai),' represented by Nishimura Shuhei and positioned as the root of the movement; Kanetomo Takayuki's New Society for Expelling Foreigners ([Shin joi undo] Haigaisha),[29] which shifted their form of activism from a right-wing movement to an action conservative movement; the NPO Movement to Eradicate Foreigner Crime (NPO gaikokujin hanzai tsuiho undo) (President: Arikado Daisuke), which became an incorporated NPO; Yeomen of the Guard (Shin'eitai) led by 'Yeomen,' which conducted training in mountainous areas with a view to starting a revolution; and Citizens' Group to Protect Japan (Nippon o mamoru shimin no kai (Nichigokai)), represented by Kuroda Daisuke and focused on criticizing the lay Buddhist organization Soka Gakkai.

The postwar Japanese conservative movement had started by building collaborative relationships with politicians and bureaucrats and focused on negotiation, lobbying and elections. From the 1970s into the 1980s, multiple groups merged, reorganized, and expanded into a 'national movement.' In the 1990s, along with the organized conservative groups, citizens launched grassroots campaigns in their local areas, and began activities; and from the late 2000s until today, various grassroots

---

29 In 2012, the New Society for Expelling Foreigners issued a "Declaration of dissolution" and disbanded (http://haigai.exblog.jp/. Accessed January 17, 2015).

60

conservative groups became increasingly radicalized and made the streets their site of action.

The emergence of conservative women's groups

In this chapter I have sketched the development of the conservative movement in postwar Japan. What position do the conservative women's groups occupy in this history? The Japanese conservative movement was traditionally led by male participants, but in recent decades numerous women-centered groups have been formed, largely triggered by opposition to gender equality. Between 2000 and 2006, when criticism of the Basic Law for a Gender-Equal Society and feminism was prevalent, many new groups and bodies of conservative women were established. Japan Conference formed the Japanese Women's Association (Nihon josei no kai) in September 2001, spelling out three objectives: 'Let's build Japanese households,' 'Let's make schools ones that nurture children's abundant sensitivities,' and 'Let's draw together the power of women who devote themselves to the country and to society' (Nihon Josei no Kai 2007). In a similar vein, Japan Conference's Osaka Women's Division conducted 'signature-collecting campaigns demanding a sensible gender-equality ordinance.'[30] Grassroots groups with the word 'women' in their title formed in all areas to oppose the establishment of gender-equality ordinances: Ube City in Yamaguchi Prefecture spawned two: Women's Forum Ube and Ube Women's Group to Think about Gender Equality (Koshiba 2008), while in Osaka City, the Osaka Women's Group for Thinking about 'Gender-Free' (Jenda furī o kangaeru Osaka josei no kai) held a 'citizen's gathering to think about gender equality' at Creo Osaka Nishi, the Osaka Municipal Gender Equality Center, in October 2002.[31]

In the late 2000s, numerous groups with a few select members coalesced in the action conservative movement, and female-centered groups were prominent. The most energetic campaigners were Gentle Breeze, Flower Clock, and Justice and Peace. The latter were also known as 'Nadeshiko Action,' with '*nadeshiko*' both referring to dianthus

---

30 'Regional focus: Osaka Prefecture success in branch activities and women's movement closely connected to the area,' *Nippon no ibuki*, June issue, 2003, p. 25.

31 '"Citizens' gathering to think about gender equality' held in Osaka,' *Nippon no ibuki*, December issue, 2002, pp. 24–5.

Chapter 2

flowers and evoking an ideal of modest Japanese femininity. Formed in 2007, the objective of Gentle Breeze was to become a 'group of women that loved Japan,' who 'shared a sense of crisis at such things as the biased reporting in the mass media, and at the classes that took a masochistic historical view in the educational space.'[32] Its estimated membership was 877 (of whom 307 were men).[33] It focused on holding demonstration marches in collaboration with male-centered groups, as well as activities such as streetside speeches and soliciting signatures. Flower Clock was established in April 2010, primarily for 'women aged from their twenties to forties such as housewives in the midst of child-rearing,' with a published membership of 1040.[34] Flower Clock mainly engaged in political protests, and regularly delivers speeches on topics such as 'Beware of the lies of South and North Korea!' and 'Beware of the lies of the mass media!' Justice and Peace specialized in the comfort women issue. It was created in 2011 to protest against the '1000th Commemorative Wednesday Demonstration' held in front of the Foreign Ministry to pressure the Japanese government to settle the comfort women issue. Its representative, Yamamoto Yumiko, enjoyed extensive exposure in the conservative media and stands out for lobbying the United Nations on the issue.

In the 2010s, numerous books were published by women connected with conservative movement groups, with titles emphasizing the links among 'women,' 'patriotism' and 'Japan,' including Sanami Yuko's *Women and Patriotism* (Joshi to aikoku) (2013); Kawasoe Keiko et al.'s *National Defense Women on the Go: What is wrong with dianthus flowers [Japanese women] loving their country?* (Kokubo joshi ga yuku: nadeshiko ga kuni o omou ten ani ga warui) (2014); Justice and Peace's Yamamoto Yumiko's *Japan's Pride that Women Protect: A chronicle of activities of the Nadeshiko [action group] that invokes the truth of the comfort women issue* (Josei ga mamoru Nihon no hokori: 'ianfu mondai' no shinjitsu o uttaeru nadeshiko katsudo roku) (2014); Sugita Mio's *The Revival of Nadeshiko: What female politicians can do* (Nadeshiko fukkatsu: josei seijika ga dekiru koto) (2014);[35] and Kawasoe Keiko and

---

32 http://www.soyokaze2009.com/index.php (accessed August 27, 2019)

33 http://www.soyokaze2009.com/soyokaze.php (accessed August 27, 2019)

34 http://www.hanadokei2010.com/hanadokei.php (accessed August 27, 2019)

35 House of Representatives member Sugita Mio attracted attention in 2018

Sugita Mio's *The 'History Wars' are a Women's Fight* ('Rekishi-sen' wa onna no tatakai) (2016).

In the context of the Japanese conservative movement, it was not until the 2000s that groups structured around women began to emerge. In this period, gender gradually came to be recognized as a social issue and a contentious matter within the conservative movement. There was a precursor movement in the late 1990s that had protested and criticized proposals for a system of optional separate surnames for married couples, but the tendency for multiple groups to collaborate in a new grassroots movement only arose in opposition to gender equality.

From a movement perspective, it could be argued that the changes in the conservative movement itself strongly influenced the activization of the women's conservative movement in this period. The organization of the various conservative groups that had continued to be pursued from the 1970s, starting from the movements for official visits to the Yasukuni Shrine and era-name legislation and ending at Japan Conference, and the emergence from the late 1990s of a grassroots movement as elucidated by Oguma and Ueno (2003) which took a similar form to that of traditional civic movements, arguably could have led to hastening formation of a conservative movement by women themselves. Women with a shared problem-consciousness gathered to create small grassroots activist groups through networking with organized conservative groups and forming connections with religious groups and bodies in their respective localities, or by exploiting the new medium of the Internet. We must not forget that changes in the circumstances surrounding women in Japanese society, including the Basic Law for a Gender-Equal Society, also prompted women to expand the conservative movement.

Emphasizing the fact that they are 'grassroots' women not from the intelligentsia – being neither academics nor journalists – is a new phenomenon since 2000. Moreover, although this phenomenon has not received much attention, from the perspective of the history of the Japanese conservative movement, it might presage a huge change.

---

for her discriminatory statements vis-à-vis sexual minorities including LGBT people, and for fiercely criticizing researchers who had been selected to receive Grants-in-Aid for Scientific Research (*kakenhi*) for studies on the Japanese military comfort women system. The latter behavior came to be called '*kakenhi* bashing,' and a complaint was filed against Sugita for defamation by the researchers on February 12, 2019.

PART II
The Conservative Movement and The Family

Part II

In Part II, I focus on the conservative women's movement that bases its position on the status of 'mothers.' Conservative movements are generally thought to place more importance on the family and norms like the gendered division of labor than on individual (women's) freedom or rights. However, the words of their female participants suggest that the conservative movement's idealization of the family based on stereotypical gender roles is not monolithic.

Throughout each of the chapters in Part II, I look at the claims and activities of women in the conservative movement who engage in action from their position as 'mothers.' I examine the opposition to gender equality as an example of a women's conservative movement that takes a 'maternal' position. As discussed in the previous chapters, the opposition to gender equality expanded in the early 2000s, making gender a contentious issue for the first time in the conservative movement. Moreover, as we saw in Chapter One, women's activity was mobilized within the conservative movement, and numerous grassroots groups with 'women' in their name were established from this period onwards.

The Basic Law for a Gender-Equal Society was enacted in 1999 and was universally opposed by conservative groups. In 1985, Japan ratified the Convention on the Elimination of all Forms of Discrimination against Women, but for a long time, the administration of women's affairs continued to be conducted independently by each government ministry in a 'vertically segmented administrative system,' and the Basic Law was intended to establish a national mechanism for deciding on an inclusive, long-term gender equality policy. The Council for Gender Equality (Danjo kyodo sankaku shingikai) set up in 1994 released its 'Vision of gender equality' report in July 1996, and the 'Plan for Gender Equality 2000' in December 1996.[1] When the 'Vision of gender equality' was compiled, in particular, unprecedented initiatives were implemented, including the first appearance of the word 'gender' (*jendā*) in Japanese official documents (Osawa 2002).

These steps led to the creation of the Basic Law for a Gender-Equal Society. Although various shortcomings in this legislation have

---

1 See Suzuki, Seki and Hori (2014) on the precursor to the Basic Law.

The Conservative Movement and the Family

been pointed out,[2] it is nevertheless deemed to be a 'historic victory for feminism' (Muta 2006: 202–4).

The opponents of gender equality criticized the Basic Law and called for its repeal, arguing that gender equality and the idea of 'gender-free' would 'do away with proper masculinity (*otokorashisa*) and proper femininity (*onnarashisa*),' 'destroy the family,' 'repudiate housewives,' and 'repudiate traditional culture'. That movement, which expanded with the involvement of media such as the *Seiron* and *Shokun!* magazines, and the *Sankei Shinbun* newspaper, began to be called a 'backlash' among Japanese feminist scholars and the feminist movement.[3] As discussed in Chapter Two, Susan Faludi (1991) used the term 'backlash' to refer to the 'reaction' or 'rebound' against feminism and advances in gender equality policies. She was specifically referring to the advance of so-called family-values policies during the Reagan administration of the 1980s which sought to stem the tide of second-wave feminism, and the growing tendency for entertainment media (film, TV, books) to portray women who were successful in the workforce as being 'hysterical' or suffering from mental illness. The term 'backlash' came to be used widely by feminist scholars and activists. Ann Cudd (2002) theoretically refines the definition of 'backlash' to mean an attempt by people who have been deprived of certain advantages or privileges through changes in the social system to attempt to recover their losses by using such means as the distortion and misinterpretation of facts, or groundless labeling.

---

2   The feminist critiques include: 'Doesn't overemphasizing "*danjo* (males and females)" make it heterosexist? (Muta 2006); and the fact that the expression 'women's human rights' used in the 'Vision of gender equality' was not employed in the Basic Law (Kaino 2006).

3   Scholars differ as to how to determine the 'backlash' period, but in this book, I deem the phenomenon of rebound vis-à-vis gender equality and 'gender-free' from 2000 to about 2006 to be a 'backlash.' To the best of my knowledge, Ito (2002) was the first in Japan to use the term 'backlash' in the initial sense of a reaction or rebound against gender equality. Writers such as Seki (2016) and Wada and Inoue (2010) criticize the 'selective surname system' for married couples proposed in the late 1990s, while others view the historical revisionism that emerged around the time of the founding of the Textbook Society as being a 'backlash,' but I would not call these pre-2000 incidents as 'backlash' because I consider that moves by the various conservative factions since the 1990s have been retrospectively called 'backlash,' based on a frame of recognition that the movement and critical discourse against gender equality constituted 'backlash.'

Part II

Of course, the Japanese feminist movement was strongly criticized and condemned long before this 'backlash.' In 'The Politics of Teasing,' Ehara Yumiko analyzes magazine articles on Japanese women's liberation in the 1970s (Ehara 1985). When women's lib emerged in Japan, the mass media and journalism reported on it with curious eyes. Ehara points out that expressions used to ridicule and tease the women who took part in women's lib were effective in invalidating its political claims. However, such 'teasing' that was directed at feminism was not called a 'backlash.' The reaction of the 2000s is considered to be the first 'backlash' in Japan because it was only then that the feminist movement began to move the authorities, and to have a presence and influence that left no room even for teasing.

The opposition to gender equality by conservative activist groups came together with 2006 as a turning-point, after the opposition movement had achieved some measure of success in the form of a 'reversal' by the gender equality authorities. In the 2005 'Second Basic Plan for Gender Equality,' a new note was added saying that 'denial of difference between genders [and] repudiation of the family or such traditional cultural practices as the Dolls' Festival differed from the gender-equal society sought by nationals.' Furthermore, in 2006 a directive was issued by the Cabinet Office to each prefecture, ordering authorities to refrain from using the expression 'gender-free' from then on. Subsequently, the number of articles criticizing gender equality gradually dwindled in the conservative media and in the newsletters of activist groups.[4]

The movement to oppose gender equality was an opportunity for women to step forward in the conservative movement, but why did these women oppose a policy which aimed for participation in a gender-equal society, and why did they agree with the conservatives' glorification of a 'family' based on orthodox gender roles? And for what reasons and under what circumstances did they take part in the movement? In Chapters Three to Five, while focusing on the discourse of the movement against gender equality that extolled the 'family' based on fixed gender roles, and

---

4   As of 2006, the movement against gender equality arguably had achieved a certain measure of success, but the gender equality administration's initiatives also continued steadily after that, with, for example, 'eradication of all forms of violence against women' being included in the priority areas in the 2010 'Third Basic Plan for Gender Equality,' and 'reformation of male-orientated labor practices' similarly being inserted in the 2015 'Fourth Basic Plan'.

which opposed women's human rights, freedom, and their advance into the public domain, I will discuss the women's conservative movement that bases its position on the status of 'mothers.' In Chapter Three, first, using the example of Japan War-Bereaved Families Association, Incorporated, which has been active since immediately after Japan's defeat in World War II, I pursue the sequence of events whereby the rhetoric that emphasizes 'the family' came to be central to the conservative movement. In Chapter Four, I analyze articles critical of gender equality carried in the conservative media and organs and bulletins published by conservative groups. I show that the logic for opposing gender equality differs according to the gender of the speaker, and that the women's claims can be interpreted through a feminist lens. Finally, in Chapter Five, from my fieldwork with a grassroots women's conservative movement group, I clarify the differences between the women's conservative movement and feminism, despite their having a shared problem-consciousness.

Chapter 3

Changes in the family discourse: Image of the 'suffering mother'

What is meant by 'family values' discourse?

'Family values' were energetically extolled by those opposed to gender equality in the early 2000s. Ito Kimio (2003a) sorts the conservative movement's arguments against gender equality into three main types, namely that gender equality would: 1) repudiate 'proper' masculinity and femininity and destroy both traditional culture and relationships between the sexes; 2) repudiate full-time housewives; and 3) destroy family ties. In this book, I employ the term 'family values' for the discourse that draws correlations between the state, patriotism and the family, as in statements such as 'the sentiment of loving one's family is concentric with the sentiment of loving one's country,'[1] and 'the collapse of the wholesome family is directly linked to the collapse of the state.'[2] In this chapter I investigate from when, and how, the 'family values' discourse began to appear in the conservative movement.

In Japan, there is little research covering the 'family values' discourse in the conservative movement and conservative media, but studies on the conservative movement in the fields of history, politics, sociology, and others have been conducted for many years in the U.S., including research that examines the expression 'family values.' In the U.S., the legalization of same-sex marriage became a point of contention at every presidential

---

1 Hayashi Michiyoshi and Yamatani Eriko (2003), 'Kazoku hokai o yurusu na (Do not permit family breakdown),' *Shokun!*, vol. 35, no. 4.

2 Nihon Seisaku Kenkyu Senta (Japan Policy Institute), 2003, 'Jendā furī kyoiku no osoru beki "heigai" (The "evils" of fearsome gender-free education),' *Ashita e no sentaku* (Choices for tomorrow), April issue.

Chapter 3

election since the 1990s,[3] with those identified as the 'conservative faction' opposing same-sex marriage in the name of so-called 'family values' (Koizumi 2011a, 2011b, 2015).[4] Some authors have observed that the U.S. conservatives take pains not to allow sexist inferences to surface in their appeals to 'family values.' Josephson and Burack, for example, argue that the family composed of a heterosexual couple and their children, along with a gendered division of labor, is deemed to be ubiquitous and 'natural' in the name of 'family values.' They call this the 'neo-traditional family:' 'traditional' in its assumption of a gendered division of labor, and 'new' (neo) in that it does not associate the gendered division of labor with men's control or domination of women (Josephson and Burack 1998).

Japanese studies, in contrast, have frequently identified the discrimination and oppression inherent to the 'family values' discourse employed by the Japanese conservative movement. The 'backlash' of the 2000s quite explicitly claimed to be in defense of 'traditional ('proper') masculinity and femininity; gender roles; full-time housewives; the role of the family; and Japanese traditions, culture, institutions, and customary practices' (Ida 2005: 126). Furthermore, Japanese conservatives contend that the 'basis for the shape of the family is that both parents are present, and any other type of family is taken to be the exception' (Tsuruta 2005: 158).

It is also notable that the 'family values' discourse evoked by the conservative movement were complementary to the promotion of neo-liberal policies, positioning the family as 'a crucial unit constituting society' (Ida 2005: 136). It both imposes an obligation on the individual to support the family and thus serve the region and state, and it assumes that the state will bear responsibility for protecting the family (Ida 2005). For that reason, the movement opposed to gender equality has been described as 'a product of the neo-liberal and authoritarian state line (new conservatism)' (Ida 2006: 181).

---

3   In the late 1970s and into the 1980s, opposition to homosexuality became a focus of the U.S. conservative movement (Sasaki 1993), while in the 1990s 'social issues' such as same-sex marriage and abortion became watersheds dividing 'conservatives' from 'liberals' in presidential elections (Nakayama 2013).

4   In terms of the categories in the U.S. conservative movement discussed in Chapter Two, those advocating 'family values' are social conservatives.

Other research, however, indicates that the 'family values' discussed in the conservative movement are not merely ideological, but rather have been presented with a topology that is close to people's 'ordinary' feelings. Nakajima Michio, who analyzed the picture-book *Twelve Vows to Learn Enjoyably* (Tanoshiku manabu juni no chikai) (from the Imperial Rescript on Education) published by the conservative Society for the Protection of Japan, states that, based on the book's explanation of the Imperial Rescript on Education by employing educational and childrearing discourse that is readily accepted by people in general, 'it succeeds in presenting issues in a context not very far removed from today's ordinary national consciousness and mental state' (Nakajima 1981b: 82).

Each of these studies points out that in the 'family values' discourse, the ideal family is taken to be composed of a heterosexual couple and their children who are related by blood, in which the woman cares for her children as a full-time housewife, yet research in family sociology has made clear that such a family configuration is neither ubiquitous nor even common throughout history. Ochiai Emiko identified the 'postwar structure of the family' as one in which: 1) 'women have become housewives;'2) [there is] 'reproductive egalitarianism' with two or three children in a majority of households; and 3) 'the ones in charge are of the generation from the period of demographic transition' born between 1925 and 1950 (Ochiai 2004: 101), and argues that this structure was built up in Japan between 1955 and 1975. The 'family' extolled by the conservative movement – in which 'women bear children, breast-feed them, and tenderly foster the lives of the next generation,' while 'men shoulder responsibility for their mission as the supporter or defender of such a home, with their minds and bodies moulded in masculine ways for that purpose'[5] – is an example of an 'invented tradition' (Hobsbawm and Ranger eds. 1983). It is no coincidence that this invented tradition conforms to neo-liberal policy.

However, while it is generally agreed that conservative movements and members emphasize the importance of the '(traditional) family,' it is worth investigating more closely when the image of the family composed of a heterosexual couple and their children became the prevailing ideal.

---

5 Fusayama Takao (2002), "Seishonen hanzai no onsho wa katei hokai da (The hotbed of youth crime is family breakdown),' *Nippon no ibuki* (Breath of Japan), March issue.

Chapter 3

As this family discourse had already been identified in the conservative movement in the 1980s by Nakajima (1981b), as mentioned above, we need to look at earlier discourses to discover the circumstances in which 'family values' began to be talked about in that movement.

As such, in this chapter, I will elucidate the changes in the family discourse in the conservative movement through analysis of the bulletins from the Japan War-Bereaved Families Association. As stated in Chapter Two, although the association's heyday of activity had passed, it had been active since immediately after the war. If we include its forerunner, the Japan Bereaved Family-Welfare Federation, we have access to longitudinal data in the form of it bulletins published continuously from 1949, which reveals its family discourse prior to the 1980s. Moreover, it is safe to assume these bulletins contain narratives of the family because the association is for families.

Japan War-Bereaved Families Association and war widows

I discussed the establishment of Japan War-Bereaved Families Association and the expansion of its activities in Chapter Two. In this chapter, I will focus on the activities of members who were wives and children of fallen soldiers and civilian army employees. As previously mentioned, the bereaved families of soldiers and civilian army employees who died in World War II have continually pressured the government for improvement in their economic and spiritual treatment. The Bereaved Families Association's initial demands were realized in the 1950s, with the implementation in 1952 of the 'War-injured and War-bereaved Families Support Act' and the 1953 amendment of the Pension Law which reinstated bereaved families' pensions and survivors' benefits.

While the association's early activities were mainly under the leadership of men – the fathers and brothers of the war dead – in the 1960s the association mobilized war widows and daughters as well. Certain moves by the war widows deserve special mention. In 1948, in the days of the Family-welfare Federation, a Women's Division (*fujinbu*) was created, and in 1954 the Bereaved Families Association established the Women's Division Council (Nippon izokukai fujinbu ed. 1995). Then, in 1959, the Women's Division Council was scrapped and the Women's Division was

74

Changes in the family discourse

formed. The war widows played a large role in the association's activities: 'The age when the wives' generation took over from the elderly parents and energetically participated as the nucleus of Izokukai was one when Izokukai was most active' (Oku 2009: 73). In December 1962, activity by the surviving children of the war dead formalized with the launch of the association's Youth Division (*seinenbu*) (renamed Young Adults' Division (*seisonenbu*) in 1982).

Oku Kentaro cites the 1963 enactment of a private member's bill, the Act on Special Benefits for Wives of the War Dead, as the trigger that activated war widows. This law stipulated payment to war widows of government bonds worth 200,000 yen (average redemption period: 10 years) and stipulated an extra allowance to recipients who had dependent family, but by the 1960s a majority of surviving children of the war dead had reached adulthood, and termination of the additional payments was anticipated. War widows who wanted to avoid a reduction in income – many wanting to be able to support their children's transition into adulthood – passionately engaged in 'repeated lobbying, or making round-robin appeals to their locally-elected Diet members, bearing their "last requests"' (Nippon izokukai ed. 1987: 46); and the Bereaved Families Association decided to make the preservation of these special allowances a priority agenda item at their fourteenth to seventeenth all-Japan rallies from 1960 to 1962 (Nippon izokukai ed. 1987). This sense of responsibility towards children and livelihood anxiety 'strongly connected wives' with the association in this period (Oku 2009: 78).

In the 1970s, the association began to campaign for state maintenance of Yasukuni Shrine Bill. On that occasion, the surviving children's generation began to take responsibility for action in place of the now elderly fathers, siblings and wives of the war dead. Today, the generation of surviving children has also become elderly,[6] but its members continue

---

6 According to surveys conducted by Mainichi Shinbun Co. vis-à-vis prefectural branches of the Japan War-Bereaved Families Association, of the twenty-seven prefectural branches that responded, membership numbers fell by a third from 2009 to 2019. The reasons given to explain this trend were the death of elderly members, delay in joining by surviving children and grandchildren, and withdrawal from the association due to advanced age (Mainichi Shinbun 2019). At the National Memorial Ceremony for the War Dead on 19 August 2019, 80 percent of the survivors scheduled to attend were aged seventy or older, including five widows.

75

Chapter 3

to pursue projects including repatriating the remains of the war dead overseas and visiting overseas cemeteries to console their spirits.

Analytical methodology

My targets of analysis in this chapter are the newsletters from the Japan Bereaved Family-Welfare Federation years (1949–50, hereafter, *Kaiho*), and the Japan War-Bereaved Families Association (from 1950 on; hereafter, *Tsushin*). Both publications were tabloids, with each issue of *Kaiho* having eight pages, while *Tsushin* had four, and these were published monthly from the fifth issue. Moreover, after the switch to *Tsushin*, the issue numbers continued where *Kaiho* left off. The format was similar to a newspaper, with reports on activities and editorial commentaries, legal advice, readers' contributions, and the like. Of the articles from 1949 until March 2007 that could be perused at the National Diet Library in 2013, I chose those that referred to the family on visual inspection. Each of the 675 issues I initially chose included one or two applicable articles, giving me a total of 910 articles for analysis.

Figure 3.1 charts changes in the number of articles over four periods. I divided the articles into four periods in accordance with qualitative changes which I will elaborate later. The four periods are 1949–1955 (80 instances), 1956–75 (204 instances), 1976–93 (366 instances), and 1994–2007 (260 instances).

There were two important points I had to bear in mind throughout my analysis: 1) as it was an association for bereaved families, I needed to differentiate narratives concerning the family in general from those specifically concerning bereaved families; and 2) as the data covered a long time frame, to be aware of the social contexts in which each article was published, as well as changing ages and relationships of the members.

To supplement my second point, I have included the estimated ages of the widows and surviving children at the beginning of the discussion of each period. I have referred to Oku's estimations of the average ages of war-bereaved families, and any mentions of members' ages seen in the newsletters or bulletins. Oku attempts to estimate the average ages of war-bereaved families by utilizing the 'Statistical Table of a Survey of Bereaved Families of Fallen Soldiers and Civilians in Military Employ'

Changes in the family discourse

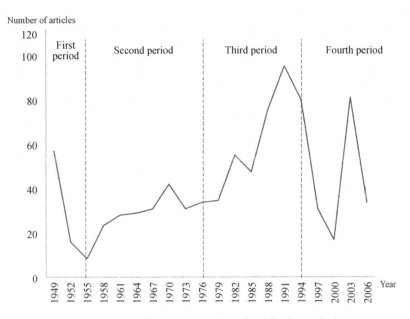

Figure 3.1 Changes in numbers of articles for analysis

(1951),[7] and statistics on public assistance recipients from 1956. The average age of war widows receiving public assistance in 1956 was 42.0 years. The average age of children is estimated from the 1951 Statistical Table. The reason for employing a different method of calculation from that of the wives' age is that wives were given priority over minors and adult children in terms of eligibility to receive survivors' benefits, and the average age of children calculated from statistics on recipients does not include children when the wife was receiving the benefit. According to the Statistical Table, as of 1951 there were 1,016,000 surviving children of fallen soldiers and civilian army employees, with the 6–12 years age bracket accounting for the largest proportion, with approximately 558,000 persons, followed by the 12–15 years bracket with approximately

---

7 This survey is included in *Collected Works of Aoyagi Ichiro* (Aoyagi Ichiro Bunshu) (Oku 2009). Aoyagi Ichiro (1900–1983) became a House of Representatives member in 1949 after having been a bureaucrat in the Home Affairs Ministry. Aoyagi also contributed an essay entitled "Memories of the Bereaved Families Issue (2)' to the August 1952 issue of the *Tsushin*, and thus is assumed to have had some connection with the War-Bereaved Families Association.

Chapter 3

232,000 persons (Oku 2009: 69). In this chapter, exercising my authority to a certain extent, I set the age range of children as of 1951 to be 6–15.

Next, I use bulletin articles to check whether these preliminary estimations match the ages of Bereaved Families Association members. A February 1985 article, 'Starting point: expectations and requests to the future young adults' division,' reported that in the Women's Division, which was mainly composed of war widows, the 'average age [is] more than seventy,' and in regard to children, 'the surviving children of the war dead, too, are now full-fledged members of society in their forties and fifties.' According to our previous estimates, as of 1986 the average age of the wives would be seventy-two, and the children forty-one to fifty, which roughly corresponds to the *Kaiho* article.

From here on, then, I conduct my analysis mindful of members' ages and life-courses, assuming a model with war widows aged thirty-three, and children aged between two and eleven as of 1947 when the Japan Bereaved Family-Welfare Federation was established.

Two family discourses in the War-Bereaved Families Association

The first period (1949–55): Construction of the "suffering mother' image

The first period was from 1949 to 1955. The average age of war widows was thirty-five to forty-one years, and their children who had been between four and thirteen years old at the beginning were between ten and nineteen years old at the end of the period. This was called the period of postwar revitalization, when Japan began its journey toward democratization and demilitarization under the guidance of the GHQ. The Japanese economy was reinvigorated by special procurements for the Korean War which broke out in 1950. Despite the beginnings of accelerating growth, though, ordinary people suffered extreme poverty, with continuing shortages of goods and loss of buildings from the war, difficulty in finding employment due to large numbers of demobilized soldiers, and postwar inflation.

Mothers, sisters, wives, and daughters of the war dead took part in the Japan War-Bereaved Families Association, but at the time of the association's launch there was debate about who would be the center of

78

the Women's Division. In the early days of the first period, mention can be seen of both mothers and wives of the war dead. An article about an informal get-together of women representatives from across the country (*Zenkoku fujin daihyo kondankai*) held in 1949 at Yasukuni Shrine makes reference to both wives and mothers of the war dead, saying: 'In this gathering, compelling voices were raised not only from the standpoint of wives who had lost their husbands, but also from that of mothers who had lost their sons and had no-one to turn to in their remaining years,' and who had 'stayed up all night with their dead sons, and their dead husbands.'[8]

In contrast, the September 1949 newsletter printed a piece by a mother of the war dead addressing the association, saying: 'We want you to think hard not only about young widows, but about old women like me,'[9] which infers that at least some of the bereaved mothers believed that the war widows had become the center of the movement. In later newsletters, mention of mothers of the war dead gradually declined. In 1952, a special feature was compiled spanning two pages, entitled 'The seven years we have thus lived through: A record of the war dead,' but it only included memoirs of 'surviving children,' 'elderly fathers' and 'widows.' There were no stories included about mothers of the war dead.[10]

Thus, early on, the Women's Division was primarily associated with war widows, but they were treated as both wives and mothers in relation to their children. At a rally in 1952 marking the establishment of a women's division in the Tokyo Metropolitan Bereaved Family-Welfare Association, there was 'a statement of opinion from the respective representatives from the standpoints of widows and mothers.' The two resolutions adopted that corresponded to a 'mother's perspective' were 'to give priority to assisting job placement for widows and surviving children' and 'to work towards increasing the amount and expanding [the availability] of scholarships for surviving children,' which clearly

---

8 'Informal gathering of all-Japan women's representatives: attendance from 38 prefectures,' *Kaiho*, no. 8, August 1949.

9 'Women's Division informal gathering, July 19,' *Kaiho*, no. 9, September 1949.

10 'The seven years we have thus lived through: A record of the war dead,' *Tsushin*, no. 40, October 1952.

Chapter 3

indicates that the 'widows and mothers' in these cases are assumed to be war widows.[11]

Articles concerning war widows in this period emphasize the hardship suffered after the death of their husbands. Many headlines emphasize the misery of war widows' living conditions, such as: 'With 1.88 million widows nationwide, livelihood subsidy insufficient even to buy rations, and remarriage harder than winning the lottery,'[12] and 'Widows' "road to hell that destroyed their happiness".'[13]

A similar tendency can be seen in articles which appear to have been submitted by war widows themselves. They complain of their harsh living conditions, writing, for example: 'In the old times, I lived my days lightheartedly, being oddly flattered to be called a 'Yasukuni home,' but 'since the defeat, I encounter many unpleasant things that I can only think are due to people's giving me the cold shoulder, as if they had completely changed their minds,'[14] and 'Why aren't jobs given to someone like me who has to live with her responsibilities as a mother at any cost?'[15] and:

> If I were an ordinary mother, I'd want to tuck my children snugly under the *kotatsu* [a low table with a heat source beneath and a quilt to keep in the warmth], or give them a sweet, but if I had done so, the next day's livelihood would have been impossible, and I toiled for my children's sake with filthy, chapped hands.[16]

In the initial days after its formation, the Women's Division seems to have widely sought collaboration with other groups that campaigned on the issue of poverty in single-female-parent households. On 20 July 1949, it formally participated in the Central Council on Mother-and-Child Welfare (*Boshi fukushi chuo kyogikai*) which was set up by a 'civic

---

11 'Rally for establishment of Women's Division of Tokyo Metropolis Bereaved Family-Welfare Association,' *Tsushin*, no. 38, August 1952.

12 *Tsushin*, no. 2, April 1949.

13 *Tsushin*, no. 40, October 1952.

14 'Listening to the voice of heaven,' *Kaiho*, no. 3. August 1949.

15 'I'm only happy when I am asleep: The cry of a widow at her wits' end,' *Tsushin*, no. 12, 1950.

16 'Determination pervades second all-Japan rally: Earning from manual labor while leading an infant by the hand. But after the talk, have cheerful days!' *Tsushin*, no. 30, June 1951.

group with deep connections to the welfare of mothers and children,'[17] and later published two related articles about the collaboration. However, in the second and later periods, there were no reports of cooperation with other women's groups in the bulletin. There was potential at that time for the Women's Division to forge a path to broader solidarity in combatting the problem of poverty in single-female-parent households, but this did not eventuate, probably because the Pension Law amendment in 1953 provided relief to the association's members, but also because the stakeholders and the association wanted recognition not as 'single-female-parent households,' but as the fatherless households and bereaved families of 'fallen soldiers and civilian army employees.'[18]

There are three notable characteristics in the articles about war widows in the first period: first, bewilderment at the about-face in public attitudes to war-bereaved families, as the mood switched from extolling them as national heroes during the war to giving them the 'cold shoulder' after the defeat; second, anger at the lack of economic support from state and society in spite of their pressing need to look after their small children; and third, shame at being unable to adequately care for their children, as their economic situation was dire even if they were employed. I call this

---

17 'A new stage for the Alliance movement: board and Diet member policy committee,' *Kaiho*, no. 4, September 1949. The Central Council on Mother-and-Child Welfare was composed of seven groups: Compatriots' Welfare Society (Doho engokai), Japan Social Work Association (Nippon shakai jigyo kyokai), Japanese National League for Commissioned Welfare Volunteers (Zenkoku minsei iin renmei), Welfare Association for Widowed Mothers with Children (Boshi aiikukai), Japan Bereaved Family-Welfare Federation, National Federation for Protection of Mothers-and-Children (Zenkoku boshi hogo renmei), and National Federation of Vocational Industries (Zenkoku jusan renmei), and in 1950 it established the All-Japan Council of Widow's Groups (Zenkoku mibojin dantai kyogikai). That council worked towards the realization of mother-and-child welfare policy and exerted a heavy influence on the enactment of the 1964 Single-Parent-Family Welfare Act (Otomo 2006). It became the All-Japan Council of Mothers-and-Children's and Widows' Welfare Groups (Zenkoku boshi kafu fukushi dantai kyogikai) in 1982.

18 According to Imai Isamu, 'the establishment of support as war-bereaved families that differed from regular livelihood support' lay at the 'core' of the organization from its initial launch as the Japan Bereaved Family-Welfare Federation, which suggests that it had a stratified 'victim mentality making bereaved families the war's greatest victims' (Imai 2017: 69).

Chapter 3

symbol of the war widow the 'image of the suffering mother,' and for the remainder of this chapter will focus on how this image has been discussed.

The second period (1956–75): Establishment of the 'suffering mother' image

In the second stage, from 1956 to 1975, the average age for war widows was forty-two to sixty-one years, and the children who had been eleven to twenty years old in the first period were now aged thirty to thirty-nine. As mentioned, the widows began to take charge of Bereaved Families Association's activities and a youth division was formed by their grown children. From 1954, Japan entered a period of rapid economic growth, and in 1956 the Japanese economy had recovered sufficiently for people to say: 'It is no longer the postwar.' In 1955, the two main conservative parties amalgamated, making the LDP the primary party in power and the so-called 1955 system began. It was around this time that the 'postwar structure of the family' was formed (Ochiai 2004), and the economic, political, and social institutions that became the basis of postwar Japanese society took shape.

In the second period, the expression 'Yasukuni wives' made its first appearance in the bulletin, albeit rarely. It appeared more frequently at the time of the enactment of the 'Act for Payment of Special Allowances to War-bereaved Wives,' including an explicit reference to 'implementing treatment as Yasukuni wives.'[19] At the seventh Women's Division workshop in 1963, the 'entrenchment of a new direction for advancement, along with firmly maintaining self-awareness and pride at last as "Yasukuni wives" as the Women's Division, and striving for the solidarity of the Women's Division' was proposed.[20] However, after the special allowance was implemented, the term 'Yasukuni wives' was again rarely used.

The image of the 'suffering mother' that had often been invoked by war widows in the first period began to be used by surviving children in

---

19 'Petitioning in waves for implementation of special allowances: Hopes for enactment in Diet regular session. National meeting of women's representatives held,' *Tsushin*, no. 143, November 1962.

20 'Seventh Women's Division workshop, with renewed resolve,' *Tsushin*, no. 150, June 1963, emphasis added.

Changes in the family discourse

the second period. Around 1960, young people's divisions began to be created one after another at regional association branches. The following statement by a third-year junior high school student at a rally for bereaved youth was published in a 1959 *Kaiho* and clearly illustrates how this discourse was structured:

> My mother cried and cried intolerably when my father died in the war, and with four children who did not understand anything being entrusted to her, she *apparently wondered* how she was going to live... In the shadows of our upbringing there was an inexpressible sadness. Not even knowing my father's face, I do not feel much sorrow, but for my mother, that *surely* was a source of worry..., so much that we cannot thank our mother enough.'[21]

Here we can see how the wives' tales of hardship as mothers that were told in the first period, were repeated from their children's perspective in the second period. The clear and emotive expressions of gratitude for their mothers' pain is a common theme. From 1960, discourse with this structure began to appear frequently.

The rise of this discourse is no doubt partly due to the fact that the generation of surviving children had reached an age when they could personally express themselves, but it also appears that the Bereaved Families Association quite intentionally sought to win over the surviving children's cohort. The organization began to notice a generational change in its membership from around 1960, but with its primary focus being 'on pressuring the state,' it seemed to struggle to attract the surviving children's generation, as evidenced by remarks such as: 'There is somewhat sparse interchange between us and the surviving children,' and 'there is a huge gap between the way the young generation thinks and the way we do.'[22]

Proactively positioning the bereaved women in the Women's Division as 'mothers' appears to have been a strategy to overcome this gap between the generations. And it was successful. At the June 1961 Niigata

---

21 '[Let's make] a peaceful world without war: impassioned plea from a fifteen-year-old girl' *Tsushin*, no. 109, August 1959.

22 'Strengthening the cultivation of the young generation,' *Tsushin*, no. 102, November 1958.

Chapter 3

Prefecture rally for a confederated Youth Division of the association, a resolution was adopted with the following wording: 'Let's thank our mothers and build cheerful households.'[23] Similar resolutions were soon adopted by Youth Divisions in all areas. A 1962 'mothers and children's gathering' organized by the Shizuoka Prefecture Bereaved Families Youth Division aimed to be 'an opportunity for young people from war-bereaved families to offer their heartfelt gratitude to their mothers.' It involved 'the presentation of bouquets of thanks from the young people to representatives of the mothers, and a chorus of "The song of happiness".'[24] Such gatherings were subsequently held in all areas, and seem to have become a regular event staged by the Youth Division.[25]

In 1975, the image of the 'suffering mother' took tangible form as a statue. From 1973, the Youth Division initiated a campaign to erect a 'statue of a mother' on the grounds of Yasukuni Shrine, and in 1973–74 made it a priority project. The 'statue of a mother' which was dedicated in 1975 (see Figure 3.2) was created based on a 'visualization of the image of the mother as perceived by members of the Youth Division.'[26] Inscribed on the statue are the words: 'Mother, who was strong, strict and gentle; I exist because of you; Thank you, Mother; May our sorrow never be repeated.' An article on the completion of the 'statue of a mother' reported: 'The shared sentiment of surviving children all over the country, "Thank you, Mother," has now taken physical form.'[27]

Changes in the social conditions of families cannot be ignored. As previously noted, this was the period in which 'the postwar configuration of the family' was formed (Ochiai 2004), and women returned to the home as full-time housewives. The surviving children's narratives of

---

23 'Drawing 500 young people. Platform and action policy also decided. Niigata,' *Tsushin*, no. 117, April 1961.

24 'Mother's joy!! May it last forever. Shizuoka Prefecture Izokukai gathering of mothers and children. Huge parade of 31 buses,' *Tsushin*, no. 137, May 1962.

25 Articles on 'Mothers and children's gatherings' were published in a total of 12 instances until the 'Regional news: "Mothers and children's gathering" commemorating the 50th anniversary of the war's end' in *Tsushin*, no. 544, April 1996.

26 '[Let us build] a statue of the "image of the mother",' *Tsushin*, no. 267, May 1973.

27 'Erection of mother's statue begins on schedule,' *Tsushin*, no. 287, December 1974.

Figure 3.2 Statue of a mother
Source: Nippon izokukai (1974)

'cheerful households' and 'thanking mother' perhaps reflect the ideal family image current at the time by those survivors who were about to start families of their own.

The third period (1976–93): The ambiguous turn of the 'suffering mother' image

The third period lasted from 1976 to 1993. The widows' ages were between sixty-two and seventy-nine, and their children, aged thirty-one to forty in the previous period, were now between forty-eight and fifty-seven. The miraculous economic growth of the 1960s had given way to a period of stable growth, triggered by the oil crises of the early 1970s. A Japanese conservative swing began to be feared, as the history textbook controversy erupted, sparking tensions with China and South Korea in 1982, and the then Prime Minister Nakasone made an official visit to Yasukuni Shrine in 1985. Moreover, it was a time when 'the family' became widely discussed,[28] with the rising divorce rate, bullying and domestic violence coming under close scrutiny, and the family

---

28 Hayakawa Takashi, 'Policy series: Guidelines on measures relating to the enhancement of the foundations of the family,' *Gekkan Jiyu minshu* (Monthly liberal democrat), September issue, 1979.

Chapter 3

being positioned as the means by which 'ethnic culture, tradition and experience would be purified and handed down to the next generation,' as in the 'Guidelines on measures relating to enhancement of the basis of the family' published by the LDP in 1979.[29]

In the third period, there were three significant changes in the image of the 'suffering mother.' The first was that the narratives of bereaved wives and children became much more similar in their deployment of that image. Let us examine the following two passages, as examples.

> For the twenty-six years since I returned from Yokosuka to my parents' home with my daughter, then aged four, I have worked at the village post office and concentrated on raising my daughter to full adulthood.[30]

> To support our livelihood, my mother endured blood, sweat and tears, sometimes going to Osaka to sell rice with me on her back, with as much rice as she could possibly pack tied around her middle, and two huge bags in her hands, or working at a textile factory from early morning until late at night.[31]

The first example was written by a war widow, and the second by an orphaned child. Despite their different perspectives, though, the descriptions of their mothers' hardship is similar. The child's narrative is remarkable for its declarative tone, as the writer experienced it personally, and is not reporting hearsay in a conjectural tone as in the second period.

The second change was in the essence of the hardship invoked by the image of the 'suffering mother.' The Youth Division, changed its name in 1982 to the Young Adults' Division and was called upon to play

---

29 Ochiai Emiko and Joshita Ken'ichi analyzed the allusions to the 'family' made by prime ministers in the Diet since the 1970s, and found that Prime Minister Nakasone's family discourse of the 1980s, especially, imagines a family with a breadwinner husband and a full-time housewife-mother; and despite this family configuration being a fully modern family, a 'traditionalization of the modern' was achieved which enabled it to be conceived as the Japanese traditional family (Ochiai and Joshita 2015: 218).

30 Yoda Kiku, 'Living a heave-ho life 11) "It's okay to cry now, isn't it?"' *Tsushin*, no. 441, September 1987.

31 Nakaoka Takako (or Ryuko), 'Living a heave-ho life 1) "[I became] a 33-year-old senior high school student through the cooperation of the family",' *Tsushin*, no. 430, October 1986.

Changes in the family discourse

a more central role in the association. Its members were admonished not to 'forever take advantage of their mothers, who [were] working painfully hard for the Yasukuni Shrine issue and the continuity of special allowances, which constituted [an] important organizational strategy.'[32] They were also called upon to 'thank their mothers for their past and present suffering, and to lighten their burden as much as possible.'[33] Invoking mothers to win over the surviving children was already common in the second period, but while the earlier strategy had focused on the mothers' historical suffering – having raised their children in the poverty of the immediate postwar – the new strategy highlighted their 'present suffering' and especially their painful efforts to pursue the Bereaved Families Association's objectives.

The third change was that the image of 'mothers' beyond the bereaved war widows which had been the central focus in the pages of the *Kaiho* and *Tsushin* until then, became more inclusive of 'mothers' in general. That tendency is clearly visible in the passage below.

> I cannot remember when, but I had no choice but to consult my mother. All she said was: 'You are my child. I trust you.' She gave me no other answer. Even now, I can hear my mother's voice as she spoke resolutely. From my experience of travelling the world, too, I believe that Japanese mothers are strong. When I think about the current condition of society, I cannot help praying for the good health of 'Japanese mothers.'[34]

The author of this passage was an LDP Diet member, Otsuji Hidehisa, recounting an episode with his own war-bereaved mother, from the perspective of a surviving child. However, in this passage, immediately after talking about his own mother, the narrative jumps to 'Japanese mothers,' in the transition from his 'experience of travelling the world' to 'Japanese mothers are strong.' Moreover, the only description of his mother's hardship is in the general terms of the 'mother who tried her utmost to protect and raise us all by herself,' with no mention of the pain

---

32 'Starting-point: Young Adults' Division members [need to] rouse themselves for their hardworking mothers!' *Tsushin*, no. 383, December 1982.

33 'Report on "the ethos of heroic spirits" (part 2 of 2),' *Tsushin*, no. 425, May 1986.

34 Otsuji Hidehisa, 'A roughneck's life, part 4,' *Tsushin*, no. 456, May 1986.

Chapter 3

私たちを必死に護り育ててくれた母

Figure 3.3 'Our mother, who tried her utmost to raise and protect us'
Source: Otsuji (1988)

and poverty which had until then been portrayed in *Kaiho* as unique to bereaved women.

This article was also accompanied by an illustration (see Figure 3.3) entitled 'Our mother, who tried her utmost to protect and raise us,' but the impression of the 'mother' depicted there is quite different than the 'statue of a mother' (Figure 3.2) created in the second period. Of course, we cannot make a simple comparison between a statue and a line drawing, but in the statue, the mother's gaze is not directed at her children, but straight ahead, and her facial expression is stern. In contrast, in the illustration both the mother and the children are smiling, and the mother is firmly embracing her children with both arms. While both are symbolic representations of a 'mother and child,' the impressions from each are entirely different.

Thus, in comparison with the 'suffering mother' images of the first and second periods, in the third period the mother image has gradually become ambiguous, and begins to open towards a maternal discourse that is not limited to war-bereaved families. This can be seen in the phrase 'Japanese mothers.'

The fourth period (1994–2007): The appearance of the 'family values' discourse

The fourth period was from 1994 to 2007, when the wives' average age was from eighty to ninety-three, and their children, who previously had been between forty-nine and fifty-eight, were now aged sixty-two to seventy-one. The surviving children were becoming elderly, as well. The Japanese economy declined from 1991, the beginning of what came to be known as the 'lost decade.' In the 1993 general election, the LDP lost its majority, and with the birth of a coalition of the Liberal Democratic Party, Japan Socialist Party and New Party Sakigake the following year, the longstanding 1955 system collapsed. At the same time, as we have seen, numerous new conservative groups formed across the country.

Among these, the Textbook Society, which fostered a new type of grassroots movement, and Japan Conference, the largest domestic conservative organization, were established in 1997. Then, in the 2000s, as previously discussed, the movement opposed to gender equality burgeoned around these two groups.

In the fourth period, there were only six articles referring to the image of the 'suffering mother.' Similar to the third period, the narrative style became increasingly standardized, and few articles referred specifically to 'mothers' hardship,' except in historical terms such as:

> With infant me in tow, my mother [endured] a series of troubles. My mother's suffering was my suffering, too.[35]

> As [in the path] traced [by] all the wives of the war dead, my mother raised my elder brother and sister and me amid great hardships.[36]

The 'suffering mother' invoked in this period appears to be an historical artifact rather than the lived experiences of the organization's members. For example, an article introducing a traveling exhibition held by the National Showa Memorial Museum on life during the Asia-Pacific War and its aftermath, 'Memories we want to hand down forever: Life in wartime and the postwar,'[37] was accompanied by a photograph with the caption: 'Mother and child walking through the burnt ruins, Tokyo' (see Figure 3.4). Although it is unclear whether the mother and chil-

---

35 Inoue Chiyo, 'Presentation of opinion (summary),' *Tsushin*, no. 553, January 1997.

36 Mizuochi Toshiei, 'On receiving endorsement,' *Tsushin*, special edition, January 2003.

37 'Showakan traveling special exhibition held in Akita [and] Gifu Prefectures,' *Tsushin*, no. 670, October 2006.

Chapter 3

dren photographed constitute a bereaved family, pictures of mothers and children taken during the war or in the immediate aftermath were published in *Tsushin* for the first time during this period. The figure of the mother looking ahead, leading her child by the hand, is similar in atmosphere to the 'statue of a mother' (Figure 3.2) erected in the second period. However, the photograph is not mentioned in the text, and the only reference to life in the postwar period mentions 'people making a fresh start towards recovery from the devastated land.' The article's generally forward-looking language is a distinct departure from the cruel and harsh experiences frequently described in articles of the first period. The image of the 'suffering mother' was already being discussed more as a historical fragment than as a family narrative in the testimonials of the Bereaved Families Association's members.

While the image of the 'suffering mother' had almost disappeared, articles about the 'family' began to appear in the fourth period, often making no mention of mothers. For example, a 1996 article reporting on a testimonial rally of people who had experienced the war said:

> When letters addressed to families from the battlefield were introduced, many of the young people became tearful, [probably because] their close relatives, including their fathers, who were prepared to die, were thinking of their country in a faraway foreign land, and worried about their family's future. These words expressing enormous love for their family [must have] struck the young people's hearts [and demonstrate a] great love for their Japanese family.'[38]

Here, the person with a 'great love for their Japanese family' was not the mother, but the father.

Furthermore, the 'family' narrative in this period is characterized by its direct connection to the state in a 'family values' discourse previously unseen in *Tsushin*, using the word 'family' to discuss the state and patriotism, as in:

> The Japanese spirit that thinks [affectionately] of family, of neighbors, and of the state.[39]

---

38 Koga Makoto, 'Politics that protects "love for the family",' *Tsushin*, no. 549, September 1996.

39 Koga Makoto, 'Cherish the Japanese spirit,' *Tsushin*, no. 662, February 2006.

Changes in the family discourse

Figure 3.4 Mother and child walking through burnt ruins, Tokyo
Source: Nippon izokukai (2006)

> If we do not teach about Japanese culture and traditions, and the importance of the family and the household to the children who will shoulder responsibility for Japan's future, and implement the kind of education that will enable them to love Japan and have pride in their own country, then this country's future will be at risk.[40]

It is plausible that this discourse began to appear in these bulletins because other activist groups had started to invoke 'family values' as a critique of moves towards gender equality. However, rather than indicating that the Bereaved Families Association was itself strongly opposed to gender equality, it appears to have been politicians and intellectuals linked to the association who criticized gender equality in these terms, and their comments were printed verbatim in *Tsushin*. This seems the best explanation for the apparent change in position of previous articles that were critical of policies based on 'family values.'

For example, articles in the third period expressed opposition to the 'Day of the Family' proposed in the LDP's 'Guidelines on Measures relating to the Enhancement of the Foundations of the Family:'

> Those who bravely stepped forward and gave their lives in difficult times ... made a noble sacrifice for preservation of the peace and safety

---

40 Mizuochi Toshiei, '[A call for] revision of the Basic Law on Education,' *Tsushin*, no. 662, February 2006.

Chapter 3

of the country, and as an expression of patriotism, that sacrifice deserves gratitude that transcends the changing times.[41]

Here, it was the 'heroic spirits' who were connected to the state, not the family.

In addition, although the family values discourse was becoming more prevalent in the fourth period, an alternative 'family' discourse was also gaining traction, albeit in a smaller way. Articles in 1997 that touched upon the problem of a declining birthrate mentioned:

> If women cannot fully exercise their abilities because of childrearing and cannot be involved in society, and are left behind by their husbands, then they will probably stop having children. In order to bear children and raise them with delight, the establishment of a support system in society as a whole for working women is necessary.[42]

Bearing in mind that both war widows and their children had firsthand experience of the suffering of single-working mothers, this demand for social support for working women is clearly derived from the image of the 'suffering mother' constructed in the Bereaved Families Association's historical family discourse.

Thus, during the fourth period, the family values discourse became dominant and the association's image of the 'suffering war widow' was replaced by a more abstract and decontextualized family values discourse.

Discord between the 'suffering mother' and family values discourse

Why did the family discourse change?

Reviewing our analysis of the Bereaved Families Association's family discourse, we arrive at the following. In the first period, hardship as mothers in the immediate aftermath of the defeat was recounted by war widows and bereaved mothers. That hardship included society's disregard for war-bereaved families, the harsh economic situation, and shame over

---

41 '"Heroic spirits" and nature of war-bereaved families,' *Tsushin*, no. 424, April 1986.

42 'Voiceless voices,' *Tsushin*, no. 563, November 1997.

their inability to look after their children properly. I refer to such narratives and images as the 'suffering mother.' In the second period, it was the turn of surviving children to define the 'suffering mother.' In the third period, the image of the 'suffering mother' constructed by war widows and their children became the dominant discourse, even as it became somewhat more ambiguous and transformed into a narrative about mothers in general. Then, in the fourth period, the image of the 'suffering mother' was historicized, and a family values discourse hitherto unseen in the pages of the *Kaiho* and *Tsushin* began to appear.

On the printed page, the transition from the image of the 'suffering mother' to the family values discourse appears to have been smooth. Certainly, both the image of the 'suffering mother' and the family values discourse comprise a 'convenient' family for the state and for advocates of patriotism. The 'suffering mother' is a discourse about the woman who, after the death of her husband, protected her home and raised her children. During the war, mothers who sent their husbands and sons to the battleground were lauded as 'Yasukuni wives.' The family values discourse, in contrast, invoked women who 'did not depend on the state,' shouldering responsibility for home-based care, such as housework, childrearing, and nursing care for elderly or disabled family members.

These two images of the family emerged from different socio-historical contexts, and whatever their similarities, there is a difference between them that cannot be overlooked, namely that the 'suffering mother' discourse is first and foremost about a single-parent family consisting of a mother and her children. The father is by definition absent from this image of the 'suffering mother.' The household is economically dependent upon the mother, perhaps with some assistance from her parents and extended family. When the mother, especially, became the economic provider in severe conditions – as portrayed by the 'statue of a mother' (Figure 3.2), with her stern expression – she did not have the opportunity to provide the kind and loving childrearing glorified by the family values discourse. In the first place, prior to the economic boom, especially in agricultural communities and not only in war-bereaved families, the unambiguous role demanded of mothers was not childrearing but productive labor (Watanabe 1999); even if both the father and mother were present, the kind of warm care idealized today was not provided. In contrast, the family values discourse was underpinned by rapid economic growth, and invokes a family with both a father and a mother present,

Chapter 3

a family in which the father enjoys economic power and dignity, while the mother is economically dependent upon her husband and devotes herself as a full-time housewife to rearing her children with overflowing affection. In short, the two types of family invoked are vastly different.

So, what dynamics were at work to shift the Bereaved Families Association's discourse from the image of the 'suffering mother' to family values? Let's turn again to the family discourse and children's ages in the third period. Between 1976 and 1993, the surviving children were aged approximately between their thirties and fifties. We assume that many of them had established families of their own, and their offspring were either about to become independent or had begun to create families of their own. In social terms, this coincided with the breakdown of the 'postwar structure of the family.'

From this perspective, the symbolic significance of the illustration 'Our mother, who tried her utmost to protect and raise us' (Figure 3.3) comes to the forefront. This illustration, depicting a mother warmly embracing her children with both arms, mixes elements from both the 'suffering mother' and the 'family values' discourses. It depicts a family that the surviving children created or construed as the ideal at the time, with the 'suffering mother' underlying it. The absence of a father might imply either that the husband or father is a 'heroic spirit' enshrined at Yasukuni, or that childrearing is a woman's role in the family values discourse and thus it is sufficient to depict a woman and her children to evoke the 'domain of women and children,' with the father's absence from the private domain taken-for-granted. In that sense, this illustration marks the transition point when the association's family discourse shifted from the 'suffering mother' image to family values.

Thus, the family values discourse which seemed on first inspection to have suddenly appeared in the fourth period had gradually begun to take form in the pages of *Tsushin* in the third period. The image of the war-bereaved single mother gradually gave way to the mother in general – no doubt informed by the changing life experiences of the war-survivors themselves – and this mother was then easily incorporated into the new 'traditional-modern family'. When the 'suffering mother' image became historical, the family values discourse was already firmly rooted and ready for rapid growth.

The conservative movement's family values discourse

In this chapter, I have examined the Japan War-Bereaved Families Association, reportedly the LDP's largest support group. From analysis of its bulletins, I have elucidated how the family values discourse initially took shape in the conservative movement. The family values discourse is not the product of any one group, though, but rather must be understood to have been produced and reproduced while being mutually referenced by various media and multiple activist groups. I therefore cannot draw any general conclusions about the family values discourse in the conservative movement.

However, this analysis does enable me to present two partial findings on the family values that are so central in today's conservative movement. First, family values have not always been extolled in the conservative movement; today's conservative family values discourse appears to have first achieved its current prominence in the 1990s. Recall that Nakajima (1981b) pointed to a family values discourse apparent in other groups in the 1980s, which might suggest that the adoption of this discourse by the Bereaved Families Association was comparatively late. We can attribute this to the association's long and firm attachment to the image of the 'suffering mother,' but even here the values shifted in the 1990s. And following that shift, it is safe to say that since the 1990s, the family values discourse has become a defining characteristic of the conservative movement in Japan.

Second, it is clear that the 'family' in the conservative movement's family values discourse is not a depiction of actual individual families living in the present moment, but an idealization inseparable from notions of state and nation. It was only after the very real experiences of its members became things of the past that the association began to express a family values discourse; and, furthermore, it coincided with a time when the historical shape of the family, composed of a heterosexual couple and their children, began to waver. Hence. while the rhetoric of the family values discourse is ostensibly to defend the family, the family it seeks to defend bears little resemblance to the families in which people actually live. This is perhaps most vividly demonstrated by the fact that the conservative movement has been unable to offer any realistic answers to contemporary social issues such as childrearing and care, domestic violence, and child poverty.

Chapter 4

The politics of 'family values': An analysis of conservative magazine articles

Opposition to gender equality

In the previous chapter, from analysis of the bulletins released by the Japan War-Bereaved Families Association, I showed how the family configuration constructed of a heterosexual couple with fixed gender roles comprising a husband as breadwinner and a wife as full-time housewife and their children came to be widely depicted as the ideal family in conservative movement groups from the 1990s onwards. Having ascertained how the family discourse changed in the conservative movement, in this chapter I will focus on the opposition to gender equality that arose in the early 2000s and analyze the family values discourse which pervades articles in conservative magazines and conservative activist groups' bulletins and newsletters, with a focus on the gender of the speakers. What motivates women to actively oppose gender equality from the perspective of 'mothers'? And what significance does their opposition have for a feminism that aims for gender equality?

Housewives opposed to gender equality

As previously mentioned, from around 2000 fierce criticism was directed at the Basic Law for a Gender-Equal Society (hereafter, the Basic Law) that was enacted in 1999, and an opposition movement began to grow. Criticism of the Basic Law and the planned promotion of policies relating to gender equality erupted from the conservative media and conservative activist groups, suggesting that gender equality would 'do away with "proper" masculinity and femininity,' 'destroy the family,' and

Chapter 4

'disavow traditional culture.' Such moves subsequently came to be called a backlash.

Leading this backlash were conservative magazines such as Sound Argument (*Seiron*) and Everyone! (*Shokun!*), and the *Sankei Shinbun* newspaper,[1] and activist groups including the Textbook Society and Japan's largest conservative body, Japan Conference. As we have seen, the anti-gender-equality movement, boosted by major media, also influenced central and regional authorities, and arguably achieved a measure of success.

Both men and women participated in the activist groups that were driving the opposition to gender equality. As we saw in Chapter One, the movement opposing gender equality arose in a context in which women were becoming increasingly active in the conservative movement. In Japan Conference, for example, a subsidiary, Japanese Women's Association was created in 2001 and unique activities by women opposing gender equality began to expand.[2] Moreover, in Ube City, Yamaguchi Prefecture, where a gender equality ordinance based on gender trait theory was enacted, a grassroots women's group called Ube Women's Group to Think about Gender Equality was formed, reportedly backing the ordinance (Koshiba 2008).

The presence of these women, assumed to be 'housewives,' has often been alluded to in prior studies. Okano Yayo, for example, having used a combination of the male and female variants of the Japanese pronoun 'they' to describe the leaders of the backlash, summarizes the women's challenge to gender equality with the question: 'Are you denying my value as a full-time housewife?' (Okano 2005a: 56). Furthermore, citing housewives and young people as examples of 'ordinary people' who condemn feminism, Sato Fumika suggests that such people harbor 'feelings of alienation' and 'frustration' 'as if the value of their own life were being repudiated' by societal changes (Sato 2006: 216), and argues that

---

1   In this chapter I mainly deal with articles from *Sound Argument, Everyone!* and similar magazines. See Wada and Inoue (2010) regarding changes in the content of articles relating to gender equality policy published in the *Sankei Shinbun* from the 1990s to 2000s, and the influence this had on the conservative movement.

2   Official membership numbers are unclear, but there were reportedly 1000 attendees at the 2001 launch rally, and several hundred participants at subsequent lecture meetings (Nihon josei no kai ed. 2007).

The politics of 'family values'

it is inappropriate to make gender equality and feminism the target of such feelings.

Why do housewives oppose gender equality?

Previous research has proffered numerous possible explanations of the people responsible for this backlash. Let us briefly review that research to assess their explanations of why housewives took part in the movement against gender equality.

According to previous studies, we can roughly divide the leaders of the backlash into three main models. First is the traditional conservative model: people whose ideal is the patriarchal family based on gender roles which 'connect to the view of the prewar state-as-family' (Ito 2003b: 15). Typical examples of this are conservative groups like Japan Conference. This traditional conservative model is the most frequently evoked characterization of those who lead the backlash.

It is clear that the housewives who participate in the movement opposed to gender equality belong to conservative movement groups, and have some conception of the 'traditional' family as ideal. But it is not clear whether they oppose gender equality because they belong to a conservative movement group, or if they connect with the conservative movement because they oppose gender equality for some other reason.

The second model is the loss-of-vested-interests model. According to Ann Cudd (2002), backlash against progressive social movements, including feminism, is an expression of resistance by people who fear they will incur a personal loss from the changes wrought by such social movements. Some writers have suggested that the backlash is primarily driven by people who benefit from the assignment to women of responsibility for caring, such as housework, childrearing and nursing care (Takenobu 2005).

Debate certainly arose in Japan in the early 2000s under the Koizumi regime about what was dubbed the 'structural reform of the housewife,' which proposed abolition of special tax deductions for spouses and reconsidering the 'third insured person' system in the pension system. Sato (2006) considered this move to be one of the factors triggering women's participation in the movement opposing gender equality.[3] No

---

3 Much more broadly than the tax system, around 2000 a heated public debate

Chapter 4

doubt, the proposed 'structural reform of the housewife' might mean loss of vested interests for women who had lived as housewives. But we are still left to wonder why criticism of the social security system should translate into criticism of gender equality.

The third model attributes the backlash to 'anxiety,' and is called 'new conservatism' (Ito 2003b: 15). The 'newness' of this conservatism is not in the direction of their thinking or political ideology, but in their active participation in response to a variety of social 'anxieties' that they harbor. It has been suggested that they have positioned gender equality and feminism as hypothetical enemies to distract themselves from things such as insecure employment due to a protracted economic slump, and the neo-liberal reforms of social security (Ida 2005).

This third model is frequently invoked as an explanation for housewives' opposition to gender equality. Ehara Yumiko posits 'people's apprehension and horror vis-à-vis injury to their own gender identity' as the context for the backlash (Ehara 2007: 192), and suggests that housewives who resist gender equality had 'lost self-confidence in being full-time homemakers and become anxious due to most married women having begun to work outside the home' (Ehara 2007: 190). The explanation that they are mobilized by anxiety seems to be the most common explanation for the participation of women in the conservative movement who take the position of housewife, but doubts remains as to whether vague anxiety is a strong enough driving force to launch grassroots groups and sustain them in the short- and medium-term.

Thus, as we can see, although there is some merit to these explanations for why housewives participate in the backlash against gender equality, they do not go far enough. In what follows, then, through analysis of articles in conservative magazines and various organs, bulletins and newsletters from conservative movement groups that have led the backlash, I will shed light on the reasons presented by women who reject gender equality, and what they perceive to be problematic about it.

---

began about the housewife's way of life, which had for decades been the principal life-course for women. This roughly coincided with the publication of a series of books by Ishihara Risa: *Fuzakeru na sengyo shufu* (Full-time housewives, don't you fool around!) (1998), *Kutabare! Sengyo shufu* (Full-time housewives, drop dead!) (1999), and *Sayonara sengyo shufu* (Farewell to the full-time housewife) (2000).

Outline of the data

Before starting my analysis, I will define the terms. Hereafter, I will employ the word backlash instead of the 'movement opposed to gender equality' in order to deal not only with articles in activist group organs, bulletins and newsletters, but also from other conservative organizations. I will use the expression 'housewife backlash' for articles whose author identifies herself as a 'housewife,' and 'mainstream backlash' for others. As it is not possible to clarify whether a writer is actually a housewife simply by analyzing the magazine articles, from here on I will write 'housewife' in brackets. I call articles other than those by 'housewives' 'mainstream' for the following reasons. Women who support backlash and participate in the movement are positioned as auxiliaries. For example, in each of the magazines and organs discussed below, pieces contributed by 'housewives' typically take the form of essays or roundtable discussions, and the allotted space is small compared to that allocated to the 'mainstream backlash.' Hence, to reflect whether such housewives are mainstream or non-mainstream, I have decided to designate articles that are not written by self-identified 'housewives' as 'mainstream backlash.'

I selected data for analysis from five publications: *Sound Argument*, *Everyone!*, Breath of Japan (*Nihon no ibuki*), Japan Current Review (*Nippon jiji hyoron*), and Choices for Tomorrow (*Ashita e no sentaku*). All of these have produced arguments criticizing gender equality (Ida 2006; Yamaguchi 2006; Yamaguchi, Saito and Ogiue 2012).[4] I selected articles that alluded to gender equality or 'gender-free' from among those carried in these magazines and organs in the period from 2000, when the backlash first animated, to 2008, after its demise. Furthermore, I also included any that were published in special features addressing gender equality, even if these terms did not explicitly appear in the article. I collected the articles at the National Diet Library, and personally confirmed their applicability.

---

4 Breath of Japan (*Nippon no ibuki*) is an organ of Japan Conference. Japan Current Review (*Nippon jiji hyoron*) is a newspaper published by a company affiliated with the New Buddhism Religious Organization (Shinsei bukkyo kyodan) based in Yamaguchi Prefecture. Choices for Tomorrow (*Ashita e no sentaku*) is a magazine published by the private think tank, Japan Policy Institute. Considering that the differences in their articles reflect their different audiences, I chose them as a target of analysis. Moreover, *Everyone!* has currently suspended publication, with the June 2009 issue being its last.

Chapter 4

Table 4.1 Number of articles analyzed

Name of magazine		2000	2001	2002	2003	2004	2005	2006	2007	2008	Total
Sound Argument (Seiron)	Mainstream	5	0	14	15	6	15	9	5	0	69
	Housewives	0	0	1	0	0	0	0	1	2	4
Everyone! (Shokun!)	Mainstream	2	1	3	4	0	1	5	0	0	16
	Housewives	0	0	0	1	0	0	1	0	0	2
Breath of Japan (Nippon no ibuki)	Mainstream	0	11	16	16	6	8	7	14	7	85
	Housewives	0	0	0	0	2	2	0	0	0	4
Japan Current Review (Nippon jiji hyoron)	Mainstream	28	27	45	51	23	24	17	9	9	233
	Housewives	3	0	0	0	0	0	0	1	0	4
Choices for Tomorrow (Ashita e no sentaku)	Mainstream	0	0	2	13	9	5	6	4	0	39
	Housewives	0	0	0	0	0	0	0	0	0	0
Dianthus (Nadeshiko tsushin)	Mainstream	NA	NA	NA	NA	1	3	2	2	1	9
	Housewives	NA	NA	NA	NA	6	29	29	27	23	114
Total		38	39	81	100	53	87	76	63	42	579

Moreover, in addition to these five publications, I also targeted the newsletter *Dianthus* (Nadeshiko tsushin) for analysis, on the grounds that 'housewives' are the main agents in grassroots movements. *Dianthus* is a small publication issued every second month by Association A, a civic group formed in opposition to gender equality in Ehime Prefecture in Shikoku. As well as reproducing essays by conservative intellectuals from other publications, reports on the group's activities, articles on local government affairs, and debate about topical newspaper articles, this newsletter contained a relatively large number of essays by 'housewives.' As of November 2010, it had published 37 issues from its launch in 2004, and of these, the first 25 issues fit the period I had set as my target for analysis, as mentioned above (see Table 4.1 for the number of articles per publication).

There were two main reasons for choosing Association A and its newsletter, *Dianthus*, as raw material for analyzing the backlash by housewives. The first is that among the fairly large number of grassroots conservative groups formed in opposition to gender equality which have remained active until the present day, the group in question had maintained the same activity focus since its initial founding, and was accessible in 2010 when I was conducting my survey. The second was that as Association A was conducting activities with a strong emphasis on people's status as 'women,' there was a high likelihood of observing a grassroots 'housewife backlash.' Women served as president and

102

secretary-general in Association A, and women were central to its activities. Its policy was to allow anyone to join, regardless of gender, but its regularly-held study groups 'often were related to women's way of life, [so] it ventured to [schedule them] in the daytime when it would be easy for women to gather' (*Dianthus*, no. 3, 2005).[5] For these reasons, I considered *Dianthus* to be apt for exploring the claims of women participating in the grassroots movement opposed to gender equality.

A comparative analysis of family values

The non-political nature of articles submitted by housewives

First, there are similarities across many articles submitted by 'housewives,' namely that such articles include 'non-political' content that at a glance appears to be unrelated to criticism of gender equality. In an essay criticizing gender-free education for the potential 'disappearance of teachers who would teach a sense of gratitude to mothers,' for example, the following episode was also recounted.

> I have memories of 'Mother's Day' that remain in my heart. Every year, at elementary school, when 'Mother's Day' was approaching, orders were taken for the purchase of brooches adorned with artificial carnations. They only cost a few coins, so could be bought with children's pocket money, and every year, I would buy one and give it to my mother. My mother would always be very pleased and would wear it on her breast all day that day.[6]

Articles by contributors who self-identified as 'housewives' that were explicitly critical of gender equality also included numerous specific episodes about their individual families that appeared unrelated to that criticism. There were references to family in sixty-nine out of 128 articles by 'housewives.' Breaking this down by magazine, there were such descriptions in one out of four article in *Sound Argument*, two

---

5   Association A is discussed in more detail in Chapter Five.

6   Mie no shufu, Emiko (Emiko, a housewife from Mie [Prefecture], 'Mothers' ordeals,' *Sound Argument*, no. 425, 2007.

Chapter 4

out of four in *Breath of Japan*, and in all four articles in *Japan Current Review*. Furthermore, of the nineteen articles in *Dianthus* that qualified as 'housewife backlash,' there were eleven essays composed solely of family episodes without mentioning gender equality.

As such, from here on, I will focus on episodes relating to the family which appear in articles submitted by 'housewives,' and conduct a comparative analysis of 'mainstream backlash' and 'housewife backlash' from the perspective of 'family values.' In mainstream articles, as well, 'family' is a vital keyword, and has been identified in prior studies, the 'mainstream' has criticized gender equality with expressions such as 'family breakdown,' 'disavowal of the family,' and 'dismantling the family.' By focusing on descriptions of 'the family,' I may be able to shed light upon the similarities and differences between the two types of backlash.

The 'family' discourse in the 'mainstream backlash'

References to 'the family' were found in 332 of 451 'mainstream back-lash' articles. In these articles, 'family crisis' was frequently explained, with 'commonality (*kyodosei*)' in the family, expressed as 'family ties' especially emphasized.

In the early 2000s, the introduction of a system of optional separate surnames for married couples was harshly criticized. Critics argued that such a system would 'dismantle the family,' 'make the parent-child relationship brittle, and weaken ties,' and individuals would 'become isolated' as a result.[7] Similar arguments were published in *Japan Current Review*,[8] and *Choices for Tomorrow*.[9]

However, although a 'family crisis' was declared in the 'mainstream backlash' articles, the importance of 'the family' was asserted at the macro level of social order or state structure rather than from the

---

7   Hayashi Michiyoshi, 2002, 'Do they so want to destroy the family? Stupefying statements again emerging in droves from the faction promoting "separate surnames for married couples",' *Sound Argument*, no. 353.

8   For example, 'Time to determine the direction of gender equality – whether to trust nationals' good sense, or to follow feminists' extreme ideas!!,' *Nippon jiji hyoron*, no. 1463, 2002.

9   For example, Japan Policy Institute, 2003, 'The "evils" of fearsome gender-free education,' *Ashita e no sentaku*, April issue.

individual, tangible experiences of the contributors. Let us examine an article published in *Current Review* in 2000 as an example. In the article, the logic of 'family breakdown,' and 'dismantling of the family' (and thus the 'collapse of the social order') is evoked.[10] At the time, there were moves in Yamaguchi Prefecture to pass a gender equality ordinance, and the article claimed that if women's workforce participation were promoted there would be no one in the household to take charge of childrearing, which they argued would mean authorizing the 'dismantling of the family.' Furthermore, that 'dismantling' was seen as synonymous with 'breaking down the social order,' because the wellbeing of the 'family' was considered to be directly connected to the wellbeing of 'society.' In this manner, a logic that perceives the family, society, and the state to be in concentric circles was specified in ninety-six of the 'mainstream' articles.

The underlying premise of this line of argument is an understanding of the family as a necessary 'foundation' for a viable society and state. This logic is explicit in the criticisms of the proposed separate surnames for married couples; for example, in the argument that the case for separate surnames stems from 'an ideology that would undermine the family, which is the basis of the state,'[11] and 'there is a risk lurking in its endeavoring to destroy the family, which is the most crucial unit of society – its very cells, one might say.'[12]

As above, the family is central to the 'mainstream backlash' articles, but it clearly differs enormously from the family found in the 'housewife backlash.' 'Family values' are invoked in the 'mainstream backlash' because the family is understood to be the foundation of society and the state, which is the writers' primary concern.

---

10 'Turning "gender equality" into ordinances is dubious! Risk of inducing "dismantling of the family" and "decline of state power",' *Nippon jiji hyoron*, no. 1361, 2000.

11 Yagi Hidetsugu, 2001, 'Let us resist the introduction of separate surnames for married couples,' *Nippon no ibuki*, October issue.

12 Hayashi Michiyoshi, 2002, 'The revolutionary strategy hidden in "gender equality:" what squirms behind the ideology of dismantling the family and morality,' *Sound Argument*, no. 360.

Chapter 4

The 'family' discourse in 'housewife backlash'

The 'family' described in articles by 'housewives' has different characteristics to those found in the 'mainstream backlash.' Among other things, as mentioned, housewives describe the family in the concrete terms of specific incidents that happened in the writers' own households, rather than in the abstract terms of society and state.

> Our third daughter has a disability. This was said to be severe when she was ten months old, but with the encouragement of my parents and husband, I have made her education and support my highest priority. Her older sisters have grown up cheerfully, overcoming their loneliness. She still has a disability, but it has grown mild... Thanks to my third daughter's birth, I have come to have an even greater appreciation of the preciousness of family: the blessing of parents, the affection for my ancestors that link to my parents, and above all, the reliability of my husband, who did not turn a hair at my third daughter's disability. With gratitude, I want to protect this family to the very end.[13]

While the essay is titled 'What family means,' it does not offer any definition of what a family comprises, nor is there any discussion about the family's role and function in society and the state. Instead, the story is recounted through family episodes of the writer's personal experience.

Furthermore, each of the articles by 'housewives' describes human relationships through narratives about the family. One essay, for example, explains that the 'merit of being a full-time housewife' is that a housewife 'has plenty of time to relate to her children and husband,' such as listening attentively to what her children say, as in this anecdote: 'My eldest son, who is in second grade in elementary school, and my second son, in first grade, came home from school and spent about an hour telling me about school; and once they were satisfied, they started on the next thing.'[14] Here an anecdote of the writer's personal experience is used to make her point. Another essay, discussed a mother-in-law's death, describing how multiple generations with different food preferences cooperated, as in 'the children put up with eating a bland stew of greens and simmered

---

13 Forty-year-old woman, 2005, 'What family means,' *Dianthus*, no. 4.

14 Housewife, Matsuyama City, 2000, 'In the end, it's up to my husband,' *Nippon jiji hyoron*, no. 1367.

106

The politics of 'family values'

eggplant when we were living under the same roof as my mother-in-law and grandmother-in-law, and my grandmother-in-law and parents-in-law ate my mince patties and grilled meat without complaint.'[15]

The narratives about interpersonal relationships in 'housewife backlash' articles have two distinctive characteristics. First, the human relationships are described from the contributor's subjective perspective. Discussions of 'family' employ nomenclature that defines any characters who appear in relationship to the writer, using terms such as 'my daughter,' 'my grandmother-in-law,' 'my eldest son,' and 'my third daughter.' In contrast, 'mainstream backlash' articles employ objective relational terms such as 'mothers,' 'fathers,' or 'children,' because 'the family' is being discussed in general and abstract terms. The specificity of the 'family' experiences in the 'housewives' testimonials do not readily lend themselves to a generalized norm that says 'mothers should be like this,' which we find in the 'mainstream backlash.'

Second, interpersonal relationships within the household are depicted as being cemented and maintained through the media of care: housework, childrearing, and nursing. In articles by 'housewives,' relationships between the writer and other family members are not attributed merely 'blood' or legal ties, but rather are built through the housework, childrearing and nursing that the authors' undertake or have undertaken, as evidenced by descriptions such as: '[They] ate my cooking,' and 'I listened attentively' to their stories. And as we saw in the description of the family meal, mutual consideration and compromises are necessary to maintaining interpersonal relationships in 'the family.'

Taking these characteristics of 'family' narratives into account, it is clear that the criticisms of gender equality in the 'housewife backlash' articles are different than in 'mainstream backlash' articles. While most of 'housewife backlash' articles are concrete 'family' narratives, there are a small number of 'housewife backlash' articles that directly criticize gender equality. For example, a special feature article in *Dianthus* objected to a gender equality guidebook published by a local authority, arguing that to be a married couple or a family means 'to have a relationship of mutual support and help, bound by mutual affection, as fellow members who share the same lifestyle and destiny,' and 'if husbands and wives do not depend on each other, both in terms of livelihood and economics,

---

15 Umeoka Noriko, 2006, 'Life relay,' *Dianthus*, no. 14.

Chapter 4

in fact we cannot call them a married couple.'[16] Here, gender equality is understood as promoting women's workforce participation and economic independence, which in turn is perceived as a threat to the family 'bound together by affection' and 'supporting and helping each other.'

Although there are similarities in the centrality of 'the family' in the 'housewives' critiques, their emphasis is different from the 'mainstream backlash.' The 'housewives' focus on the preservation of interpersonal relationships within the household for their own sake, rather than as a focal point for raising concerns about society or the state.

The discursive structure of 'family values'

Relations of latent hostility

In the previous section, I divided articles relating to gender equality carried in conservative magazines and conservative group publications into two categories: 'housewife backlash' and 'mainstream backlash,' and elucidated differences in the ways 'the family' was portrayed in those respective articles. By contrast with 'mainstream backlash,' which discussed 'the family' in normative terms, always treating society and the state as the main points, the 'housewife backlash' articles prioritized human relationships within the household that were established and maintained by the performance of housework, childrearing and nursing, and expressed fear that 'prompting women's social and economic independence' (gender equality) would destroy the family in which people of different genders and generations lived together. This is a significant difference in the way 'the family' has been discussed in different kinds of article. Let us now look for connections in the logic underpinning the two discourses.

The first thing to note is that they complement each other. From the perspective of the 'mainstream,' a 'housewife's' 'moving story' about her family demonstrates her commitment to the kind of family that is based on the gendered division of labor and confirms that the family image which 'mainstream' proponents defend is supported not only by men, but by women, also. 'Housewives,' too, can interpret the social significance

---

16 "What?? That gender equality studies guidebook – it is so strange,' *Dianthus*, no. 7, 2007.

108

The politics of 'family values'

of the housework, childrearing, and nursing that they have hitherto undertaken as being able to appeal widely to society by connecting those functions to a 'mainstream' context of discussing the state.

However, beneath the surface appearance of complementarity, upon deeper examination we find significant differences and inconsistencies in the logics of the 'housewives' and the 'mainstream' critiques of gender equality.

The central tension between the two positions is undoubtedly the recognition given to 'housewives.' The 'mainstream backlash' articles tend to claim that full-time housewives are socially 'advantaged' rather than oppressed, arguing that housewives enjoy economically abundant circumstances, and that 'unequal power relations' do not apply because in Japan, 'where the housewife holds the purse strings and controls the entire household economy,' wives often manage the household budget,[17] and 'many housewives have their husbands buy them clothing and jewelry, and take them out for meals and entertainment and the like, and therefore, far from being "slaves," they are enjoying their lives to the full.'[18]

'Mainstream' articles presume equality in the family and the absence of control and oppression within it, and present extremely optimistic descriptions of the housewives' situation. By contrast, frequent reference to the discord and distress of being 'housewives' can also be found scattered through the 'housewife' articles. An essay in *Dianthus* entitled 'Hoorah for full-time housewives!' pushed back against the idea that 'the full-time housewife is a sparkling presence,' describing the way she 'spends all day on housework' every day without a break, and 'from a young girl's perspective, that might appear to be the figure of a woman without dreams or hopes.'[19] Furthermore, a 'housewives' article in *Japan Current Review* describes the author as having been so busy when serving as a school officer that she 'had no choice but to cut corners with the cooking, cleaning, and keeping things neat and tidy,' which left her family 'dissatisfied,' and she 'personally started to have pangs of conscience

---

17 'The Beijing Conference and gender equality: Attacking its validity (part 2 of 2),' *Nippon jiji hyoron*, no. 1531, 2003.

18 Japan Policy Institute, 2003, 'The "poison" of gender-free that undermines education,' *Ashita e no sentaku*, April issue.

19 Tanaka Naoko, 2006, 'Hoorah for full-time housewives!,' *Dianthus*, no. 13.

Chapter 4

and build up stress.'[20] Thus, even articles in which housewives sang the praises of the full-time housewife, highlighted negative aspects of the situation, such as frustration and guilty consciences.

Moreover, 'mainstream backlash' and 'housewife backlash' offer conflicting descriptions of the cooperation in the family which both have identified as the crucial constituent of 'family ties.' In 'mainstream' articles, the gendered division of labor is the nucleus of a married couple's relationship, commonly expressed as 'a difference in the roles in a married couple' and 'if a married couple's awareness of the division of roles disappears completely, then the meaning of marriage will almost vanish.'[21] Furthermore, gender equality is criticized for suggesting 'the idea of making men do the housework and childrearing in the same way as women, in order to create a society where two-income couples are a matter of course,'[22] indicating a refusal to accept a situation in which men would perform housework, childrearing, and nursing alongside their wives. Thus, according to the 'mainstream backlash,' family 'cooperation' requires conforming to the gendered division of labor.

In contrast, it is much less common for the 'housewife backlash' articles to directly mention the gendered division of labor. This could be because their discursive structure does not readily connect to generalized social norms, tending instead to recount specific family episodes. However, even personal family narratives that may seem at a glance to be trivial reveal important differences from 'mainstream backlash.' For example, an essay about the relationship in a married couple describes how the writer's husband enthusiastically cared for her after she had surgery: 'Little by little, my husband's cheeks grew thinner, and though he did not say it in words, I realized how much he was worrying about me.'[23] Another essay recalled the writer's father when she was a child, recounting an event when her father had rebuked a man for directing abusive language to her mother, saying: 'What are you doing to a woman

---

20 Housewife, Hiroshima City, 2000, 'Full-time housewives should be appreciated,' *Nippon jiji hyoron*, no. 1361.

21 Japan Policy Institute, 2003, 'The "evils" of fearsome gender-free education,' *Ashita e no sentaku*, May issue.

22 Hayashi Michiyoshi, 2000, 'Feminism's fascist turn: interrogating the fearsome ideas of Yamaguchi-ken's Deputy Governor Oizumi,' *Everyone!*, vol. 32, no. 4.

23 Saito Takae, 2006, 'The ties of a married couple,' *Dianthus*, no. 13.

The politics of 'family values'

and child?!'[24] This essay, entitled 'Memories of my father,' suggests that her strongest impressions of her father stemmed from his thoughtfulness and affection towards her and her mother, rather than his gendered role of economically supporting the family. This is typical of the way that articles by 'housewives' depict mutual connections among family members that pivot on heartfelt communication, not gender roles.

The family based on the gendered division of labor which 'mainstream backlash' imagines is very different than the 'family values' championed by 'housewife backlash.' The cooperation based on the gendered division of labor which the 'mainstream' advocates does not invoke the heartfelt 'consideration' and 'thoughtfulness' in the home that the 'housewives' discuss. To take the argument to its extreme, in the family of the 'mainstream backlash,' all a married couple needs to do is perform their respective gender roles, regardless of whether someone suffers or is conflicted by the arrangement. Why, then, is this disparity and antagonism between the two discourses not recognized, leaving the 'housewife backlash' being seen as complementary to the 'mainstream backlash?'

The dual nature of female intellectuals

In pondering the connections between the logics of the 'mainstream' and 'housewife' backlashes, I will focus on female intellectuals[25] who I classified with the 'mainstream backlash,' and investigate the dual nature of the logic that they employ, and its role. Male intellectuals comprise a majority in the 'mainstream backlash,' but no small number of women are present, too. They are conservative female politicians like Yamatani Eriko, Takaichi Sanae and Nishikawa Kyoko, and conservative female culturati like Hasegawa Michiko and Ichikawa Hiromi. Since the 1990s, conservative female politicians' exposure in general commercial media has been notable (Kaizuma 2017), and fifty-four articles with those women as opinion leaders were carried in the five magazines that I analyzed: *Sound Argument, Everyone!!, Breath of Japan, Japan Current*

---

24 Miyoshi Kanako, 2006, 'Memories of my father,' *Dianthus*, no. 12

25 To identify the symmetry and similarity among the 'housewives' speaking from their everyday experience, I designate female Diet members, regional assembly members, university instructors, journalists, culturati and the like who speak from an expert's perspective as 'female intellectuals.'

Chapter 4

Review, and *Choices for Tomorrow*. Association A, which published the *Dianthus* newsletter, also supported them, with six of the nine lecture meetings held by Association A as of 2011 presenting female intellectuals including Mrs. Yamatani as speakers. Association A also invited male intellectuals like Takahashi Shiro to lecture at meetings, but a special feature spanning the fifth and sixth issues of *Dianthus* was devoted to the times when Mrs. Yamatani was the featured guest, suggesting that the reaction was huge.

These female intellectuals have a dual nature in being both conservative intellectuals and housewives, and thus play an important role in the discursive structure surrounding family values. While having composed articles opposing gender equality as intellectuals, they speak of themselves as housewives at the same time. Nishikawa Kyoko, for example, announced at a lecture meeting: 'As I have been a full-time housewife all along,'[26] and Yamatani Eriko has said: 'In my case, as I had no parental leave, I quit my job and became a full-time housewife.'[27] Even while being intellectuals, they were simultaneously claiming that they were housewives.

The female intellectuals who make this claim criticize gender equality using two logics for different purposes. On the one hand, from the standpoint of intellectuals, they employ a logic that deems the family to be the basis of society and the state in the same way as mainstream male intellectuals. The claims that 'the family is the smallest unit of society,'[28] and 'the foundation of Japanese society is the household, and we should respect it,'[29] are common with mainstream male intellectuals. Criticisms of the proposal for separate surnames for married couples also argued that it relates to the state: 'transcending private aspects and

---

26 Nishikawa Kyoko, Yamamoto Kazutoshi, et al, 2003, 'Symposium on education: Children will be destroyed: The problem of gender equality. "Socialization of childrearing" will destroy children,' *Nippon no ibuki*, October issue.

27 Yamatani Eriko, 2004, 'My mission is to fix education, family and country,' *Ashita e no sentaku*, March issue.

28 Ichida Hiromi, 2003, 'Now, proper masculinity and femininity,' *Nippon no ibuki*, September issue.

29 Nishikawa Kyoko, Sakurai Yoshiko et al., 2007, 'The revitalization of the state and education begins from 'the family:' National resolution is also being questioned,' *Sound Argument*, no. 420.

The politics of 'family values'

technical issues, even to the extent that each individual's view of the state actually will come under question.'[30]

On the other hand, female intellectuals also discuss their personal experiences of housework, childrearing and their heartfelt interactions with their families from the perspective of housewives. In almost all of her articles, Yamatani Eriko alludes to episodes with her husband and children, or her own mother and father.[31] Hasegawa Michiko also discusses her experience of having suffered maternity neurosis.[32]

In this manner, individual, tangible family episodes are directly linked to the macro contexts of society and the state in a discourse unique to female intellectuals that facilitates the coexistence of the two distinct logics.

> In my family, my mother used to make me *chirashi-zushi* [sushi rice with a variety of toppings] at the time of the Girl's Day, and she would put iris petals in the bathwater to celebrate Boy's Day... The [five] annual festivals are all a kind of 'prayer.' Through the traditional events, I pray not only for my own child's happiness, but also for the happiness of the Japanese ethnos that has continued without interruption.[33]

In the above passage by Yamatani Eriko, traditional events held within the household to pray for 'one's own children's happiness' are 'naturally' connected with 'the happiness of the Japanese ethnos.' This pronouncement

---

30 Yamatani Eriko, Takaichi Sanae and Nishikawa Kyoko, 2002, 'Drop dead, "separate surnames for married couples:" Don't be hoodwinked by "gender equality" said in a honeyed voice,' *Everyone!!*, vol. 34, no. 3.

31 Yamatani Eriko and Yagi Hidetsugu, 2003, 'Roundtable discussion to criticize feminism: Don't use taxes for the dismantling of the state, social norms and the family!' *Sound Argument*, no. 366. Others include Yamatani Eriko and Ino Sumire, 2006, 'The objective is a "family[-centered]" society with joint [participation] by men and women,' *Sound Argument*, no. 407; Yamatani Eriko and Nakajo Takanori, 2005, 'The deception of gender equality and shocking sex education,' *Sound Argument*, no. 402; and Yamatani Eriko, Takahashi Shiro et al., 2003, 'Destroying the country by its own means: The great folly of child-rearing support policy,' *Sound Argument*, no. 370.

32 Hasegawa Michiko and Yamatani Eriko, 2004, 'Talking about women's dignity in a time of falling birthrates and "loser dogs [unmarried and childless older women],"' *Sound Argument*, no. 389.

33 Yamatani Eriko and Hayashi Michiyoshi, 2003, 'Do not permit family collapse,' *Everyone!*, vol. 35, no. 4.

Chapter 4

uses a similar logic in relation to childrearing by breastfeeding. Although she says: 'There were times when I was impatient at my child's taking nearly an hour to breastfeed,' she claims that 'breast milk and lullabies are truly precious things,' and 'the feeling of respect for life is the most fundamental element for [people] all over Japan to retrieve.'[34]

Some of the female intellectuals' also cited examples of the care and psychological interactions they received as infants. Below is a passage from a presentation Nishikawa Kyoko gave at a symposium commemorating the fifth anniversary of the founding of Japanese Women's Association, the women's branch of Japan Conference.

> When I was little, every day I was told embarrassingly often by my grandparents, neighbors, and all kinds of people: 'The Sun is watching, so you mustn't do anything bad.' At those times, I wished they would shut up, but actually those words were implanted firmly into my heart. Whenever I have to make some decision, they spring to mind. I regard them as an expression that brings together Japanese moral and religious views, and lifestyle customers.[35]

Although not from the perspective of a housewife, the speaker's experience of having been the recipient of care from her family is connected to the state.

As such, what role is being played by the logic of female intellectuals in connection with the two different logics of the 'mainstream' and 'housewife' backlashes?

To repeat, the disparity between the logic of 'the mainstream' and that of 'housewives' is significant. While the ultimate target of the mainstream is the abolition of the Basic Law, the significance of housework, child-rearing and care and the social recognition of values that housewives advocate could not be achieved only by the mainstream's means and objectives.

---

34 Yamatani Eriko, Nishidate Yoshiko and Kobayashi Michiko, 2007, 'Special three-member talk: Now is the time for reinstatement of the rights of "women" (Special feature: Is the Japanese family all right as it is?),' *Sound Argument*, no. 425.

35 Sakurai Yoshiko, Nishikawa Kyoko, Yamatani Eriko and Hasegawa Michiko, 2007, 'Symposium abstract: The revitalization of the state and education starts from "the family." The people's resolution is also being questioned,' *Sound Argument*, no. 420.

The politics of 'family values'

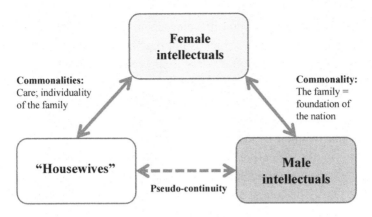

Figure 4.1 The structure of conservative 'family' discourse

The differences between the two views are significant enough to undermine the claims of family values put forward to criticize gender equality. I posit that female intellectuals' function to mediate between these contradictory positions and make them appear to be continuous. Figure 4.1 illustrates the discursive relationship among female intellectuals, the mainstream backlash, and the housewife backlash. The intellectuals' claims, which position the experiences of housework, childrearing, and nursing within the logic of the mainstream, are similar to the logic of housewives who allude to specific family episodes and experiences of caring. Hence, the conservative women who have influence because they are intellectuals seemingly render the logic of housewives as complementary to the family understood as the foundation of society and the state, which is, in turn, central to the mainstream perspective.

Housewife backlash and the 'ethic of care'

Traditionally, people opposed to gender equality have been treated as monolithic, and housewives who oppose gender equality have been considered to have aligned themselves with mainstream proponents. However, as we have seen, when we compare the way housewives and the family are discussed in their respective discourses, there is clear potential for antagonism between the mainstream and housewife cohorts. Mediating between these opposing sides were the female intellectuals, with their dual roles as intellectuals and housewives, whose individual experiences of caring were directly connected to the state. Structuring the

115

Chapter 4

backlash discourse around family values in this manner renders the family discourse of housewives – which is not itself intrinsically conservative – as complementary and supportive of mainstream family discourse.

From this perspective, we can say that although the housewife backlash criticizes gender equality in defense of care work in the home, it has been absorbed into the logic of the mainstream which sees it as self-evident that women should shoulder responsibility for such care work, resulting in the effective silencing of the conservative housewives' demands for social recognition of the significance and value of care work.

The family discourse in the mainstream backlash reflects the family-state view. In the Meiji era, the ideology of the family-state was used for 'mobilizing and justifying the people's loyalty to the emperor and the state by melding "family" and "nation" together' in order to build a modern state, establishing 'a continuum in which feelings towards the family, if expanded and extended, would lead to patriotism by making people regard the nation as one family' (Muta 1996: 81). The family-state ideology strove to subordinate children's 'filial piety' to their parents to their 'allegiance' as subjects to the emperor. In that sense, the family discourse in the mainstream backlash is typical of the discourse used to inspire nationalism in Japan.

In contrast, I suggest that the family discourse in the housewife backlash raises some critical issues. According to political thinker Okano Yayo, the family appears to be 'natural' to the state because it incorporates and reproduces various values and social structures in the society in question. However, the family, politics, and the state are not identical, and their interests frequently conflict. Okano describes the potential in such a scenario, as follows:

> It is in the very scenario where the political nature of the family 'and' politics being 'different' is exposed that we can hear the voices of political dissent calling for better political values, norms, and social structures. (Okano 2000: 867)

From this perspective, the housewife backlash which emphasizes caring interpersonal relationships in the family may in fact express valid concerns that cannot be dismissed as backlash. Although they are not making explicitly political claims, articles by housewives that have been presented as criticisms of gender equality in the conservative media could

The politics of 'family values'

perhaps be reinterpreted as objections to the low status of care work undertaken by women in the private domain. Moreover, if this is a valid reading of the arguments of housewives who oppose gender equality, perhaps it opens possibilities to find common ground for dialogue in feminist debates.

Feminist literature includes a rich vein of what might be called a 'feminist ethic of care' which reexamines social institutions and structures through the lens of care and dependence. Carol Gilligan (1982) first proposed an 'ethic of care'[36] in her book, *In a Different Voice*. Gilligan argues that the prevailing theories in developmental psychology are androcentric, relegating women to a low stage in moral development and proposed that the moral development of women should hinge on an 'ethic of care.'[37]

Gilligan juxtaposes an 'ethic of care' against an 'ethic of rights,' where the latter is based on concepts of law and rights which have been considered the standard for human moral development. Clement (1996) summarizes the characteristics of an 'ethic of care' in three points: 1) emphasis on maintaining human relationships; 2) a humanistic view of people as being connected to others; and 3) context dependence. An 'ethic of care' places unequivocal value upon the maintenance of human relationships. In the care-versus-justice debate that exploded after Gilligan, the question has been whether an 'ethic of care' and the 'logic of justice' should be integrated, and if so, how it would be possible. While the 'logic of justice' refers to abstract laws and rights in making decisions, an 'ethic of care' is based on preserving human relationships. To that end, an 'ethic of care' seeks to address problems from the perspective of how to respond to the needs of others in situations of conflict between others, or between another and oneself, with the aim of maintaining relationships with others with whom one has ties.

---

36 Gilligan referred to this as an 'ethic of responsibility' rather than an 'ethic of care' The 'different voice' that Gilligan articulated would be hugely influential in philosophy and political thought, sparking a long running debate about a 'logic of justice' versus an 'ethic of care.'

37 Gilligan's argument has been criticized by feminists for being essentialist, despite her qualification: 'The different voice I describe is characterized not by gender but theme' (Gilligan 1982: 2). Critics such as Catharine MacKinnon (2005) object to a normative theory of social gender construction in which the moral development of women *must* revolve around human relationships.

Chapter 4

The 'ethic of care' thus has a different view of human beings than the 'logic of justice.' While the latter assumes free and independent/ autonomous individuals, the former regards a person not in isolation, but as a being who is always connected with others. Thus, the 'logic of justice' is concerned with 'how one can meet one's obligations to others without infringing on individual autonomy', while an 'ethic of care' asks,' how can one achieve individual freedom without violating one's moral responsibility to others?' (Clement 1996: 13).

An 'ethic of care' is context-dependent in contrast to the universalized abstractions of justice. The need to answer others' needs sometimes creates friction between competing needs, or between oneself and another. To resolve such friction, Gilligan suggests that 'the moral problem arises from conflicting responsibilities rather than from competing rights and "requires for its resolution a mode of thinking that is contextual and narrative rather than formal and abstract"' (Gilligan 1982: 19). When specific others with whom one is connected have difficulties, an 'ethic of care' seeks solutions appropriate to the specific context.

Arguably, the housewife backlash reflects aspects of this 'ethic of care.' The housewife backlash speaks of the family primarily in terms of how to respond to the needs of others, especially family members such as children, spouses, and parents, and reflects on how those responses were made in the past. Articles by housewives differed from the mainstream backlash in that while they expressed the frustration and difficulties that the authors experienced as caregivers, they also placed supreme importance on the interpersonal relationships built through care.

The housewife backlash also expressed a view of humans as beings who are connected with others. As we saw earlier, *Dianthus* criticized individual independence. The housewife backlash authors considered it meaningless to view the dependent and caring relationships within the household from the perspective of individual independence. They considered it impossible for there to be individual independence within the family. Their narratives about family clearly portray the context-dependent nature of care. Although the housewife and the mainstream backlash both discuss the family without questioning the gendered division of labor, they differ in how they imagine the family. While the mainstream backlash portrays an abstract and normative 'family that all should conform with,' the housewife backlash presents diverse families through concrete descriptions of everyday life. Moreover, the format of

The politics of 'family values'

such narratives was confined to essays, and were not abstract narratives about the 'value of the family' in society or the state.

Previous research and commentary has suggested that women who support the backlash against gender equality and participate in the conservative movement: 1) have a political consciousness of patriarchal familism; 2) fear the loss of vested interests due to changes in legal institutions that might affect full-time housewives; and 3) are 'worried' that 'their way of life as housewives will be denigrated.' Reconsidering these points in light of the findings presented in this chapter: 1) the housewives did not express strong political views in discourse, which tells us little about their political consciousness; 2) can be discounted because they did not speak of vested interests; and 3) it is certainly possible that a sense of crisis about the social valuation of their identity as homemaker has fostered 'antipathy' among housewives towards gender equality. However, as we have seen, the housewives' criticisms of gender equality were not driven by negative motivations such as 'self-defense,' but rather by a positive motivation similar to an 'ethic of care'. In other words, regardless of the circumstances by which they became housewives, from the perspective of those responsible for care the primary motivation appears to be appealing for recognition of the significance of 'dependence labor' (Kittay 1999).

Nevertheless, the critical political position of the 'housewife backlash' that calls for recognition of the social value of care in the private domain has been obscured by the discursive structure of the 'family values backlash', aided in no small part by female intellectuals'[38] whose claims connect with the logic of the 'mainstream backlash' which regards women's assumption of the burden of care as 'natural.' Thus, the 'housewife backlash' is placed in this kind of paradoxical situation.

---

38 I indicated in this chapter that 'care' might be considered to underpin the housewife backlash discourse, but as I could not sufficiently establish such a feature appearing in female intellectuals' discourse, this remains a challenge. Kaizuma Keiko's arguments offer abundant clues whenever we are considering Japanese conservative female politicians. From her analysis of articles by conservative female politicians in general commercial media since the 1990s, while touching on their diversity, Kaizuma points out that because 'those women have at least something that can resonate with or seem familiar to a broad range of people,' therefore 'they have the ability to lessen people's feelings of resistance towards xenophobia, hardline militarism, historical revisionism and the religious right-wing' (Kaizuma 2018: 148).

Chapter 5

The women's movement against gender equality

The grassroots movement against gender equality

In the previous chapter, my analysis of various communications media from conservative activist groups revealed that women who identify as 'housewives' in their opposition to gender equality tend to believe that the achievement of equal social participation regardless of gender would negatively influence human relationships within the home. It also showed that such women positively value the social significance of the domestic care work they perform.

Their argument overlaps with the feminist ethic of care which, since Carol Gilligan, has criticized the very foundations of modern society, which assumes that individuals are independent/autonomous from the perspective of care. However, it remains unclear why these women think that interpersonal relationships in the household will be 'destroyed' by gender equality and support a 'backlash.'

In this chapter, therefore, I will focus on a civic group, Association A, which spread the movement against gender equality in a regional area. Through interviews with members of that group, I will investigate those women's rejection of gender equality while revealing the on-the-ground situation in a grassroots conservative movement.

The campaign against gender equality which expanded nationwide in the early 2000s was led by a variety of activist groups. As we have seen, Japan Conference has been identified as the largest conservative organization in Japan, and along with its female version, Japanese Women's Association, and the Textbook Society, have been the central players in that movement (Ida 2006). Other fierce opponents of gender equality were the Japan Conference League of Local Assembly Members (Nippon kaigi chiho giin renmei);' the 'Extreme sex education and

Chapter 5

gender-free education fact-finding survey project team,' a group of parliamentarians within the LDP; and religious bodies including the Shinto Political Alliance , and Unification Church (Toitsu kyokai), now renamed the Family Federation for World Peace and Unification.

After the enactment of the Basic Law on Gender Equality, local government bodies began to enact ordinances for the promotion of gender equality,[1] and local movements opposed to such ordinances arose across Japan (Yamaguchi, Saito and Ogiue 2012). Whenever moves by regional assemblies to enact those ordinances were seen, groups campaigning against them formed grassroots civic associations to block them. However, these groups were characterized by weak continuity of action, seeing that their activity wound down once ordinances were either enacted or rejected, or, if they continued activities, their aims shifted from opposition to gender equality to other contentious issues such as children's education or family problems.

The battle over gender equality was fierce in regional assemblies and, in no small number of local authorities, the opposition movement achieved some measure of success. Chiba, the sole prefecture yet to have a gender equality ordinance today, began to actively implement gender equality measures after Domoto Akiko took office as Governor of Chiba Prefecture in 2001. Although a draft ordinance was tabled at the September 2002 prefectural assembly, after being carried over three times, it was rejected in April 2003 (Kashima 2018). Furthermore, some local authorities have also adopted petitions aimed at limiting the effects of the ordinances.

The Kagoshima Prefectural Assembly adopted a petition opposing gender-free education in July 2003, and in October 2003, a petition was adopted by the Ishikawa Prefectural Assembly to the effect that

---

1 According to the Cabinet Office's Gender Equality Bureau, as of 2018, ordinances relating to gender equality had been enacted by forty-six prefectural governments (i.e., all but Chiba), and in 645 municipalities (accounting for 37.1% of the total). There is great disparity in the rate of adoption by local government bodies by prefecture. While on the one hand there were prefectures in which all local government authorities had created the ordinances (e.g., Ishikawa, Tottori, and Oita), there were others with low rates: Wakayama (6.7%), Aomori (5.0%), Yamagata (8.6%), Gunma (8.6%), Chiba (13.0%), and Kanagawa (15.2%) (Gender Equality Bureau, Cabinet Office, 'Status of promotion of measures relating to the creation of a gender-equal society or women in local government bodies (2018–19).'

the ordinance 'must not be utilized by radical ideological movements calling themselves "gender free",' while a resolution was adopted by Tokushima Prefectural Assembly declaring that 'the realization of a truly gender-equal society that deems the position of removing all distinctions between genders to be a mistake.' Moreover, in Ube City in Yamaguchi Prefecture, a gender equality ordinance was enacted that included promises not to 'disavow "proper" masculinity and "proper" femininity.' nor to 'disavow full-time housewives,' but it was also pointed out that this might be departing from the spirit of the Basic Law (Ito 2003a; Kanai 2008).

Association A is a women-centered grassroots group campaigning in opposition to gender equality in Ehime Prefecture, one of the areas where the battle over the ordinance was most ferocious. Based on fieldwork I conducted with Association A from May 2008 to March 2011 and interviews with twenty-three of its members, as well as articles in Association A's bulletins, I investigate the experiences and attitudes of women who oppose gender equality. Association A publishes the bulletin called *Dianthus*, which I discussed in Chapter Four.

There were three reasons for choosing Association A for this investigation. First, it was a women-centered group; second, although grassroots groups' campaigns opposing gender equality are generally short-lived, Association A had continued activities from its establishment in 2004 until the time of my survey in 2011, and so was a relatively stable activist group; and third, Oguma and Ueno's (2003) study of grassroots conservative movements had surveyed a volunteer organization called History Circle, the Kanagawa Prefecture branch of the Textbook Society, and as that group was active in the suburbs of a large city, I conjectured that a grassroots group operating in a regional area might exhibit different characteristics and tendencies.

To elaborate on my third point, Oguma and Ueno (2003) summarized the five distinguishing characteristics of History Circle as follows. Its mode of activity featured: 1) emphasis on members' voluntary participation; 2) loose ties among members, with no hierarchical relationship between fixed office-bearers and ordinary participants; 3) a semi-independent relationship with its parent organization (Textbook Society); 4) use of communication technology such as the Internet; and 5) self-identification as a movement by 'ordinary citizens' that distanced itself from political parties. On these bases, Oguma and Ueno argue that History Circle has

Chapter 5

the characteristics of network-type civic movements, and represents an 'urban populism' in which individuals isolated from a community come together, in contrast to the traditional conservative movement grounded on a 'village-communitarian "power base"' (Oguma and Ueno 2003: 3). Bearing the characteristics of History Circle in mind, I will consider whether such characteristics are also found in groups operating in regional areas.

The battle over gender equality in Ehime Prefecture

Amendment of the Matsuyama City gender equality ordinance

Ehime Prefecture was the site of a particularly intense battle over gender equality.[2] In Matsuyama City, especially, debate over a gender equality ordinance expanded in a confused mixture involving authorities and regional assemblies, and citizens both for and against. At the March 2002 city assembly meeting in Matsuyama, a policy for establishing a gender equality ordinance was decided, and the ordinance was passed by a majority vote in favor at the assembly's regular sitting in June 2003. It was enforced from 1 September 2003, but it immediately came to light that the city authorities were intending to submit a proposed amendment at the September regular sitting of the assembly which would start on the seventeenth of that month. At the same time, Matsuyama City also proposed a 'Basic ordinance for the wholesome development of children.' This draft ordinance trumpeted such ideas as the cultivation in children of a 'spirit of love for and pride in [their] native place,' and for them to 'inherit a warm, considerate heart and hand it on to the next generation.' It stipulated that guardians should treat children 'with deep affection' and that citizens should 'call upon [children] to stop saying and doing things that violate social norms, and to support and guide [them] with enthusiasm,' but critical voices were raised from civic groups that this

---

2 Notably, Ehime Prefecture was a relatively early adopter of initiatives for gender equality. In 2001, a gender equality plan called 'Partnership Ehime' was formulated, and in March 2002, the Ehime Prefecture gender equality ordinance was decided. See Sasanuma (2004) for details of the ordinance and the process of its formulation.

would 'constrain childrearing by law.'[3] Partly because these two draft ordinances concerning women and the family were submitted at the same time, they drew attention from citizens.

The proposal to amend the gender equality ordinance contained the following two amendments. First, it was proposed that the English terms 'gender (*jendā*),' 'sexual harassment (*sekushuaru harasumento*),' and 'domestic violence (*domesutikku baiorensu*),' which had been simply transliterated using the Japanese *katakana* syllabary, be translated into Japanese. Specifically, 'gender' was to be replaced by a phrase meaning 'awareness of a fixed division of roles according to sex,' and 'sexual harassment' by 'words or actions of a sexual nature against the wishes of the other party.' These alterations were problematic in that much of the original meaning of each of the terms would be pruned away. In the case of the word 'gender,' there was a likelihood that it would be trivialized to an issue of awareness, such as in an 'awareness of a fixed division of roles,' whereas for 'sexual harassment,' suspicions were raised by those promoting gender equality, suggesting that this would underestimate the social and economic harm and disadvantage that arose from having been on the receiving end of so-called '*seku-hara*' (the Japanese abbreviation of 'sexual harassment').

The second amendment was a more substantial change to Article Ten. In its original preamble, Article Ten stipulated 'respect for sexuality and consideration for lifelong health,' and specified reproductive health and rights, including 'men and women shall respect each other's sexuality,' and '[women's] own decisions on pregnancy, childbirth, and other matters relating to reproduction and sexuality shall be respected.' In the revised version proposed by the city, 'respect for ... sexuality' was changed to 'men and women shall deepen their mutual understanding of each other's physical characteristics,' while mention of sexuality and reproduction was proposed to be amended to 'each other's will shall be respected with regard to pregnancy, childbirth, and so forth,' thus limiting women's right of self-determination in sexuality and reproduction.

Furthermore, the lack of transparency about how this revision came to be proposed was questioned by citizens' groups promoting gender equality as well as some members of the municipal assembly. While the original ordinance formulated in June 2003 had been compiled in an

---

3 *Ehime shinbun*, morning edition, 11 September 2003

Chapter 5

open manner, was debated at a 'Matsuyama Gender Equality Meeting' that included members of the general public, and was discussed in public hearings,[4] the submission of the reform proposal happened suddenly. Its apparent justification was that the city received 'faxes, letters and emails from all over Japan, expressing the opinion that "the right to self-determination on sexuality and reproduction will authorize abortion and free sex, and lead to the corruption of morality"' (Shin 2004: 52).

Deliberation of the proposed amendment led to confusion in the municipal assembly. After citizens both for and against the proposal were called as material witnesses and the motion was repeatedly carried forward,[5] a revised amendment passed in December 2003 following the submission of further proposals by assembly members affiliated with the LDP. As a result, the terms transcribed in katakana remained unchanged, but the wording regarding sexuality and reproduction was altered to say: 'Men and women shall deepen their mutual understanding, and their own decisions shall be respected.' The revisions arguably rendered the perspective of women's reproductive health and rights less substantial. Perhaps unsurprisingly, citizens who had originally promoted gender equality opposed the revisions, while citizens who opposed gender equality legislation approved of it.

Establishment and activity of Association A

In 2004, after the Matsuyama City's revised gender equality ordinance passed, volunteers from the pro-amendment faction who had been observers at the municipal assembly debates established Association A, a civic group opposed to gender equality. Its principal activities comprised lectures (annually, with 150 participants), study groups (twice a month, with about ten participants), and the publication of a bulletin, *Dianthus* (every second month). Its annual membership fees were set at 1000 yen, and it had 764 members as of 2011. Association A had entered its seventh

---

4 *Ehime shimbun*, morning edition, 30 September 2003

5 The carrying forward of an ordinance proposal in the Matsuyama City assembly was 'the first such incidence on record since 1947,' (*Ehime shinbun*, morning edition, 3 October 2003), and it was the first time material witnesses had been summoned since that program was instituted in 1991 (*Ehime shinbun*, morning edition, 21 October 2003). These precedents indicate how contentious the issue was in Matsuyama City at the time.

126

year when the survey began. As mentioned, I decided to survey Association A because it was an example of a female-led grassroots organization opposed to gender equality that had been active over a long period.

Association A has always aspired to be a female-centered group. To win members, Association A appealed to a variety of other groups, as I will discuss later, but it neither answers to any higher organization, nor supports any particular political party. The current president, Ms. Y (female, in her fifties) explains this, saying: 'We wanted to make it a group that was easy for any sort of woman to join,' and considers it to have avoided presenting any specific character. Furthermore, Association A is led by women, and its bulletin reports that 'the majority of members are women, and they are all sorts: some have jobs, and some are full-time housewives.'[6] Its study groups, too, are described as 'gatherings where members, most of whom are women, can seek advice on and study about issues that are close at hand.'[7]

Association A, which was established after the amended Matsuyama City ordinance passed, has augmented its awareness-raising activities with frequent appeals to authorities. In August 2005, it had a face-to-face meeting with Ehime prefectural officers, soliciting opinions about the prefecture's gender equality policy.[8] In 2006, it held a study meeting, inviting nine LDP-affiliated members of the prefectural assembly in addition to a journalist, Sakurai Yuko,[9] and in September 2007, Association A members petitioned the Matsuyama City Civic Engagement and Community Development Division to implement an 'appropriate' gender equality policy.[10]

Association A's submission of Petition no. 35 deserves special mention: 'As to a request for clarification of the basic policy for operation of the Matsuyama City gender equality promotion ordinance.' This petition was submitted in December 2007 to Matsuyama City by seven members of Association A, with three assembly members as sponsors. The petition included items such as 'give consideration to the differences between men's and women's physical and mental characteristics,' and

---

6 *Dianthus*, inaugural issue, 2004

7 *Dianthus*, inaugural issue, 2004

8 *Dianthus*, no. 7, 2005

9 *Dianthus*, no. 9, 2006

10 *Dianthus*, no. 19, 2006

Chapter 5

'to value full-time housewives' social contribution, and support them.' It also included items such as 'not to encourage learning or research in gender studies or women's studies,' which drew strenuous objections from scholars of women's studies and gender discourse.[11] The petition was adopted 17 December 2007 after one member of Association A had been summoned as a material witness.

The fundamental assertions of Association A

Association A touts six basic reasons for its opposition to gender equality: 1) respect for 'proper' masculinity and femininity; 2) emphasis on family ties; 3) re-examination of sexual self-determination; 4) sex education that considers children's stage of development; 5) freedom of speech; and 6) respect for traditional culture.[12] These claims aligned with the criticisms of gender equality spread by the 'mainstream backlash' through conservative magazines and the organs of activist groups, as discussed in Chapter Four. In 2004, when Association A was established, these critiques of gender equality were already widespread in the conservative media, and Association A took up the cause with claims such as: '"gender-free" will disavow any difference between genders,' 'it will deny proper masculinity and femininity,' 'it will destroy the family,' 'reproductive health and rights, and sex education, will encourage free sex,' 'it criticizes such terms as "husband" and "wife" as being discriminatory,' and 'it will destroy such traditional culture as the Doll Festival [to celebrate Girls' Day] and carp streamers [to celebrate Boys' Day].'

Association A has utilized these accumulated resources to conduct its activities. For example, it invited conservative intellectuals such as Yagi Hidetsugu, Takahashi Shiro and Sakurai Yuko as well as politicians such as Yamatani Eriko as keynote speakers to its annual lecture meetings. Moreover, it endeavored to demonstrate the legitimacy of its assertions by reprinting in its bulletins essays that these intellectuals had published in other magazines, alongside information specific to Ehime Prefecture and articles written by its own members.

---

11 In response, the Japan Association of Gender and Law issued a 'Statement deploring the trend in some regional local government bodies of hindering gender equality and social development' (7 February 2008).

12 *Dianthus*, Inaugural issue, 2004

And yet, Association A's claims differ from the nationwide criticism of gender equality. An article in the inaugural issue of its bulletin, entitled: 'In order for both men and women to be *happy*' (emphasis added), states that the association was launched 'due to simple doubt' as to whether gender equality/gender-free, which 'tries to do away with "proper masculinity" and "proper femininity" and tries to ban Girls' Day and Boys' Day celebrations, and even folk tales,' is 'after all something that will make people and society *happy*.' When its bulletin called for new members, it said: '"The family" and "children" are the last strongholds for society now, when many things are crumbling away from people's hearts,' and it expressed the wish for people to join 'in order to protect the family and children from the offensive of gender-free.'[13] Two years later, an article entitled: 'The path we have trodden: Upon reaching our second anniversary'[14] criticizes gender equality, saying: 'We cannot help doubting its worth if it will invite discord into and resistance to *real life*, as well as intergenerational conflict and confusion in the values system.'

From such assertions, we can see that Association A raised different issues about gender equality than the major conservative media and groups discussed in Chapter Four. Association A presents gender equality as a family issue, as in 'protecting the family and children from "gender-free",' and its suggestion that gender equality 'does not accord' with individual 'happiness' and 'real life' is not about meta-level social systems or social structures, but with a topology closer to everyday concerns. These claims are characteristic of Association A, a grassroots activist group.

Overview of the respondents and analytical methodology

How does Association A's critique of gender equality at the level of everyday concerns address the circumstances of its members' participation in their movement? I first want to use my interviews with Association A members from February to March 2011[15] to identify the factors that led members to become activists.

---

13 *Dianthus*, no. 2, 2004

14 *Dianthus*, no. 13, 2006

15 See Suzuki (2019) on my survey of Association A.

Chapter 5

I interviewed twenty-three members (eighteen women and five men), each of whom were introduced to me by the president, Ms. Y.[16] As Association A was specifically centered on women, I asked Ms. Y to introduce female members. However, Ms. Y wanted to ensure I heard from members of diverse backgrounds in terms of, for example, age, area of residence, group affiliation, and religious belief, which enabled me to interview members from diverse cohorts, albeit mainly women.

Of my respondents,[17] twenty-two were aged fifty and above, and nine (the largest number) identified their occupation as 'housewife' (in an open question). Importantly, many respondents answering 'housewife' had previously been employed and were describing their post-retirement situation with the term 'housewife,' while others identified as 'housewives' even though they were employed in part-time or non-regular work. Nine respondents had graduated from a four-year university course or higher, including all five men. Moreover, all respondents, bar two, also belonged to other groups, including: eight in Japan Conference, five each in Institute of Moralogy and Ehime Branch of the National Association for the Rescue of Japanese Kidnapped by North Korea (Rachi higaisha o sukuu kai Ehime) (hereafter, 'the Rescue Association'), three each in Textbook Society and House of Growth, two each in Learning from Japanese History Group (Nihon no rekishi ni manabu kai), Original Gospel Bible Seminary (Kirisuto no makuya) and the Ehime Branch of the Association of Sound Argument (Ehime Seiron no kai), and one each in New Buddhism Religious Organization, the Association of Shinto Shrines, Gathering to Study the Eastern Thought of Yasuoka Masahiro, the Association to Think about Matsuyama (Matsuyama o kangaeru kai) and a volunteer group. Eleven of the respondents belonged to two or more groups besides Association A (see Table 5.1 for the attributes of the respondents cited in the following discussion). Ms. Y claimed that their demographic details were more or less representative of Association A's

---

16 In implementing the survey, I first negotiated with the president, Ms. Y, by telephone and email, and explained in writing the purpose of my research vis-à-vis people who would cooperate in my interviews, and how I would handle the data. I obtained prior permission from some individual respondents for audio recordings of their interviews, and I took written notes while interviewing those who did not consent to recordings.

17 I obtained data on base attributes such as age, sex and occupation via a questionnaire administered after their interview.

130

The women's movement against gender equality

Table 5.1 Respondent profiles

Name	Sex	Age	Occupation	Highest completed educational level	Affiliated group/s
B	M	50s	Teacher	4-year university	Japan Conference; Textbook Society
C	M	70s	Unemployed (researcher)	Graduate school	None
D	F	60s	Self-employed	4-year university	Japan Conference; New Buddhism Religious Organization
E	F	50s	Housewife	4-year university	Japan Conference; Textbook Society; Gathering to Study the Eastern Thought of Yasuoka Masahiro
F	F	70s	Unemployed (teacher)	4-year university	House of Growth
G	F	50s	Farmer	Senior high school	Volunteer group
H	F	30s	Housewife	4-year university	Japan Conference
I	F	50s	Welfare worker	Junior college	None
J	F	70s	Farmer	Senior high school	Institute of Moralogy
K	F	50s	Self-employed	Senior high school	Institute of Moralogy
L	F	60s	Housewife	Senior high school	House of Growth; Rescue Association
M	F	60s	Welfare worker	Senior high school	Original Gospel Bible Seminary
N	F	70s	Housewife	Technical college	Original Gospel Bible Seminary
O	F	50s	Housewife	Senior high school	Institute of Moralogy
P	F	70s	Housewife & commissioned welfare volunteer	Senior high school	Institute of Moralogy; Learning from Japanese History Group; Rescue Association
Q	F	60s	NA	Senior high school	Rescue Association
R	F	60s	Housewife	Junior college	Institute of Moralogy; Learning from Japanese History Group
S	M	60s	Foundation officer	Graduate school	Association to Think about Matsuyama
T	M	80s	Unemployed (teacher)	4-year university	Japan Conference; Ehime Branch of the Association of Sound Argument
U	M	70s	Shinto priest	4-year university	Japan Conference; Association of Shinto Shrines
V	F	60s	Housewife & Welfare worker	Senior high school	House of Growth; Rescue Association
W	F	70s	Housewife	Junior college	Japan Conference; Ehime Branch of the Association of Sound Argument
Y	F	50s	Self-employed	NA	Japan Conference; Textbook Society; Rescue Association

(* Brackets indicate former occupation)

Chapter 5

membership, but I was unable to access the data necessary to confirm that claim. Furthermore, as Ms. Y introduced the respondents, we can assume that they belonged to her personal network.

Degrees of involvement varied widely among respondents to my survey. To analyze their narratives, including any correlation between their degree of involvement and the circumstances of their joining the association, I assessed the twenty-three respondents according to Hasegawa Koichi's (1991) categories of social movement participants. Using the anti-nuclear power movement as an example, Hasegawa classifies social movement participants into five cohorts, namely: a 'leadership cohort' at the center; a 'full-time activity cohort' who always participate in regular activities; a 'peripheral activity cohort' who participate irregularly in large-scale meetings and signature-gathering events; a 'positive support cohort' who pay membership fees, receive bulletins and contribute to fundraising; and the 'peripheral support cohort' who only irregularly participate in signature-collecting, fundraising and meetings. When we apply this to the respondents, we get one person from the 'leadership cohort,' two from the 'full-time activity cohort,' two from the 'peripheral activity cohort,' eighteen from the 'positive support cohort,' and none corresponding to the 'peripheral support cohort.' Two reasons could be considered for the absence of members of the peripheral support cohort: 1) as Association A has a membership-fee system, basically all members pay membership fees; and 2) as I had asked the president, Ms. Y, to choose the respondents, it is likely that members with a low level of involvement in activities were overlooked.

I will now examine the narratives of respondents in each category. Please note that the age and status specified are as of 2011, at the time of the survey.

Circumstances of members' participation in the movement

Leadership and full-time activity cohorts

The leadership cohort is represented by the president, Ms. Y (female, fifties). Ms. Y was the central figure in Association A's activities, involved in everything from planning lectures to compiling and distributing bulletins. When Ms. Y was posted overseas for work, she was motivated by how the people she met in various countries regarded their own countries with pride. After her return to Japan she started to read the author Kobayashi Yoshinori, a cartoonist and conservative commentator famous for his criticism of the left, and later began to attend events by conservative groups. She reports having previously participated in Japan Conference, House of Growth, and the Textbook Society. Ms. Y launched Association A along with Mr. B whom she met at the Textbook Society.

Mr. B (male, fifties) and Mr. C (male, seventies) comprised the full-time activity cohort. Mr. B was a foundation member of Association A and was serving as the coordinator at the time of the survey. However, Mr. B's main activity was with Textbook Society, where he had given lectures. He had also given lectures at the Learning from Japanese History Group, Institute of Moralogy, Shinto Youth Association (Shinto seinenkai), and "Let's protect the imperial house" Okayama prefectural residents' group (Koshitsu o mamoro Okayama kenmin shukai). Mr. B had a strong interest in history education issues, and said that he participated in Association A because gender equality was an issue that effected all people. He explained that interest in history textbooks was limited to the field of school education, and for most people 'it was like looking up from below at enemy planes having dogfights.' In contrast, gender equality was 'the kind of issue that had to do with the family, like fathers, or mothers, or suchlike.' Mr. B compared it to 'a land battle' because it involved all people.

Mr. C's primary role was explaining administrative and political trends to members. Soon after establishing the association, Ms. Y paid a visit to Mr. C 's workplace, and Mr. C reportedly joined the association on the spot. Mr. C had learned of the terms 'gender equality' and 'gender' from the magazine *Sound Argument*, to which he subscribed, and apparently had no hesitation in joining because he had felt 'slight discomfort' at the number of books on gender discourse on display in bookshops.

Peripheral activity cohort

The peripheral activity cohort comprised Mrs. D (female, sixties) and Mrs. E (female, fifties). Both had at different times been the association's treasurer, but had retired from office while remaining irregular participants.

Mrs. D is a member of the New Buddhism Religious Organization, where she was once responsible for providing home-visit counseling to

Chapter 5

devotees. In that connection, when the amendment of the Matsuyama City ordinance was proposed, she was approached by Japan Conference to be a material witness for the pro-amendment faction. She prepared for her testimony by studying gender equality materials provided by the New Buddhism Religious Organization. In that process, Mrs. D became acquainted with Ms. Y and got involved in launching Association A.

Like Mr. B, Mrs. E was primarily interested in historical issues. Mrs. E was originally passionate about international exchange, having hosted international students from the Philippines, Australia, South Korea, and elsewhere. She became more deeply engaged in historical issues following an argument with a South Korean acquaintance during the 1980s textbook controversy.[18] Due to her anxiety over the deteriorating Japan–South Korea relations, Mrs. E had been learning Korean from her South Korean acquaintance, thinking that 'it would be nice if we could get along at a grassroots level.' However, triggered by the textbook controversy, Mrs. E felt that 'grassroots get trampled quite flat through political moves.' In arguing with her Korean acquaintance about using the term 'invasion' in history textbooks, Mrs. E found she was completely unable to answer back. She subsequently began to study history, reading books and speaking to her parents and relatives and developed a new understanding of prewar Japan, which she describes as follows.

> I thought that it was the kind of era when Japan was full of people that did nothing but bad things, like the rich exploiting the poor, and men oppressing women, but when I look at our parents, they are quite carefree, right? Sure, there were some people with money, but those sorts quite often made donations, or put their own money into repair work on the rivers and so on, so there were lots of highly respectable people. But when I wondered what the discrepancy was, I thought maybe my assumptions were wrong.

After she 'realized that Japan was not such a bad country after all,' Mrs. E joined groups such as Gathering to Study the Eastern Thought of Yasuoka

---

18 News that the word 'invasion (*shinryaku*)' would not be permitted by the Japanese Ministry of Education, Culture, Sports, Science and Technology (MEXT)'s textbook screening process triggered protests from China and South Korea in response, which escalated into a diplomatic issue (Hatano 2011).

134

Masahiro and the Textbook Society. She met Ms. Y at Japan Conference and accepted her invitation to join Association A.

Positive support cohort

Eighteen respondents, more than half, corresponded to the positive support cohort category. The circumstances which led people in this cohort to join the association can be divided roughly into: 1) previous personal acquaintance with the president, Ms. Y; and 2) having been solicited from groups with which they were previously affiliated. Moreover, significant differences in their motivation towards Association A's activities corresponded to this division.

The first category included four individuals: Mrs. F (female, seventies), who joined Association A based on her personal friendship with Ms. Y, with whom she had interacted at House of Growth; Mrs. G (female, fifties) who had become acquainted with Ms. Y at the Women's Division of Bodaiji Temple parishioners' Women's Division; and Mrs. H (female, thirties) and Mrs. I (female, fifties), both of whom were sending their children to Ms. Y's academic coaching school.

Mrs. F and Mrs. G, who also had interactions with Ms. Y independently of Association A, justified participating in the association on the grounds that they had no reason to oppose it. Mrs. F says, for example: 'Well, Ms. Y is trying her hardest all by herself, and so I should do whatever I can,' and 'After all, the family is important,' while Mrs. G says: 'I don't have any particular reason to oppose [the association], and so, er, if there is something I can do, I'd like to cooperate.'

Partly because Mrs. H and Mrs. I had joined the association after reading the bulletins handed to them by Ms. Y, they perceived Association A's bulletins as a rare and precious source of information. They positioned Association A as a medium for obtaining information that could not be gained from the mass media, with Mrs. H surmising that 'it is quite hard to get 'right[-leaning]' information … because newspapers, television and so on try to be neutral.' Moreover, Mrs. I said that through reading the association's bulletins, she had begun to recognize that certain newspaper articles were 'a bit dubious.'

In contrast, fourteen of the remaining respondents categorized as positive support cohort had joined Association A following solicitations at other groups with which they were affiliated. Mrs. J (female, seventies)

Chapter 5

and Mrs. K (female, sixties), who belonged to the moral cultivation group, Institute of Moralogy reportedly joined when Association A's former president, Mrs. Z, had encouraged everyone at a Moralogy meeting to join (Mrs. K). One joined after a leader of House of Growth (Mrs. L: female, sixties) requested her cooperation with the association, while others were approached at Original Gospel Bible Seminary by an acquaintance who was active in Association A (Mrs. M: female, sixties; Mrs. N: female, seventies).

Respondents who had had been solicited at other groups almost all limited their participation in Association A to simply paying the membership fee. As Moralogy member Mrs. K (female, sixties) lived some distance from Matsuyama City, Association A's activity base, she said she was often unable to attend lectures or study groups, and only read the bulletins when she had time. Mrs. M (female, sixties), in turn, who said it was only a year since she had joined, seemed to have little idea what Association A's activities actually were, saying: 'Frankly speaking, I am not sure at all what they are doing, who publish this newsletter.'

In this manner, Ms. Y and the respondents who were prior acquaintances willingly engaged with Association A's activities as much as they could, either based on trust in Ms. Y or a desire to support her efforts. In contrast, those respondents who had been mobilized through other groups had low motivation to participate in its activities.[19]

Members' reasons for supporting Association A

People associated with a variety of groups participated in Association A, but there were vast differences in participant's knowledge about gender equality. Having had doubts or a critical awareness vis-à-vis gender equality *prior to joining* was not necessarily the reason for their participation in Association A. Nonetheless, respondents frequently expressed empathy with Association A, as in Mrs. E comments that the association had 'almost the same *values* as I had had beforehand,' while Mrs. O (female, fifties), upon hearing Ms. Y talk about gender equality,

---

19 The president, Ms. Y, appeared to be cognizant of this tendency. When I asked her about it, she admitted that this cohort was contributing to the group's finances, saying: 'I think it is amazing that they kindly keep on paying even 1000 yen every year.'

thought: 'It *has something in common* with the situation here, too.' Let us turn now to examine the sort of assertions from Association A its members endorse.

The realities of gender equality

First, let us look at the narratives of respondents who were aware of gender equality as an issue before joining Association A. This included eleven of the twenty-three respondents, some of whom had learned of the term 'gender equality' during the public debate over the amendment of the Matsuyama City ordinance, and had been involved in launching Association A. Even among people involved in the women's movement, in 2000, there were not many who knew about the Basic Law for a Gender-equal Society.[20] Under those circumstances, what common ground did the members of Association A have with gender equality policies?

Arguably, the members of Association A, most of whom had affiliations with other groups, would have found it comparatively easy to access information about gender equality. When Mrs. J (female, seventies), who had been involved with Moralogy for many years, first heard the expression 'gender equality (danjo kyodo sankaku),' she thought it probably meant 'men and women would help each other,' 'be able to participate in all kinds of events,' and could 'endeavor to build a society where [people] could make their best efforts.' She then said: 'When I read magazines and such, there were wrong things written about gender equality. So, I began to have suspicions, wondering if that situation would be acceptable.' Similarly, Mrs. Q (female, sixties), who had been deeply involved in the Rescue Association, recounted that she had also thought gender equality to be 'men and women cooperating' and she 'thought it almost strange that anyone would oppose it,' but 'when I looked at the documents and newspaper articles sent to me [and] all kinds of books, [I found] it was a bit different, and so I began to think, "What's going on?!"' It was not possible in the interviews to determine the sources from which respondents gained information, but it seems likely that they

---

20 On the state of the women's movement immediately following the enactment of the Basic Law for a Gender-equal Society, Ueno Chizuko expressed her incredulity at 'hearing people at women's gatherings around the country asking: "When, and who, suggested such a law?" and "What effectiveness will it have?"' (Ueno 2011a, 236).

Chapter 5

learned about gender equality from the organs and bulletins published by the groups to which they belonged and other related groups.

Some of the respondents had attended lectures concerning gender equality sponsored by local authorities. Mrs. P (female, seventies) had supported local elderly people and young people with problems such as non-attendance at school for many years as a commissioned community volunteer. Mrs. P reported receiving a request from a women's group to attend a lecture 'to raise the status of women,' where she had heard the term 'gender equality' for the first time. However, Mrs. P says that she 'gradually became annoyed' while listening to the speaker. Mrs. P explained what particularly triggered her anger as follows:

> That lecturer was saying, you know, 'When you get up in the morning, say [to your husband]: "You cook the meals today," or "When you get home this evening, you prepare dinner," or "Today it's your turn to do the washing."'
>
> And what did she say the wives would be doing? She said that ideal gender equality would be for me to watch television, or drink tea. We thought: 'Whaat?'

Of course, we do not know what the speaker said, or in what context she said it, but Mrs. P recalled feeling angry when she talked about a married couple sharing household chores. Mrs. P seems to have interpreted the speaker's message as a suggestion to 'make' a husband do housework, further describing her discomfort as follows:

> If it were me, I would say things like, 'Sorry, dear, but would you mind getting the cups out?' and rather than being annoyed at such things and kicking things around in anger, er, when the meal is cooked and the table set, wouldn't it be better to say something like: 'Sorry, but could you put the food on the table for me, please?' or 'Could you get the chopsticks ready, please?'

Clearly, Mrs. P thought it would be better to 'request her husband to do things' while repeatedly showing how apologetic she feels, by saying 'Sorry,' and was uncomfortable at what she perceived to be a suggestion to 'order [her] husband arbitrarily to do the housework.' However, rather than a reaction to the idea that her husband perhaps ought to share in the housework, her discomfort may have been due to her recognition that 'commanding' her husband to do housework was not a realistic way of getting things done in her experience.

Others were persuaded by the conservatives' critiques of gender equality, although they had no interaction with the authorities' gender equality measures. Critics of gender equality, who employed the expression 'gender-free' for leverage, as well as opposing government initiatives, also campaigned against efforts to teach gender equality in the classroom – such as coeducational classes in home economics, mixed-sex class rolls, and sex education – describing these initiatives as 'moves to erase the gender difference between boys and girls.'[21] Mrs. H (female, thirties) first learned about gender equality from Ms. Y, but says that the school her children attended had already adopted mixed-sex rolls at that time. She says that when she heard that 'after the initial introduction of mixed school rolls' at the chalkface, male and female students sharing the same rooms at outdoor education facilities, and sex education 'has been set in areas with advanced gender equality,' she thought: 'Oh, that's no good.'

While some respondents recounted having felt discomforted by administrative initiatives relating to gender equality, others reportedly had begun to develop some measure of understanding about it. Mrs. K (female, fifties) lived some distance from Matsuyama City. When policies connected to gender equality started to be implemented in her area, Mrs. K had a positive impression of it being just 'common sense' when an acquaintance told her of having gone to the city to hear about the gender equality measures. She described 'common sense' as follows.

> I don't think this locality [where I live] is much like that. As you might expect, married couples with dual incomes talk in that kind of way about the husbands helping their wives, and that's natural, right? Unless everyone works together to raise the children, too, it would be absolutely impossible for just the mother to do it. That's the sort of thing they were saying, and as I listened, I thought, 'They're not mistaken.'

---

21 See Horiuchi ed. (2006) on initiatives for coeducational home economics classes since 1994 and their backlash. On sex-education bashing, see Asai et al. (2003).

Chapter 5

Mrs. K ran a business with her husband, and knew many people who were raising children while working. From her experience, she thought that childrearing was 'absolutely impossible for just the mother to do.' In this case, first impressions of the gender equality measures seemed like 'common sense' based on personal experience of raising children in a dual income home. However, as she learned more about the initiatives for gender equality, Mrs. K became puzzled by the gap between what she had heard and what was being said in the media:

> I hear that the dolls [for Girls' Day] and the samurai helmets and May dolls [for Boy's Day] will not be allowed, but they are traditional things, and I think that girls should be like girls and boys should be like boys, absolutely... I don't know how far gender equality will go from here.

Putting gender roles into practice

Regardless of whether respondents had knowledge of gender equality or not before joining Association A, they shared a perception that gender equality would 'ignite conflict between men and women, and husbands and wives.' Mrs. R (female, sixties) commented: 'I feel it doesn't really make sense to me, as if people involved in "gender-free" are sort of making light of men, or suppressing [people's rights], rather than [promoting] equal rights.'

Respondents' primary concern about gender equality was how it would affect the family. Respondents stressed the importance of family while relating specific episodes of their own experiences and family situations. One frequently voiced concern was about the relationship with a mother-in-law. In the case of Mrs. E, for example, the mother-in-law was described as 'sort of having a one-track mind.' 'Er, she was quite strict, anyhow, but was really strict with herself, as well,' but 'in the end, she, er, was good to me.' Mrs. E's mother-in-law was deceased, but she said: 'Even now, if I'm having some sort of trouble, I sometimes wonder what my mother-in-law would have done now.' Mrs. G, also, talked about hanging out the washing the way she was taught by her mother-in-law:

> She used to say when you hang out the clothes, you need to hang them facing south, with the buttons and the trousers facing south, too. That's

140

what she told me. She said this right up to the moment of her death. I still follow her teachings.

The frequency of women mentioning their mothers-in-law, certainly does not necessarily imply that the relationship between them was amicable. Many respondents, the majority of whom lived in a regional area and who were in their fifties or older, were either currently living or had lived with their husband's parent or parents.[22] For these women who had borne responsibility for housework, childrearing, and nursing care in their husband's family, the relationship with their mother-in-law was probably the most difficult, and thus, memories of interactions with their mother-in-law had a lasting impression. Although they never directly voiced dissatisfaction with their mother-in-law, the complexity of their relationship with her exuded from expressions such as 'she was a strict person,' or from the episode of her detailed instructions about hanging the washing 'facing south.'

There was also no shortage of women who expressed the view that 'making their husband look good' was necessary for maintaining cordial relationships within the household. Mrs. G said: 'After all, I think the foundation lies in the home, in the men, you could say, or in the father,' and expressed her idea that 'it is the father who is the head in the home, and order is maintained by the family's respecting the father.' Mrs. K, who worked in the family business, said: 'We work in the same way, but it's definitely never the same. My husband is boss, after all. The children, too, see it as being that way, so men have men's work, and women have women's work.' Mrs. K also said that she had to 'make her husband look good,' but in the household, she said: 'Women are stronger. Things are always harmonious that way. In front of the children, I always butter up their father, saying he's strong and so on, but when [the children] grow up, they will realize the truth.'

---

22 According to the seventh National Survey on Household Changes conducted by the National Institute of Population and Social Security in 2014, 3.5% of married men aged twenty or above lived with their spouse's parent or parents, while 10.1% of women in the same age group did so. The proportion of people who were living with their spouse's parent or parents had shrunk in comparison with the same survey conducted in 2004 and 2009, but in all survey years, a higher proportion of women than men were cohabiting with their spouse's parent or parents.

Chapter 5

The women interviewed had hitherto performed their gender roles of housework, childrearing, and nursing care, and 'buttering up' their husband. However, the gender roles that female members imagined to be the 'guiding principles' for creating amicable interpersonal relationships within the household were not always described in glowing terms. There were some respondents whose accounts of the importance of performing their gender role included explanations of their family situation and their own distress and bewilderment. Mrs. D, for example, said that prior to being a home visit counselor, she had agonized over the couple relationship. Being a 'strong-willed woman' who 'was really working gung-ho like a man,' Mrs. D thought that her husband had stopped working because she worked so hard. After that, she says, she had started to think she 'had to make her husband look good.'

Mrs. J's narrative is similar. She described what her mother told her when she married into her husband's family:

> When you marry into that family, the father is the lintel and the pillars of that house, and because you are the one entering it, [you] will be the *shoji* [sliding doors], the ones covered with thick paper, or some other type of door. So, unless you fit yourself to those [pillars], the house will fall down if the pillars or lintels are cut [to fit you]. Sliding doors are fitted by shaving off the bits that are not right – their height, et cetera. So, the one to do the cutting is the wife, meaning you, so whatever happens, be patient, and persevere.

Mrs. J seems to have had a hard time especially in her relationship with her parents-in-law, saying that while she could not articulate what had happened, she was often 'conflicted in her heart.' Attending study meetings of Institute of Moralogy, Mrs. J says 'I heard that I must try as hard as possible not to go against my parents[-in-law] because it would cause discord in the family, so I thought I should try. So, I have persevered, all the while telling myself that time and again, in various ways.'

In this manner, the women I interviewed had lived in a way that aligned with their gender roles as mothers, wives and daughters-in-law, even while suffering at times in order to maintain harmony in the household, and to keep its interpersonal relationships cordial. In their narratives, gender roles are depicted not only as norms that people should obey, but also as behavioral guidelines for living as mothers, wives, and daughters-in-law.

The role of family discourse

Association A's grassroots anti-gender-equality campaign

As we have seen, people from many other groups became members of Association A. Most respondents had an affiliation with some other group prior to joining the association, and their narratives suggest that nationwide conservative groups such as Japan Conference and the New Buddhism Religious Organization had promptly taken action when the amendment of the Matsuyama City ordinance was being debated, which triggered the creation of Association A. Although Oguma and Ueno's (2003) study of grassroots conservative movements does not mention the History Circle's relationships with other groups, it is clear in the case of Association A that many other groups were associated by proximity, at least. So, what was the relationship between Association A and the two groups identified as the central opponents to gender equality, Textbook Society and Japan Conference?

First, the Textbook Society's accumulated activist experience influenced Association A. The leadership cohorts – Ms. Y, Mr. B and Mrs. E – had all participated in the Textbook Society. Moreover, the bulletin's recollections about the association's launch describe the enactment of the Basic Law for a Gender-Equal Society and local gender equality ordinances as a 'bolt from the blue' for 'those of us who had just been distracted by the history textbook issue and debate over historical recognition,'[23] suggesting that the founding members of Association A had become activists because of their interest in the history textbook issue. In Ehime Prefecture, the Textbook Society was already active, and in 2002, the history textbooks it had compiled were adopted for use in the prefectural combined junior-and-senior high school.[24] Immediately after its formation, Association A began pressuring administrative staff and members of municipal assemblies, and holding large-scale lectures by prominent conservative intellectuals, drawing on their experiences in the Textbook Society.

Second, many respondents belonged to the Japan Conference. Some had joined Association A upon learning of it through the Japan

---

23 *Dianthus*, no. 13, 2006

24 On the adoption of the Textbook Society's history textbooks in Ehime Prefecture, see Ouchi (2003).

Chapter 5

Conference, while others had become acquainted with each other at Japan Conference before Association A was formed.[25] In that sense, Japan Conference appears to have been a forum where people with interests in a range of issues – including history, education, the family, and gender – got to know each other, transcending religious beliefs or dogma.

Nevertheless, religious groups were also significant influences in Association A, with numerous participants affiliated with House of Growth, Association of Shinto Shrines, New Buddhism Religious Organization, and Institute of Moralogy. These groups had established roots in Association A's areas of activity, had spread widely and had many followers, and Association A's agenda arguably appealed to these groups. My survey, however, revealed that while recruiting in religiously-affiliated groups has the merit of being able to mobilize many people at one time, it also has the demerit of low potential for securing personnel to take proactive charge of its activities, as many members of Association A also live in areas far from its activity base and it is thus sometimes difficult for them to participate.[26]

A conservative movement connected through the family

In this way, Association A recruited members from the Textbook Society, Japan Conference, and various religious groups. Although its activities did not offer many opportunities for members to mingle with each other, Association A attracted people whose primary interest lay elsewhere, and who held diverse doctrines and beliefs. Thus, even if they had little knowledge about Association A's activities or gender equality, they felt 'able to support' Association A because of its way of thinking about the family. This suggests that the family connects many people, including those with different beliefs, those not affiliated with any religious group, and those who had not had much experience in social or political movements.

However, Association A's ability to mobilize these people and continue its activities for seven years was not simply because the family was

---

25 Ms. E reportedly made few new acquaintances through Association A's activities.

26 For Original Gospel Bible Seminary devotees Ms. M and Ms. N, following the path of belief was of the highest importance, and they supported Association A only to the extent that it did not interfere with their beliefs.

144

its main focus, but also because of its particular method of topicalizing the family. As we saw in Section 5.2, in its appeal to 'family values,' Association A highlighted the value and significance of the family by aligning it closely with the individual's everyday consciousness, as symbolized by the word 'happiness.'

The family narratives of the female members of Association A suggest that this framing of the family resonated with those members' own views. Although many prefaced their remarks by saying: 'I don't know much about gender equality,' they frequently invoked the family, based on their personal experiences as women in a regional community. To preserve harmony in the household, they had lived in anguish as mothers, wives and daughters-in-law. They had performed their gender roles, which were understood not only as norms, but as guidelines for achieving 'family happiness.'

For the women who gather at Association A, Mrs. G's description of there being 'no particular reason to object, either' is perhaps the most common explanation for their participation. Of course, these women were not 'ordinary citizens' in the sense that they originally belonged to religious or political groups and participated in conservative politics. However, the reason why there were no traces of hesitation in their narratives of joining Association A when they were invited to by acquaintances, even if they were not familiar with its purposes and activities, was that Association A took a 'family advocacy' stance. They have no special 'reason to object' to Association A's claims that the family they have created through many years of care is a 'precious thing,' and that 'family' is significant. Many people have had experience of family in some form or another. By appealing to that experience of family, Association A has won support from people with different ideas and creeds.

PART III

The Conservative Movement, Women's Lives and Sexuality

Part III

In Part III, I discuss women's conservative action groups that emphasize 'women' rather than 'mothers' or 'wives.' Until then, the question of whether to take a stance as mothers or as women had been considered to be a major point of divergence in the women's movement. The Japanese second-wave feminist movement, 'women's lib,' paid special attention to women as active agents, and reexamined the very meaning of being a woman, which differed from the previous women's movement that had addressed women's issues from a position of mothers or wives (Kanai 1990). This was because the women's lib movement feared that women's emphasis on the standpoint of mothers would reinforce an essentialism that depicted housework, childrearing, and nursing as a 'natural' pursuit for women. In addition, positive promotion of the positionality of women was also an attempt to transcend the sexist double standard that categorized women as either mothers or whores.[1]

As we saw in the Introduction, there are two currents in U.S. conservatism, namely 'social conservatism' and 'laissez-faire conservatism,' in which women classified as the former reportedly expound 'family values' as mothers, while the latter act from the standpoint of women. In the U.S., the progress of women's social participation, and the fact that many women have built careers in political and economic fields, are cited as factors in the growth of 'laissez-faire conservatism.' In the current situation of women's social participation in Japan,[2] it seems unlikely one might find 'laissez-faire conservative' women like those in

---

1 Tanaka Mitsu's essay, 'Liberation from the toilet (*Benjo kara no kaiho*)' (Tanaka 2001) directly tackled this point. The various thoughts fostered in the women's lib movement have not grown stale even today.

2 Women's low status in Japan is demonstrated by all manner of statistics. According to the Global Gender Gap Index published annually by the World Economic Forum (compiled from the fields of economics, education, health and politics), Japan's overall score in 2018 was 0.662 (110th out of 149 countries), and by field, the scores in economics (0.580) and politics (0.078) were particularly low. According to the Cabinet Office's *White Paper on Gender Equality, 2019 edition*, the proportion of female Diet members was 10.2% in the House of Representatives and 20.7% in the House of Councilors (as of January 2019); and in regional assemblies, women accounted for 10.0% of members at prefectural assembly level, while in more than 30% of town and village assemblies, there were still no female assembly members as of December 2018. In the occupation field, too, the proportion of non-regular workers was 56.1% for females and 22.2% for males (as of 2018).

the U.S. in sufficient numbers to organize activist groups. However, in pondering the Japanese case, it is necessary to reconsider the perceptions of researchers, journalists and leftist activists whose gaze is directed at the female participants in the conservative movement, as well as the differences in the social environment surrounding women.

There is no dearth of essays that discuss female participation in the action conservative movement, including the Association of Citizens, from the perspective of it being a mothers' movement. Yasuda Koichi, who reported on a demonstration against Fuji Television Network for 'showing nothing but Korean wave dramas,' said that 'women were an overwhelming majority' of the protestors and compared the way that 'housewives, especially those accompanied by children, showered Fuji TV with choral chanting while pushing their strollers' to a demonstration by the Association of Consumer Organizations (Shufuren), saying the two protests would be similar if the Japanese flags being waved in the former were replaced by the rice paddles on display in the latter (Kimura, Sono and Yasuda 2013: 73). Moreover, a special feature in the December 2012 *AERA* magazine, entitled 'Japan is leaning (Nihon ga katamuku),' included an article by Kinjo Tamayo: '"Protect Japan" from anxiety for the future and motherhood: The "justice" of women who drift to the right' (Kinjo 2012).

Discourses linking the family and female participants perhaps have not appropriately grasped the identity of women in the action conservative movement. Since the beginning of the 2010s, women belonging to that movement have published a succession of books. In these works, moreover, the authors' position is indicated not by the word 'mother,' but by expressions such as 'patriotic woman' (Sanami 2013), 'national defense woman' (Kawasoe et al. 2014), or just 'woman' (Yamamoto 2014).[3]

In recent times, some feminists have discussed conservative women's action groups from the perspective of women rather than housewives or

---

3   As I discuss in Chapter Six, this does not suggest that there are no women engaging in the activities of action conservatives from the position of mothers. Kitahara Minori has reported on the 'Learning about Japan infants' classes' that Flower Clock recommends (Kitahara and Paku 2014). These classes, run by Meiji Shrine, apparently hold activities for parents and children to learn about the Meiji-era Imperial Rescript on Education and Kojiki (Record of Ancient Matters). Moreover, during fieldwork I conducted on conservative women's action groups, I met women who were engaged in educational issues for the sake of their children on the brink of entering university.

Part III

mothers. Kitahara Minori and Suni Paku for example, who reported on a political propaganda activity conducted by Flower Clock in May 2013, describes the scene and her impressions as follows:

> Apart from flags printed with the name of the group, Flower Clock, everything they brought along was handmade, including the Rising Sun flags with which they had decorated their mobile phones and placards with paper flowers attached. It was obvious that they had each made these, paying [for the materials] out of their own pockets so as not to go to much expense. It was a women's handmade movement that felt very pleasant, and was overflowing with enthusiasm. (Kitahara and Paku 2014: 58)

Upon observing Flower Clock's political propaganda activity, Kitahara and Paku reportedly felt 'a strange sense of familiarity and bewilderment, rather than disgust,' and says they suddenly had the idea that 'it was a movement that we knew' (Kitahara and Paku 2014: 59). In a conservative women's group, Kitahara and Paku had thus found a resonance with women's civic movements like the feminism with which they were involved.

There are many women's groups in the action conservative movement, commencing with Flower Clock. Those that 'hammer the fact that they are women' include Gentle Breeze and Justice and Peace (Yamaguchi 2019: 184). Some organizations do not canvass widely for membership, but rather campaign with just a few female activists, so even on a small scale, women have gained entry to the action conservative movement. Such groups include Citizens' Group that will not Permit the Invasion of Japan, Modern Dianthus Club (Gendai nadeshiko kurabu), Women's Society that Denies the Lie of the Military Comfort Women (Jugun ianfu no uso o yurusanai josei no kai), Japanese Women's Study Group 'Let's Rebuild Japan' (Tatenaoso Nippon josei juku), Bracing Wind Yamato/ Lion's Society (Shishi no kai), and Company of Fighting Women on the Brink (Tatakau josei gakeppuchi tai).

The various groups in the action conservative movement show undisguised contempt for Japan-residing foreigners and discriminatory sentiment and hostility towards Japan's East Asian neighbors South Korea, China, and North Korea, but the women-centered groups tend to focus on the comfort women issue (Yamaguchi 2013b). In fact, an article labelled 'Big roundtable discussion' of female members of Flower Clock and Justice and Peace was published in the September 2013 issue of *WiLL* magazine, which mentions the comfort women issue.

As such, an investigation of conservative women's action groups would be difficult without discussing the comfort women issue. Hence, before proceeding to the next chapter, I will provide a brief outline of the Japanese military comfort women. During World War II, so-called sexual 'comfort stations' were established to service Japanese soldiers. Many women from countries and territories under Japanese control, including the Korean peninsula, Taiwan, Okinawa,[4] and China, as well as women from mainland Japan, became comfort women. The processes by which someone became a comfort woman varied; although some had been working as licensed prostitutes and became comfort women either voluntarily or through deception, most were abducted and confined by the Japanese military, and continually subjected to sexual violence.[5]

However, it was only in the 1990s that the system of comfort stations during the war started to attract international attention. The direct trigger was a South Korean woman named Kim Hak-sun 'coming out' as having been a Japanese military comfort woman in 1991. That coming-out, in turn, was prompted by the burgeoning international recognition of wartime sexual violence as a war crime, and the growing movement to eliminate violence against women based in 'women's human rights.' Following Kim Hak-sun's revelations, initiatives began to attempt a resolution of the comfort women issue: in 1993 the Japanese government

---

4   A full discussion of comfort women from the perspective of colonialism is beyond the scope of this book. Tamashiro (2022) discusses sexual violence in Okinawa from the perspective of postcolonial feminism, ranging from the comfort stations established there, to the sexual violence of the U.S. military stationed in Okinawa today, and argues that sexism and colonialism must not be overlooked.

5   Today, the comfort women issue is most commonly discussed in terms of Japanese–Korean relations, and the widely diverse circumstances in which women became comfort women makes it difficult to discuss them in simple terms. The pervasive image of comfort women having been forcibly trafficked by the Japanese military, however, has prompted some researchers to express alarm about the way Japanese comfort women, many of whom had previously been licensed prostitutes, were being rendered invisible by the Japan–Korean frame of debate. See, for example, Fujime (2015), and Kinoshita (2017).

Part III

published the Kono Statement (formally entitled 'Statement by Chief Cabinet Minister Kono regarding the Publication of Results of a Study on the Issue of Comfort Women'), which acknowledged that the military had been involved in the comfort women system during the war; while in 1995 the semi-governmental Asian Women's Fund was established.[6]

However, at the same time that the government recognized a need to address the comfort women issue, an historical revisionist social movement rose to prominence, typified by the Textbook Society, as discussed in Chapter Two. So-called comfort-women bashing – arguing that 'comfort women did not exist' – erupted in this period, led by Textbook Society and the conservative media. Suzuki Yuko divides comfort-women bashing claims into four categories, citing the arguments of Fujioka Nobukatsu, the founder of the Textbook Society, as examples: 1) that 'comfort women were licensed prostitutes,' which deems the activities of comfort women to have been commercial transactions; 2) that the military's involvement was restricted to having facilitated the establishment of comfort stations, and that the managing agents were civilian business people; 3) that they cannot be called comfort women unless it can be proven that they were 'forcibly trafficked;' and 4) the 'authorization of sexual violence' argument that says 'sexual violence always accompanies war' (Suzuki 1997: 42).

In this manner, a discourse that disavowed the existence of Japanese military comfort women and the harm they experienced predated the action conservative movement, but groups from that movement actually had also engaged in comfort-women bashing (Yamaguchi 2016). A special exhibition entitled 'Korea and Japan: A century since the Japanese annexation of Korea' was held in January 2011 at the Suiheisha History Museum in Nara Prefecture. The organization known as Suiheisha (Levelers' Society) was founded to counter institutional and social discrimination against the lowest caste in feudal Japanese society, known in highly derogatory terms as 'Eta,' meaning 'much filth.' This term was spat by Association of Citizens at a protest rally it conducted in response to the exhibition, saying: 'They say that comfort women equal sex slaves, but they are idiots. If you have any complaints, come on out, you filth!'

---

6   The 'Asian Women's Fund' was wound up in March 2007, and all that remains is a digital museum, 'The comfort women issue and Asian Women's Fund,' which summarizes the project's content (http://www.awf.or.jp/).

(Yasuda 2015: 135). Thus, it can be seen that activist groups from the action conservative movement had been using the comfort-women bashing discourse which had been produced since the 1990s, mainly in conservative forums.[7]

However, if we focus on female participants in the action conservative movement, we must consider the possibility that their emphasis on the comfort women issue might differ from the male critics. Any mention of the comfort women issue, whether direct or indirect, implicitly refers to women's sexuality, as well. Why do women activists focus on the comfort women issue, despite its implicit sexuality, which is difficult to broach? And what dynamics are at work in women's condemnation of those who were comfort women? In the two chapters in Part III, I turn my attention to the comfort women discourse found in women's groups aligned with the action conservative movement. To examine why women in the conservative movement are critical of the comfort women, a topic inseparable from gender but unrelated to the family, as we saw in Part II. I will also ponder the significance of their bashing of comfort women.

---

7 In the early 1990s, conservative factions' arguments to repudiate the comfort women were primarily directed inside Japan, but more recently they have been energetically transmitting them outside Japan, as well. For details, see Yamaguchi, Nogawa, Morris-Suzuki and Koyama (2016).

Chapter 6

The contentious comfort women issue

Women of the action conservative movement

From this chapter onwards, I discuss female-centric activist groups associated with the so-called action conservative movement which appeared in the late 2000s. In 2013, a video posted on a free Internet site provoked wide public discussion. It features a female middle-school student holding a microphone, making the following speech near Osaka's Tsuruhashi station, close to the largest residential concentration of resident-Koreans in Western Japan.

> **Speaker:** Hello, all you shit Japan-residing *Chonko* [an insulting slang term for Koreans] living in Tsuruhashi, and all you Japanese people here now.
>
> **Audience:** Hello!
>
> **Speaker:** All those [Koreans], I hate them, I really hate them!
>
> **Audience:** Right!
>
> **Speaker:** I want to kill them [as a favor to you]! If they keep on pushing their luck, I'll give them not a Nanking massacre, but a Tsuruhashi massacre!
>
> **Audience:** Right!
>
> **Speaker:** If Japanese anger explodes, that'll be what we'll do.
>
> **Audience:** Right!
>
> **Speaker:** This is Japan.
>
> **Audience:** Right!

Chapter 6

> **Speaker:** It isn't the Korean Peninsula!
>
> **Audience:** Right!
>
> **Speaker:** Get back there now!
>
> **Audience:** Get back there![1]

Surrounding this junior high school student, who is shouting in a childish tone the pretentious words: 'I'll give them … a Tsuruhashi massacre!,' are people presumably from the group organizing this event as well as many other adults, including police monitoring the situation. Not one, however, attempts to stop or silence the girl. Far from it. Participants can be seen applauding, egging her on, and breaking into occasional laughter, apparently 'enjoying' her speech.

The sponsor of this event was the Association of Citizens against the Special Privileges of the Zainichi, abbreviated to Association of Citizens. As discussed in Chapter Two, conservative groups like the Association of Citizens that engaged in direct action such as political protests and demonstration marches are called the action conservative movement. The groups in that movement have identified a variety of hypothetical enemies, and express animosity towards these enemies at group activities. There are three broadly identified 'enemies.' The first are Zainichi (Japan-residing) Koreans. Ignoring the historical context of Korean migration to Japan during Japan's colonial rule of the Korean peninsula and subsequent Japanese policies vis-à-vis resident foreigners, all groups of the action conservative movement, including Association of Citizens, which led a new rightist movement trend called the ACM, deem institutional and social treatment of Zainichi Koreans to be 'special privileges,' and have campaigned for them to be treated in the same manner as foreign newcomers who take up residence in Japan.

The second set of enemies comprises the East Asian nations of South and North Korea, and China. Japan has numerous and diverse issues with these three countries: it has a dispute with South Korea over territorial rights relating to Takeshima/Dokdo Island; it has problems with North Korea relating to the abduction of Japanese citizens, nuclear armaments,

---

1 'Advance warning of a massacre at Osaka's largest Korean Town, Tsuruhashi (Middle school girl),' 2013. (https://www.youtube.com/watch?v=GoTBRpcaZS0. Accessed May 3, 2015)

156

The contentious comfort women issue

and missiles; while in recent times, its territorial dispute with China over dominion of the Senkaku/Diaoyu Islands in the East China Sea has received much public attention. Furthermore, Japan has not fulfilled its responsibility to these three countries in regard to the memories of its past wartime aggression and colonial rule, or for compensation for damage. Thus, the publication of revisionist history textbooks and prime ministerial visits to Yasukuni Shrine escalate into diplomatic issues. All the groups in the action conservative movement take hardline positions vis-à-vis these three countries, on the pretext of 'protecting Japanese national interests.'

The third 'enemy' is the Japanese 'left-wing.' In the Japanese case, left-wing activist groups and individuals take a critical stance towards the government, demanding the protection of freedom, equality, and human rights. Moreover, they sometimes cooperate with overseas NGOs and NPOs to settle various issues that have arisen within Japan. The groups of the action conservative movement criticize these positions as being 'anti-Japanese,' and occasionally protest against the activities of groups deemed to be left-wing.[2] The people who comprise the action conservative movement harbor animosity towards the left-wing, sentiments which have been fostered by the anti-left-wing discourse in the conservative media.

Groups affiliated with the action conservative movement began to ramp-up their activities from around 2009 (Maeda 2013). Their activities were soon problematized by left-wing activists and leftists commentators first triggered, perhaps, by the 'Calderon incident' in February 2009. When the Japanese government sought to deport the parents of a Filipino family named Calderon who had overstayed their visas, separating them from their child who had been born and raised in Japan, people who supported the government's response demonstrated near the child's junior high school. Many people first learned of the Association of Citizens from reports of this demonstration (Higuchi 2014). In August 2009, the group converged on the venue for an exhibition on the military comfort women held in Mitaka City in Tokyo, mounting a protest rally;

---

2   The fact that the communication style generated by action conservatives on the Internet has a high affinity with anything 'anti-left-wing' might be a factor in the inclusion of the left-wing and leftists among the hypothetical enemies of action conservatives (Kitada 2005).

157

Chapter 6

and in November, it obstructed a festival at the Korea University campus in Tokyo's Kodaira City. Furthermore, on 4 December that year, a group connected with Association of Citizens called 'Team Kansai' converged outside the Kyoto North Korean Number One Elementary School, and protested at the school gates in the presence of the children, claiming that the school was unlawfully occupying a local park.[3]

Since initiating this series of incidents, the Association of Citizens and related groups have continued to express extreme malice especially vis-à-vis resident-Koreans at demonstrations. Their cries such as 'North Koreans, get back to the Korean Peninsula!' and 'Throw the Zainichi Koreans into Tokyo Bay!' came to be classified as 'hate speech,' a new term which became so widely recognized in Japanese society that it was nominated for New Word and Buzzword of the Year in 2013. Hate speech has since been criminalized (in 2016, see below), defined as an attack 'based on discrimination towards racial, ethnic, sexual, and other minorities' (Morooka 2013: ii).[4] As the Association of Citizens continued to expand its activities, hate speech began to be heard almost weekly in Japan, especially in major urban areas.

Subsequently, counter-protests were organized by people who felt threatened by these activities whenever the Association of Citizens and other conservative action groups held rallies. The actions of the counterprotesters[5] severely hampered the Association of Citizens' ability to conduct streetside speeches, and when they did proceed, the events were not effective as propaganda. In 2014, Sakurai Makoto, the inaugural president of Association of Citizens, resigned and formed a new political organization, Japan First Party, further weakening the Association of Citizens' centripetal force. Although the Diet's 2016 enactment of the 'Hate Speech Law (Act on the Promotion of Efforts to Eliminate Unfair Discriminatory Speech and Behavior Against Persons Originating from Outside Japan)' further contributed to the declining

---

3 Nakamura (2014) provides details of this incident from the school's perspective.

4 On legal theory regarding hate speech and trends outside Japan, see Bleich (2011), Waldron (2012), Maeda Akira (ed.) (2013); and on hate crime, see Maeda (2013).

5 On the countermovement to action conservatives, see Tominaga (2015) and Kanbara (2014) which consider the novelty of the countermovement from the perspective of social movement theory, based on interviews with participants.

The contentious comfort women issue

visibility of Association of Citizens' activism, other conservative action groups continue their activities.

Most participants in the action conservative movement are men, but many women have also joined. Especially since 2009, many women-centered groups have been established, ranging from large organizations with members nationwide, including Gentle Breeze and Flower Clock, to small groups such as Citizens' that will not Permit the Invasion of Japan, Modern Dianthus Club, and Bracing Wind Yamato/Lions' Society, which have held panel discussions on comfort women around the country. Yamaguchi notes that 'women from various generations have made great efforts as leaders or behind-the-scenes in administration' in the action conservative movement, and 'have played prominent roles' (Yamaguchi 2013b: 88).

Just as the hate speech in Tsuruhashi mentioned above was voiced by a junior high school girl, women who participate in the action conservative movement spread their scathing, discriminatory views about resident-Koreans at streetside locations. Yasuda (2012) describes the scene of female Association of Citizens members making hate speeches, as follows:

> One interjecting, 'That's right! That's right!' in a particularly high-pitched voice was a young woman wearing a knee-length skirt and a flimsy cardigan. For the very reason that her facial features were so regular, her subdued appearance, like that of an office clerk who had raced there immediately on her way home from work, gave her a special distinctiveness among the participants in the street protest. She, too, repeated words full of loathing once she took hold of the microphone: 'Japan-residing Koreans are still talking nonsense, saying they were forcibly brought here. They are still clamoring for an apology, and for compensation! Japanese people are being made fools of by the Zainichi! If you Zainichi hate Japan that much, please go back to your ancestral land! Do the Zainichi want money so much that they will go so far as to tell lies?!' (Yasuda 2012: 5)

However, while women engage in hate speech, I suspect there is a dilemma underpinning their voicing of hate speech in public settings. Understanding 'women's language' as an ideology, linguistics scholar Nakamura Momoko reveals that women's ways of speaking and their

159

Chapter 6

choice of words have always been socially contested issues. Nakamura perceives 'women's language' not to be the words and manner of speaking women employ, but a norm that women 'should speak.' Through analyzing the 'women's language' found in textbooks and etiquette guides dating from the Edo period until the postwar Occupation period, Nakamura points out that 'women's language' is 'an ideology that has always fulfilled a political role' (Nakamura 2007: 315); and especially in the postwar period, 'women's language' came to be 'tied to an innate "stereotypical femininity"' (Nakamura 2007: 314).

From this perspective, women raising their voices and attacking others in public is a deviation from 'proper femininity.' Presumably, such deviant behavior would not have been acceptable in the original conservative movement, so how do we explain this? In this chapter, I will discuss the activities of women's groups in the action conservative movement that assert the fact that they are 'women,' in particular; using a video-content analysis approach, I will investigate the characteristics of groups that mainly consist of women, and how they differ from male-centered groups.

Analytical methodology

The action conservative movement and the Internet

Analyzing the content of videos uploaded to the Internet, I will elucidate the characteristics of women's groups in the action conservative movement. There are two reasons for choosing this methodology: first, although it is necessary to shed light on the claims of the women who participate in the action conservative movement, the groups linked with that movement do not have print media; and second, instead of print media, the various groups in the action conservative movement take videos of their activities and upload them to the Internet. Such videos have become a vital tool for recruiting new members to the movement. I will explain this in more detail below.

In social movements, the publication of newsletters and bulletins by activist groups has crucial significance. By regular production of print media, members can communicate their claims and opinions to people outside their activist group to people who are potential supporters, as well as sharing ideas and information within the group. Furthermore,

The contentious comfort women issue

writing testimonials in that media can be a process of introspection and recognition of how their experiences of hardship or sadness can connect to society. This is why many activist groups and organizations have traditionally produced paper-based media.[6]

However, conservative action groups typically do not have print media.[7] Instead, they seek to appeal to people and recruit new members via the Internet. The rise of nationalist discourse on the Internet has clearly shaped the action conservative movement.

Internet posts calling for 'patriotism' or expressing hostility and contempt towards China and the Koreas have gradually increased on message boards such as '2channel (*ni-channeru*)' (now '5channel (*go-channeru*)'), blogs and social media, which have come to be called the 'Net right-wing.'[8] It appears that these sites have mobilized some people to join the action conservative movement whose previous activism had been limited to posting comments on the Internet, with some observers commenting that 'if the "resource that is the "Net right-wing" did not

---

6 Various attempts are underway to archive materials collected and compiled amid the expansion of social movements (Arai 2014). For example, handbills compiled by women's lib groups in the 1970s have been organized and published in three volumes as *Shiryo uman ribu shi* (Materials on the history of women's lib), and at NWEC (National Women's Education Center), a Womens Archive has been established that has collected the *minikomi* (newsletters) published by groups in all areas. It is possible to browse these newsletters at the Women's Action Network site, the portal for Japanese feminism (https://wan.or.jp/).

7 One exception is 'Channel Sakura,' an organization for the production and transmission of conservative cable television programs which also publishes a digital book entitled *Ronshi* (Points of argument).

8 Numerous surveys have been conducted of the so-called 'Net right-wing.' According to the Web-based questionnaire conducted by Tsuji Daisuke in 2007 and 2014 (Tsuji 2017, Tsuji and Fujita 2011), with 'Net right-wing' defined as someone who satisfied all three of the following conditions: 1) had a negative attitude towards China and South Korea; 2) had a conservative political orientation; and 3) had expressed opinions or engaged in discussion of political and social issues on the Internet, 1.3% of respondents in 2007 and 1.8% in 2014 fell into that category. In the 2014 survey, although males accounted for a majority of the Net right-wing (79%), attributes such as age, educational background, employment situation, household income, and marital status had no apparent significance. Nagayoshi produced similar results in a 2017 survey of men and women in the Tokyo Metropolitan Region (Nagayoshi 2019).

Chapter 6

exist, then Association of Citizens probably would not exist, either' (Yasuda 2012: 44).

In fact, conservative action groups exploit the Internet; most have home pages or blogs, as well as accounts on social networking sites. They post schedules, reports on their activities, opinions about current affairs, and information about other groups' activities, among other things. They also take videos of their streetside speeches and demonstrations, which are sometimes streamed live on sites such as 'Niconico video' or 'Ustream.' Videos are uploaded to YouTube at a later date, and then shared in individual and group blogs and social networking sites. It has already been standard practice these days for 'left-leaning' civic groups to make full use of the Internet, but in the late 2000s, when the various organizations of the action conservative movement appeared, they were much more adept at utilizing the Internet and were appraised as being 'far different from left-wing civic movements which are heavily dependent upon print media and interpersonal networks' (Higuchi 2014: 124).

Some studies have found that this use of Internet technology led to the mobilization of new members. According to Higuchi (2014), who interviewed conservative activists, twenty-five of his thirty-four respondents had been recruited to the movement via the Internet. Although ten respondents (the largest cohort) reported having come upon conservative action groups when searching for information, there were also some who had arrived at the Association of Citizens' site through searching keywords relating to historical or diplomatic issues and following the links, or from watching related videos on YouTube. These are common characteristics of Internet culture.

Overview of the data

The three conservative women's action groups that I selected for analysis were Gentle Breeze, Flower Clock and Justice and Peace. Gentle Breeze formed in 2009, with 570 member as of 9 July 2019, was the first one established among the groups I analyzed. Flower Clock, established in 2010, appears to have had 1040 members as of August 2015. Justice and Peace is closer to a project than a group. In 2011, a protest called Justice and Peace 2011 was mounted against a gathering sponsored by groups supporting former comfort women. For some time after that, the

The contentious comfort women issue

instigator, Yamamoto Yumiko, took the lead in holding protests and other events under the name of Justice and Peace.

I focused on these three groups because they uploaded many videos, and were able to mobilize members. My data for analysis consisted of videos uploaded to YouTube by the three groups. As previously mentioned, videos of protests and demonstrations by groups of the action conservative movement were distributed not only via YouTube but also via Niconico video and Ustream (Yasuda 2012). The three groups I analyzed also posted videos onto these sites, but I restricted my analysis to YouTube for the following reasons: first, it is difficult to obtain sample data from live-streamed videos when using Niconico video and Ustream; and second, many videos distributed via Niconico video and Ustream can also be found on YouTube.

I employed the following procedure in selecting the videos. First, in December 2016 I searched YouTube by inputting the Japanese names of the three groups. Next, I listed the search results in descending order of relevance, and selected videos capturing the groups' activities, such as political propaganda, protests and demonstrations, from the top of the list down. These included videos of activities conducted in conjunction with other groups, as well as those conducted in isolation. However, because members of the target groups often did not appear in the videos in cases of co-sponsorship, I ultimately excluded those videos. The central activity base for each group was Tokyo, but they also had regional branches. I included videos from the branches in my analysis, as well. Furthermore, my search method also produced videos of lectures, but I eliminated those in order to focus on what female activists were communicating to the outside world.

My analysis was limited to videos uploaded before July 2016. This cutoff point was decided because political activism in relation to the comfort women issue had again begun to arise due, for example, to an agreement between the Japanese and South Korean governments effected in December 2015,[9] and I anticipated being able to see reactions to it

---

9   The Japanese and South Korean governments agreed to 'confirm the final and irreversible resolution' of the comfort women. On 28 July 2016, the South Korean government established a 'Reconciliation and Healing Foundation,' to which the Japanese government contributed one billion yen. However, there was much criticism of the agreement between Japan and South Korea from South Korean domestic public opinion and Japanese

163

Chapter 6

Table 6.1 Number of videos per group

Name of group	2009	2010	2011	2012	2013	2014	2015	2016	Total
Justice and Peace	0	0	6	7	0	1	0	0	14
Gentle Breeze	45	25	2	34	43	27	7	2	185
Flower Clock	0	1	0	67	82	50	56	13	269
Total	45	26	8	108	125	78	63	15	468

from each of the groups. While the action conservative movement is always concerned with multiple topics, it is unusual for it to continuously address any topic in depth. Therefore, I thought that a six-month period would be sufficient to observe how they developed their activities around the Japan-Korea agreement and, in addition, how these activities came to an end.

I analyzed a total of 468 videos across the three groups, including: fourteen by Justice and Peace; 185 from Gentle Breeze; and 269 by Flower Clock (Table 6.1). The average length of video was 10.01 minutes. I classified the activities depicted in the videos into four categories: 1) political propaganda; 2) protests; 3) demonstrations; and 4) other. 'Political propaganda' here means appealing to the public by presenting one's principles and arguments in a loud voice or using loudspeakers on the street. 'Protests' means protest rallies at a fixed location, not marching. 'Demonstrations' means marching demonstrations. 'Other' included videos of members being interviewed by other groups, notifications of events, promotional videos, music concerts, etc.

Across the three groups, political propaganda videos were the most frequent (348 instances), followed by protests (57 instances), demonstrations (48 instances), and other (15 instances) (Table 6.2). One reason for the unusually large number of videos of political propaganda activities was that such events were conducted with great frequency; other factors included the editing format and the way videos were posted onto the

---

activists, researchers, and journalists who have been working to resolve the comfort women issue, and the foundation was dissolved by South Korean government on 21 November 2018. A contribution of 500 million yen remains, and although Japan and South Korean governments are supposed to discuss the use of the remaining funds, those talks have not progressed. On the problems with the Japan–South Korean agreement, see Maeda Akira, ed. (2016), Nakano, Itagaki, Kimu, Okamoto and Kimu (2017), and Okano Yayo (2016; 2018).

164

The contentious comfort women issue

Table 6.2 Breakdown of types of activity

Name of group	Political propaganda	Protests	Demonstrations	Other	Total
Justice and Peace	4 (28.6%)	6 (42.9%)	0	4 (28.6%)	14
Gentle Breeze	98 (62.0%)	33 (17.8%)	47 (25.4%)	7 (3.79%)	185
Flower Clock	246 (91.4%)	18 (6.7%)	1 (0.4%)	4 (1.5%)	269
Total	348 (74.4%)	57 (12.2%)	48 (10.3%)	15 (3.2%)	468

video site. During political propaganda activities, activists made speeches lasting about ten minutes each. When more than one orator spoke at an event, sometimes a separate video of each speaker would be posted. For example, when six people spoke on one occasion, it might be split into six videos, which explains the much greater number of videos of political propaganda activities. I have listed the activities recorded in the videos I used as data for analysis in Table 6.3.

Certain tendencies could be seen in types of activity among the three groups' videos. First, although Justice and Peace did not post many videos *per se*, protests accounted for forty percent of its total. Political propaganda activity videos were the most numerous in the case of Gentle Breeze (62%), but it also had the largest proportion of videos of demonstrations among the three groups, accounting for slightly more than twenty-five percent of its total. Almost ninety percent of the videos featuring Flower Clock were recordings of political propaganda activities.

In analyzing these videos, I established two policies. First, textual analysis would be my principal task. Online videos by these groups can be viewed as substitutes for the print media that progressive civic movements had traditionally utilized. Hence, rather than using quantitative analysis, which is generally used for analyzing television commercials and programs, I transcribed the words spoken by the activists in the videos and subjected those texts to qualitative analysis. Second, although I principally engaged in textual analysis, I also analyzed how the intentions and subjectivity of the camera operators or editors were expressed in the videos. According to Yasuda (2012), some male participants in the action conservative movement aim to record the various groups' activities on video camera. My aim was to deduce how the female conservative activists were reflected in the gaze of male activists and positioned by them.

Importantly, in the following discussion, I frequently quote from the videos. There is a risk that reproducing hate speech in a print medium

165

Chapter 6

Table 6.3 List of activities analyzed

Name of group	Date held	Theme of activity
Justice and Peace	Nov-11	Protest against South Korean 'Wednesday Demonstrations'
	May-12	Protest against establishment of an organ to monitor human rights violations
	Sep-12	Activity outside LDP headquarters
Gentle Breeze	Aug-09	Street propaganda activity in Shibuya's Hachiko Square (1)
	Aug-09	Street propaganda activity in Shibuya's Hachiko Square (2)
	Sep-09	Street propaganda activity from Kansai outside Navio
	Sep-09	Street propaganda activity in Hachiko Square
	Oct-09	Street propaganda activity outside Kobe's Sannomiya station
	Nov-09	Street propaganda activity outside Fukuoka Tenjin
	Feb-10	Demonstration against suffrage for foreigners
	Mar-10	Demonstration against suffrage for foreigners & separate surnames for married couples
	May-10	Shibuya demonstration
	Aug-10	Ginza demonstration
	Nov-10	Osaka demonstration
	Aug-11	Demonstration to blame Democratic Party
	Mar-12	Street propaganda activity outside Kobe's Sannomiya station
	May-12	Streetside questionnaire on military comfort women
	Jul-12	Street propaganda activity in Shinjuku
	Sep-12	Street propaganda activity outside Kobe's Sannomiya station
	Sep-12	March for cutting Japan-South Korean diplomatic relations
	Nov-12	Sapporo parade
	Jan-13	Counter-protest against demonstration against Osprey deployment
	Apr-13	Protest against Gunma-no-mori Korean workers' memorial
	Jul-13	Sapporo parade
	Aug-13	Protest against Comfort Women's Memorial Day
	Sep-13	Street propaganda event in Sapporo
	Sep-13	Protest outside House of Councilors' office building
	Mar-14	Street propaganda event outside Sannomiya station
	Mar-14	Signature-collecting for revocation of the Kōno statement
	May-14	Signature-collecting for Kōno Yōhei's summons to the Diet
	Jul-14	Street propaganda event in Sapporo
	Jul-15	Street propaganda event against AMPO
	Sep-15	Street propaganda event in Hokkaido
	Feb-16	Street propaganda event outside Maebashi district court
	Apr-16	Street propaganda event outside Maebashi district court

The contentious comfort women issue

Name of group	Date held	Theme of activity
Flower Clock	May-10	Parade against child allowances & separate surnames for married couples
	May-12	Street propaganda event in Shibuya
	Jul-12	Street propaganda event in Shibuya
	Oct-12	Street propaganda event in Shibuya
	Dec-12	Street propaganda event in Shibuya
	Mar-13	Street propaganda event in Shibuya
	May-13	Street propaganda event in Shibuya
	Aug-13	Street propaganda event in Shibuya
	Oct-13	Street propaganda event in Funabashi
	Nov-13	Street propaganda event in Shibuya
	Jan-14	Street propaganda event in Funabashi
	Apr-14	Street propaganda event in Omiya
	May-14	Street propaganda event in Shibuya
	Aug-14	Street propaganda event in Shibuya
	Sep-14	Protest at Iwanami Shoten
	Oct-14	Street propaganda event in Funabashi
	Jan-15	Street propaganda event in Shinbashi
	Apr-15	Street propaganda event in Jinbocho
	May-15	Street propaganda event in Jinbocho
	Jul-15	Protest at Ministry of Land, Infrastructure, Transport and Tourism & Foreign Ministry
	Aug-15	Street propaganda event in Shibuya
	Oct-15	Street propaganda event in Nakano (1)
	Oct-15	Street propaganda event in Nakano (2)
	Dec-15	Street propaganda event in Shinjuku (organized by another group)
	Feb-16	Music festival
	Mar-16	Street propaganda event in Ikebukuro
	May-16	Street propaganda event in front of Metropolitan Offices (organized by another group)
	Jun-16	Street propaganda event in Shinjuku (organized by another group)
	Jun-16	Street propaganda event in Shibuya (organized by another group)
	Jun-16	Street propaganda event in Shinjuku (organized by another group)
	Jul-16	Supporting speeches at Sukiyabashi

Chapter 6

might contribute to the diffusion of such speech, but I decided to quote the minimum necessary to directly address the situation that has arisen in contemporary Japanese society.

Tendencies in videos from women's groups

The oldest video analyzed was 'Gentle Breeze [at] Hachiko Square, 1) August 08.07,' uploaded on 7 August 2009. The narrator explains that this was Gentle Breeze's second political demonstration. The orator is announcing to passersby that the group was formed by 'ordinary housewives and ordinary female office workers gathering together,' and is 'not affiliated with any political party, nor with any religion.' These two claims – that they are ordinary people who are not politically or religiously affiliated – were frequently repeated in videos from Gentle Breeze and Flower Clock.

Analysis of the videos revealed two recurring tendencies in the activities of these women's groups. First, even when the women's groups had organized the event, the female activists were not always the main actors; and secondly, the assertions that they are mothers does not necessarily express their full position. I will elaborate on each of these points below.

By-standers to male participants

Scenes in which women participants hid behind male participants were common in the videos. Among the three groups analyzed, this tendency was especially notable in the case of Gentle Breeze, which often held activities in conjunction with male-centered groups. For example, a video of a Gentle Breeze protest in November 2013 records a counterdemonstration to a protest march objecting to the deployment of MV-22 Osprey aircraft to a U.S. military base on Okinawa.[10] The Gentle Breeze protest continued for about three hours, which was divided into

---

10 'Protest action that "Gentle Breeze" conducted in November 2013: Gentle Breeze counterattack in Ginza against the parade opposing Osprey deployment.' (https://www.youtube.com/watch?v=gNC2CGgdzo0, access: April 2, 2015). The titles of some of the YouTube videos referred to below include dates, while others do not because different video filmmakers and uploaders have different ways of titling their videos.

168

The contentious comfort women issue

nine videos before uploading. The first video began with an address by the president of Gentle Breeze. Subsequent videos recorded speeches by various conservative action groups delivered in the lead-up to the arrival of the protesters opposing the Osprey deployment, remonstrations when the demonstrators were passing, and closing remarks.

According to the president of Gentle Breeze, the aim of this activity was to 'protest against the parade of a ridiculous bunch of liars.' Next, she explained why she believed they were liars: 1) their claim that 'world peace will be more likely to eventuate if Japan has no armed force'; 2) their claim that 'Osprey is low-risk'; and 3) that the opposing faction comprised 'pretend Okinawans.'[11]

The proceedings up to this point had been led by women appearing to be members of Gentle Breeze, but they gradually lost control of the protest. When the protesters against the Osprey deployment approached the spot where Gentle Breeze and other conservative action groups were gathered, the chanting began, led by a woman from Gentle Breeze who bitterly shouted: 'Traitors!' (Other participants: 'Get ou—t!') 'Traitors! Get ou—t!'[12] However, once the male activists took up the chanting, they took the lead, and only after all of the marchers had passed were the women from Gentle Breeze able to take charge of the protest again.[13]

This tendency for the leadership of a women-initiated activity being snatched by male participants is also apparent in other videos such as one recording a demonstration that Gentle Breeze held in May 2010 against the Democratic Party,[14] which was in power when Gentle Breeze became active. Its activities were frequently aimed at criticizing that regime.

At this march, women took charge of the chanting at the front of the formation, and participants followed the female caller's lead when she shouted: 'We absolutely oppo—se (*Hanta—i!*) the Democratic

---

11 'Gentle Breeze: Political propaganda activity against the Osprey anti-deployment parade in Ginza, 1 (January 27).' (https://www.youtube.com/watch?v=gNC2CGgdzo0, access: April 2, 2015).

12 'Gentle Breeze: Political propaganda activity against the Osprey anti-deployment parade in Ginza, 3 (January 27).'

13 'Gentle Breeze: Political propaganda activity against the Osprey anti-deployment parade in Ginza, 4 (January 27).'

14 'Gentle Breeze demonstration, 3rd instalment! Japan will collapse if things go on like this!' (https://www.youtube.com/watch?v=0zfo4nuqy2g, access: April 3, 2015).

169

Chapter 6

Party regime that cannot manage the crisis!' Response: '*Hanta—i!*'[15] However, the further back the demonstrators were standing, the more their demeanor changed, with the male participants more aggressively chanting with megaphones: 'Toss the treacherous Hatoyama cabinet into the incinerator!' Response: 'Toss 'em in!'[16]

Furthermore, a video recording a demonstration staged by Gentle Breeze in February 2010 shows that women were constrained in response to male activists taking the lead.[17] In this protest against the Democratic Party government, kimono-clad women were walking four abreast in the front row, handing the microphone from one to another in order, and taking turns to lead the chanting. When the first woman finished declaiming: '[That] Ozawa Ichiro who's trying to escape by shedding his lizard's tail [i.e., blaming a subordinate for his own transgression], let's drive 'im out!' Response: 'Drive 'im out!', she handed the microphone to the next woman. However, in that miniscule pause, a male participant immediately behind them launched into the chant: 'The Democratic Party, we shan't forgive!' Response: 'Shan't forgive!', and other participants continue from there. In the video we can see the woman with the microphone trying to estimate when the men will stop chanting before she can address the passers-by in Shinjuku, saying: 'We are Gentle Breeze – demonstrators – that is, ordinary women who love Japan, who have taken action. These days, Japan is on the verge of being demolished.'

In the many videos of activities that Gentle Breeze undertook alongside male-centered groups, scenes like the above recur frequently, but even in women-only activities, there was a tendency for women to not take the leading roles due to harassment by male audiences or passersby. In Flower Clock's political propaganda activities on the streets, when female orators are speaking, people in the audience – presumably participants in the action conservative movement – frequently interject, and not simply expressing agreement with the speaker. Below is an interchange in a video recording of a street campaign conducted by

---

15 'Gentle Breeze demonstration, 3rd instalment! Japan will collapse if things go on like this! 1.' (https://www.youtube.com/watch?v=0zfo4nuqy2g, access: April 3, 2015).

16 Ibid.

17 '(5) Feb. 7 Gentle Breeze punishment parade ♪ in Shinjuku opposing voting rights for foreigners & rejecting multiple citizenship.' (https://www.youtube. com/watch?v=MpPUxUJRN0g, access: April 3, 2015).

Flower Clock in March 2013 on the theme of 'Beware of mass media lies!' The female orator criticized NHK (the national broadcaster) for having 'made YouTube delete a posted Diet telecast,' and in the course of that discussion, the following interchange was seen among female audience members.

> **Orator:** I wonder why they try to stop young people from watching Diet telecasts.
>
> **Woman A:** Why is it?
>
> **Woman B:** Yes, it's strange.
>
> **Woman C:** I wonder why that is.
>
> **Orator:** [Why did] NHK request the deletion of the YouTube video…?[18]

In response to the orator's question: 'I wonder why,' women in the audience echoed; 'Why?' before the orator continued her speech. This give-and-take format functions to support the orator so that she can make her speech smoothly, at a smart tempo.

In contrast, as a different female orator was speaking on the same day, we see an exchange with her male listeners with quite different connotations.

> **Orator:** Actually, until 1998, Japanese suicides numbered *twenty thousand* yen [*niman en*] or so for a—ges.
>
> **Audience (male):** *Twenty thousand people* [*niman nin*].
>
> **Orator:** Twenty thousand people. [But] after deflation started…[19]

The men at the venue corrected the orator's slip of the tongue, and she reiterated the correction as she resumed her speech. Whereas the female

---

18 'Flower Clock political propaganda activity: Beware of mass media lies! Political propaganda activity at Hachiko Square, 2 (March 26).' This video, which was uploaded to YouTube, has been removed as of August 2023. However, a video with the same content can be viewed at the following URL: https://www.nicozon.net/watch/sm20441696, access: August 5, 2023.

19 'Flower Clock political protest: Beware of mass media lies! Political propaganda activity at Hachiko Square, 1 (March 26).' This video, which

Chapter 6

audience in the previous example had interjected in a way that supported the flow of the speech, the men in the second example had interrupted the flow of the speech.

Male audience members interrupting female speakers was a frequent occurrence at other political propaganda activities, as well. At an event held by Flower Clock in October 2012, for example, the female orator was speaking sarcastically about South Korea, observing that it had not produced any Nobel Prize winners. During her speech, the following exchange was seen between her and male listeners.

> **Orator:** There's no reason why South Korea, supposed to be the most excellent ethnic group in the world, hasn't won [the Nobel Prize], right?
>
> **Audience:** Right.
>
> **Orator:** Because those guys believe that they are definitely superior to Japan.
>
> **Male audience member:** That's right. And they haven't won even one war, either.
>
> **Orator:** (Laughs) Why, then, does South Korea ...?[20]

The orator had not mentioned war and is interrupted by a man in the audience. In response, the orator momentarily laughs, as if to placate him, and then resumes her speech. In that moment, the woman's speech was suspended, and the tempo was broken by the man's interruption.

Another way that women's leadership is usurped is in the editing of videos. This is apparent in the video of the 'Japanese mothers' parade objecting to "child allowances" and "separate surnames for married couples"' organized by Flower Clock in conjunction with another group to object to the Democratic Party government's family policies. Although

---

was uploaded to YouTube, has been removed as of August 2023. However, a video with the same content can be viewed at the following URL: https://www.nicozon.net/watch/sm20441395, access: August 5, 2023.

20 'Hosted by Flower Clock: Beware of South Korean and North Korean lies! In Shibuya 2 (October 11).' This video, which was uploaded to YouTube, has been removed as of August 2023. However, a video with the same content can be viewed at: https://www.nicovideo.jp/watch/sm19094989, access: August 5, 2023.

The contentious comfort women issue

Figure 6.1 On-screen caption from a Flower Clock demonstration march

why they oppose child allowances is not made explicit in the video, a banner inscribed with the words 'Why pay allowances even to foreign children?' was displayed at the head of the parade. Thus, it seems that the groups were opposed to paying child allowances to resident-foreigners.

At this demonstration, marchers also chanted: 'Come what may, [we] mothers shall protect (*mamorima—su!*) [our] children!' with the response: '*Mamorima—su!* (We shall protect [them]!).' This chant clearly indicates that the protesters were asserting their position as mothers who would 'protect their children.' They claimed that 'separate surnames for married couples would mean parents and children would have different surnames. Let's think of children's feelings (*kangaemasho—!*),' with the response: '*Kangaemasho—!* (Let's think!).' In their opinion, if married couples had separate surnames, the children would take their father's surname, in which case, the mother and her children would have different surnames. The women in this demonstration were asserting themselves as mothers.

However, text inserted in this video by the editor reveals that it was edited from a different perspective than that of the female participants. Figure 6.1 shows a caption in a video of this demonstration, clearly written from the perspective of fathers, saying: 'What on earth will happen to the feelings of hardworking dads? To the feelings of children?' superimposed on an image of marching women.

Chapter 6

Notably, fathers were hardly mentioned in the chanting at this demonstration. The name of the account that uploaded this video was Yamato Press, Co., which was also listed in the video's end credits. Thus, it seems safe to assume that the filming and editing were both carried out by a company called Yamato Press, a conservative alternative media company with 26 columnists, only three of whom are women,[21] which suggests that it is not a women-centered media outlet.

Even documentary videos reflect the subjectivity of the camera operator and editor, who decide what to film, what to keep, what to cut, and when to insert a caption. Due to this male-dominated process, conservative female activists often end up as a mere backdrop to the male activists.

Mothers as a polite fiction

The second tendency that becomes apparent in videos of the activities by conservative women's groups is that although they proclaim the position of mothers, they do not always *act* from that position. Of the three groups studied, Flower Clock used the word 'mother' most often during its activities.[22] During the march against child allowances and separate surnames discussed above, for example, one speaker announced: 'We current moms and *future moms* oppose the child allowances that the government is pushing forward,' implying that all women can be represented by the category of 'mothers.'

However, even in the case of Flower Clock, analysis of the speeches suggests that the emphasis on being mothers is not always consistently maintained. At a Flower Clock event entitled: 'The Japanese Constitution that cannot protect [our] children's future: More dangerous than nuclear power generation!,' a horizontal banner held up behind the speaker (Figure 6.2) is framed with cartoonish faces, seemingly depicting children, as if to encircle the event's title. This banner is suggestive of the position of a mother who is 'protecting [her] children's future.'

---

21 The list of Yamato Press columnists can be viewed at the following URL: https://www.yamatopress.tokyo/columnist (access: August 6, 2023).

22 At Gentle Breeze, 'regular housewife (*futsu no shufu*)' and 'ordinary female office worker (*futsu no o-eru*)' were frequently-used terms, whereas the Justice and Peace frequently used the term 'Japanese women (*Nippon josei*).'

The contentious comfort women issue

Figure 6.2 Scene of a Flower Clock street propaganda event

However, examining the words spoken at this event reveals that only one woman out of seven was speaking from a mother's position. At Flower Clock's regular propaganda events, a title is affixed to each orator's speech. Titles from that event include: 'The logic of Article Nine of the Constitution is inconsistent,' 'South Korea's high suicide rate and sex crime rate,' '[We] Japanese will no longer be hoodwinked,' 'Is the Japanese Constitution valid?' 'Countries that wish for constitutional reform, and those that do not,' 'The origin of the South Korean national flag,' and 'Do we really have to observe Article Nine?'

The only one of these speeches to mention children from the standpoint of a mother was by a woman speaking on the topic: '[We] Japanese will no longer be hoodwinked.' This speaker, citing a female academic who had appeared in a news program, argued that 'lately, female university professors have been putting Japan down on television,' and 'children are the victims' because 'if they object, their grades might be lowered, or they might not be able to get [their professor's] assistance in finding a job,' and so '[we] must help Japanese children.'[23] However, the other speeches were either in support of constitutional reform or criticism of

---

23 'Scenes of May 29 Flower Clock political propaganda event: Japanese Constitution ... more dangerous than nuclear power generation! No. 3.' This video, which was uploaded to YouTube, has been removed as of August 2023. However, a video with the same content can be viewed at the following URL: https://www.nicovideo.jp/watch/sm23662943, access: August 5, 2023.

175

Chapter 6

Article Nine of the Constitution, and made no reference to the status of mothers.

Flower Clock's activities only involve women, and although it emphasizes that its activism is conducted from the standpoint of mothers, there is a clear tendency for little reference to be made to children. Even though the group formally claims the position of mothers, there is the perception that its assertions do not much need to emphasize this position deliberately at these events. Not only in the action conservative movement, but in the conservative movement as a whole, the status of women who are not mothers seems at first glance to be ambiguous.

Focus on the comfort women issue

The 'discovery' of the comfort women issue

Conservative female activists tend to be buried behind their male counterparts, even at their own events, and they emphasize that they are mothers even though they are not necessarily speaking as such. However, they tout the fact that their groups are women-only. There is only one topic, though, on which they can speak from the position of women rather than mothers in the conservative movement, namely, the comfort women issue.

Figure 6.3 shows the number of videos in my data that alluded to the comfort women issue by group. Gentle Breeze, the first of the three groups to be established, had campaigned on the comfort women issue from its inception in 2009, referring to comfort women in more than twenty-four percent of the videos analyzed for 2009 and twenty percent in 2010. However, after Justice and Peace mounted a protest outside the Foreign Ministry in 2011, the frequency of mentions of the comfort women issue in Gentle Breeze videos swiftly increased, to almost fifty-nine percent in 2012; fifty-six percent in 2013; and eighty-nine percent in 2014. Flower Clock, which started running regular events from 2012, alluded to the comfort women issue in sixty percent of its videos in 2012, and although the proportion subsequently declined, there were allusions to that issue each year.

One activity that could be considered a trigger for the sudden focus on the comfort women issue by conservative women's activist groups is the so-called Justice and Peace 2011 rally held in December that year.

176

The contentious comfort women issue

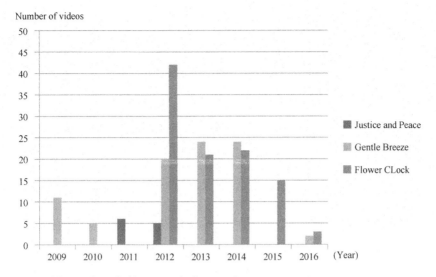

Figure 6.3 Number of videos mentioning comfort women

This was a counter-protest to the demonstrations that had been held every Wednesday since January 1992 outside the Japanese Embassy in South Korea by former comfort women and their support groups, calling upon the Japanese government to resolve the comfort women issue. The one-thousandth 'Wednesday demonstration' was held on 14 December 2011, and to mark the occasion simultaneous action was taken around the world. In Japan, a support group protested by surrounding the Foreign Ministry with a 'human chain.' Justice and Peace 2011 was planned in opposition to this worldwide action, and conservative women activists gathered across the road from the Foreign Ministry, chanting and making speeches.

In the video of that event, we see the organizers announce: 'We are Japanese Women for Justice and Peace 2011. *Japanese women* who feel anger at the comfort women's enormous lies have gathered here and are appealing [to you]' (emphasis added).[24] The term '*Nippon josei* (Japanese women)' was employed rather than 'housewives,' 'female office work-

---

24 'Japanese Women for Justice and Peace 2011: Do not forgive the lies of the comfort women! Protest action against the South Korean Wednesday demonstrations.' (https://www.youtube.com/watch?v=LR_2BS3jrUY, access: April 3, 2015). This video has been deleted as of 2023. The protest was recorded in a separate video (https://www.youtube.com/watch?v=ZQrweLCvKBU, access: August 7, 2023).

177

Chapter 6

Figure 6.4 Protest against an anti-Osprey-deployment demonstration

ers,' or 'mothers.' We can see banners announcing the presence of Gentle Breeze and Flower Clock, as well. The atmosphere is aggressive, with anger candidly expressed in such chants as: 'If you have the leisure to complain to Japan, go to Vietnam and apologi—ze!' Response: 'Apologi—ze!' 'Why are you spreading fabricated lies here, rather than apologizing to Vietnam?! Response: 'That's right!'[25]

From 2011, the comfort women issue was increasingly mentioned at both Gentle Breeze and Flower Clock events, and commensurate changes could be seen in their activities, as well. '[We] won't let you establish anything like a Comfort Women's Memorial Day! Counterattack!!'[26] was a protest held by Gentle Breeze, but observation of the participants filmed in the video yielded several points of difference between this and the counter-protest to the anti-Osprey-deployment campaign. This event was a counter-demonstration to a march advocating for a day commemorating Japanese military comfort women on 14 August, the date on which Kim Hak-sun spoke publicly about having been a former comfort woman.

---

25 In response to the South Korean government seeking settlement of the comfort women issue from the Japanese government, action conservatives frequently exclaimed that 'South Korean soldiers, too, were raping local women during the Vietnam War.'
26 'Gentle Breeze: We won't allow the establishment of anything like a Comfort Women's Memorial Day! Counterattack!! 3 (August 14, 2013).' (https://www.youtube.com/watch?v=dpDj9JLZMFE, access: April 4, 2015).

The contentious comfort women issue

Figure 6.5 Protest against a memorial day for comfort women

The five-part video shows speeches made by three men in the lead-up to the arrival of the pro-comfort-women demonstrators, but the subsequent chanting was consistently led by female participants, and protest participants are seen to be well controlled by the Gentle Breeze organizers. No male activists were seen interrupting female activists).[27]

The comfort women counter-protest is also visually different to the Osprey counter-protest, most notably in the physical positioning of participants. In the Osprey-related counterprotest, participants gathered in a straight line along the sidewalk beside the road (Figure 6.4); the male participants look excited, as if they are about to spill onto the road, while the women tended to be obscured behind the men.[28] Conversely, in the comfort women memorial protest (Figure 6.5), the female participants are standing in the front row, while their male counterparts are calling out from one step back. In this case, the camera is obviously focusing on the women.[29]

---

27 'Gentle Breeze: We won't allow the establishment of anything like a Comfort Women's Memorial Day! Counterattack!! 3 (August 14, 2013).' (https://www.youtube.com/watch?v=dpDj9JLZMFE, access: April 4, 2015).

28 'Gentle Breeze: Counter-political propaganda activity in Ginza on January 27 against a parade opposing Osprey deployment, 4).' (https://www.youtube.com/watch?v=8EnOGZux7WI, Access: April 4, 2015).

29 'Gentle Breeze: We won't allow [them] to make anything like a Comfort Women's Memorial Day! Counterattack!! 4 (August 14, 20013) (*sic*).' (https://www.youtube.com/watch?v=bn0iVe5tAWc, Access: April 4, 2015).

Chapter 6

Ambivalence about the comfort women issue

Conservative women's activist groups took the initiative in activities addressing the comfort women issue, but when we focus on what they are saying, their ambivalence on that issue emerges. To demonstrate this, let us first look at how male participants discussed the comfort women issue.

A video of Gentle Breeze and others protesting an event held by a support group for former comfort women at the office building for Upper House Diet members recorded harsh speeches and chanting directed at the support group and former comfort women from South Korea who had arrived in Japan that day.[30]

The men in the protest are spitting words full of hatred and scorn at the former comfort women, calling them 'old hags of comfort women,' 'senile old hags,' and '[You] beggars [who] call yourselves military comfort women';[31] 'Drum the lying whores into Tokyo Ba—y! Response: 'Into Tokyo Ba—y!'; '[You] whores who love, love, love money so much that there's nothing else to protect [you], get out of Japa—n!' Response: 'Get out of Japa—n!').[32] Furthermore, male participants aggressively used hate speech typically directed at Japan-residing Koreans: 'They're disgusting!' Response: 'So they are!'; 'Why have those disgusting old hag whores (*baishun babā*) come here to this office building belonging to House of Councillors members who are supposed to be the representatives of the Japanese nation?!'[33] and 'people who are holding a *disgusting, disgraceful* gathering consisting of comfort women at the Japanese national House of Councillors office building in glorious Japan.'[34]

In contrast, the female participants' allusions to former comfort women are complicated, using both aggressive and non-aggressive dis-

---

30 'Gentle Breeze: [Please] assemble at the street protest to counter the comfort women's gathering inside the Diet office building!' (September 24).

31 'Gentle Breeze: [Please] assemble at the street protest to counter the comfort women's gathering in the Diet office building!' 1 (September 24).' (https://www.youtube.com/watch?v=JcrQ9cMcUn8, Access: April 4, 2015).

32 'Gentle Breeze: [Please] assemble at the street protest to counter the comfort women's gathering in the Diet office building!' 2 (September 24).' (https://www.youtube.com/watch?v=ItQfLfK1Rzw, Access: April 4, 2015).

33 'Gentle Breeze: [Please] assemble at the street protest to counter the comfort women's gathering in the Diet office building!' 3 (September 24).' (https://www.youtube.com/watch?v=TDqT_oFS_vw, Access: April 4, 2015).

34 'Gentle Breeze: [Please] assemble at the street protest to counter the comfort

courses.[35] An example of an aggressive discourse is the claim that former comfort women gained economic advantage, which is begrudged. A recurring claim in these videos is that comfort women at the time were 'highly paid' – supposedly higher than a Japanese military officer[36] – and that immediately after Japan's defeat, 'those who had been prostitutes had savings of about one hundred million yen in today's money in their bank accounts.'[37] Moreover, at the abovementioned protest outside the House of Councillors office building, one said: 'Those old prostitutes who have won the trust of South Korea's President Park – I guess they'll fly first class to France and America to tell their lies.'[38] Expressions such as 'winning the President's trust' and 'flying first class,' indicate a perception that the former comfort women receive ample support, both politically and economically.

Another point relates to discrimination against 'prostitutes.' When women of the action conservative movement discuss comfort women,

---

women's gathering in the Diet office building!' 4 (September 24).' (https://www.youtube.com/watch?v=NIv4W8DSmc8, Access: April 4, 2015).

35 Most of what these women had to say about the comfort women was unoriginal. Assertions that comfort women 'earned such good money that they could build any number of houses,' and that former comfort women were not 'forcibly' taken away by the Japanese military, but had been 'sold by their parents;' or that the Japanese military was 'goodwill involvement for protecting the comfort women by carrying out regular health checks' can be heard in many videos, but these claims had all been previously made in publications such as Nishioka Tsutomu's 2012 book, *Yoku wakaru ianfu mondai* (The easily-understood comfort women question) (Soshisha), for example. However, even if they were simply parroting claims like these, analyzing the claims they made and the context in which they made them reveals something about the women's state of mind.

36 'Gentle Breeze: We won't allow [them] to make anything like a Comfort Women's Memorial Day! Counterattack!! 3 (August 14, 20013) (*sic.*)' (https://www.youtube.com/watch?v=xKV5-BZ3HVE, Access: April 4, 2015).

37 'Flower Clock: There weren't any military comfort women! Political propaganda dissemination event in Shibuya, 1 (May 10, 2012).' (https://www.youtube.com/watch?v=JHaUye3-5XA, Access: April 4, 2015). This video has been deleted as of 2023. The protest was recorded in a separate video (https://www.nicovideo.jp/watch/sm17785014, access: August 7, 2023).

38 'Gentle Breeze: Protest at the comfort women's gathering in the Diet offices! In front of the House of Councilors' members' office building (September 24, 2013).' (https://www.youtube.com/watch?v=8Lmpp9H4RLQ, Access: April 4, 2015).

Chapter 6

they frequently employ the word 'shame (*haji*).' For example: 'I think that maybe the South Koreans who were really prostitutes haven't come forward. That's because naturally they're *ashamed*;' 'There were more Japanese prostitutes [than others]. But are those people speaking out now like the South Korean prostitutes? They wouldn't, would they?' Response: That's right!'. 'After all, no matter how important a job it might have been in those days, I think that being too *ashamed* to come forward would be how ordinary Japanese women would feel.'[39] These statements indicate a belief that both 'engaging in prostitution' and 'having it known that one engaged in prostitution' are 'shameful things,' and the activists are criticizing the former comfort women who have come forward, saying: 'Shame on you!' Furthermore, they believed that 'ordinary Japanese women' who had been comfort women would be too ashamed to come forward.

The non-aggressive discourse seen among the female participants is not evident among male participants in the action conservative movement. This non-aggressive discourse can be roughly divided into two assertions. First, conservative female activists sometimes express empathy towards former comfort women, even if only partially. As we have seen, male participants called former comfort women 'old hags (*babā*),' but female participants seldom use this term, calling them 'grannies/old ladies (*obāsan*)' instead. Another comment recorded at a Flower Clock event was: 'As for self-styled military comfort women, the only thing we should have sympathy for is their having been sold by their parents, and so...' The suggestion here is that the women are deserving of sympathy because they were 'sold by their parents,' but no such words of 'sympathy' were ever expressed by male activists.[40] At another event, an orator who, having declared that 'there is also a way of life' that constituted 'having pride in being a prostitute,' conceded that 'the comfort women ... sold their bodies and earned money, working

---

39 'Gentle Breeze: We won't allow [them] to make anything like a Comfort Women's Memorial Day! Counterattack!! 2 (August 14, 20013) (sic).' (https://www.youtube.com/watch?v=xKV5-BZ3HVE, Access: April 4, 2015).

40 'Flower Clock sponsored: Beware of South Korean and North Korean lies! In Shibuya, 2 (October 11, 2012).' This video has been deleted as of 2023. The protest was recorded in a separate video (https://www.nicovideo.jp/watch/sm19094989, access: August 7, 2023).

The contentious comfort women issue

hard for their families' sake. I do think I'd like to say to them, "Well done. It must have been tough.""[41]

Women of the action conservative movement also began to use the expression, 'human rights.' This was especially marked in Gentle Breeze's activities, but at the abovementioned protest against the gathering of former comfort women's support groups at the House of Councillors members' office building, an appeal was made, saying: 'You Japanese, who shut off your *women's future*, and shut off [your] children's future … the comfort women's lies have been exposed. But in spite of that, you continue. That's funny, isn't it?'[42] Here, we see a tacit recognition that the comfort women issue is, above all, a problem relating to Japanese 'women's future.' A further statement was also seen at the protest at this time, as follows:

> I think their having brought a comfort woman here and having them spread their shame constitutes ignoring comfort women's *human rights* and trampling them underfoot. As *women*, we cannot forgive the Japanese and South Koreans who ignore comfort women's human rights. *As women*, we cannot forgive them.[43]

After these speeches, the crowd began chanting: '[You] Diet members who drag elderly grandmothers around and make them tell lies: protect women's human rights! Response: 'Protect [their human rights]!'[44]

Here, though, the context and use of the term 'women's rights' differ from those used in the feminist movement, as they are based on the premise that former comfort women are 'being made to tell lies' by

---

41 'Flower Clock political propaganda event: April 2, 2015. Don't teach children false history! Mr. Takeda, The Restoration Political Party – New Wind). This video has been deleted as of 2023.

42 'Gentle Breeze: [Please] assemble at the street protest to counter the comfort women's gathering in the Diet office building!' 3 (September 24, 2013).' (https://www.youtube.com/watch?v=TDqT_oFS_vw,Access: April 4, 2015).

43 'Gentle Breeze: [Please] assemble at the street protest to counter the comfort women's gathering in the Diet office building!' 1 (September 24, 2013).' (https://www.youtube.com/watch?v=JcrQ9cMcUn8, Access: April 4, 2015).

44 'Gentle Breeze: [Please] assemble at the street protest to counter the comfort women's gathering in the Diet office building!' (1 (September 24, 2013).' (https://www.youtube.com/watch?v=JcrQ9cMcUn8, Access: April 4, 2015).

183

Chapter 6

their supporters and support groups. However, even with this in mind, a plausible reason for conservative women appealing to the concept of 'women's human rights' in the context of the comfort women issue is that it allows them to make claims from the standpoint of women rather than mothers.

The intersection of sexism and ethnic discrimination

The various groups in the action conservative movement have mainly focused their activities at Zainichi (Japan-residing) Koreans, South and North Korea, China, and the Japanese left-wing. However, as we have seen, women's groups began to turn their attention towards the comfort women issue, especially from 2011.

The September 2013 issue of *WiLL* magazine included an article titled 'Big roundtable discussion,' involving female members of Flower Clock and Justice and Peace. It stated two reasons for taking up the comfort women issue. The first was linked to their defiance of feminism. Conservative women activists saw the comfort women issue as essentially an expression of 'anti-Japanese sentiment' and a 'political issue,' which, they said, had 'become a "women's rights issue" internationally' (Oka et al. 2013: 227). They also claimed that 'the comfort women issue had already become a tool of feminists [who thought that] if they evoked the term "women's rights," the facts wouldn't matter' (Oka et al. 2013: 228).

The second reason was a recognition of the strategic effectiveness of women raising their voices on an issue about which men found it difficult to speak. People demanding resolution of the comfort women issue were perceived as 'wanting to ... ignite hostility between the sexes, making women out to be victims, and men to be perpetrators' (Oka et al. 2013: 228). Yamamoto Yumiko from Justice and Peace writes: 'I think that the comfort women's issue, given its properties, is a question precisely for women to address' (Oka et al. 2013: 227). Although she offers no details about 'its properties', the 'Big roundtable discussion' article argues that 'if men vent an opposing view, this could be interpreted as "contempt for women" or "bullying of women"' (Oka et al. 2013: 228). Furthermore, the women's speaking out, saying 'That won't do!' was intended to cir-

184

The contentious comfort women issue

cumvent the creation of such a structure of 'hostility between the sexes' (Oka et al. 2013: 228).

The article clearly states that because the comfort women issue is difficult for conservative men to directly criticize, female activists began to speak and act in men's stead. It is clear that for conservative women's groups, the comfort women issue is a topic about which they can speak assertively from the position of women, rather than mothers.

The comfort women issue stands at the intersection of two types of discrimination. First, the comfort women issue is discussed in the context of ethnic discrimination. Former comfort women are ethnicized in the conservative's arguments. The women who became Japanese military comfort women were from numerous countries and regions, including Japan, the Korean Peninsula, Taiwan, China, the Philippines, Indonesia, and the Netherlands. However, comfort women are invariably imagined by conservative women to be South Korean; hardly any allusion is made to comfort women from any other country.[45]

In addition, South Korean comfort women were compared and contrasted with Japanese comfort women. South Korean comfort women, it was said, exposed their past as 'prostitutes' because they were 'shameless' women who came demanding an apology and compensation from Japan, while Japanese comfort women supposedly remained silent because they 'felt ashamed,' and were thus extolled as women who did not pursue compensation from the Japanese government. These claims have a similar structure to the chauvinism which mocks South Korea and 'bashes' Japan-residing Koreans. Noting the increasing tendency since the 1990s for 'right-wing forums' to discuss South Korea in the context of questions of historical recognition, represented by the comfort women issue, Higuchi deems historical revisionism to be 'the origin of a chauvinistic movement specifically targeting South Korea' (Higuchi 2014: 157). In that sense, the action conservative women's groups focus on the comfort women might be seen as a logical development in an exclusionary movement linked to historical revisionism.

At the same time, the discourse on comfort women seen in such groups is also sexist. As discussed in the previous section, when action conservative women's groups discussed the comfort women issue at

---

45 In the videos I analyzed, the rare mention of comfort women from anywhere but South Korea were about those from Indonesia or the Philippines.

Chapter 6

political demonstration marches and protests, there was a mixture of aggressive and non-aggressive commentary. Their aggressive assertions included that comfort women had been 'high earners' in their day, and were now 'receiving economic and social support' from support groups and the government, and that it was 'shameful' for them to talk publicly about their past as comfort women. Their non-aggressive behavior included referring to former comfort women by the polite term for grandmother (*obāsan*), and appealing to the concept of women's rights in their criticism of supporters' making former comfort women testify about their experiences.

If we arrange the arguments presented by conservative women's activist groups on the comfort women issue in this manner, we can see that their sexist utterances are complex. While such groups oppose resolution of the comfort women issue and vehemently criticize former comfort women and their support groups, they also express seemingly sympathetic attitudes and non-aggressive assertions, even if they are superficial. How do we explain this?

One reason appears to be that action conservative women's groups have strongly internalized a male-centered value system, including norms such as 'proper femininity.' Their verbal abuse of former comfort women is based on the view that prostitution is a shameful occupation, which is a manifestation of their having internalized a consciousness towards male-centered 'sexuality' which is prevalent in Japanese society. Prostitution is deemed to be 'bad' because: 1) 'sex/sexuality' itself has been regarded as abhorrent and should therefore be hidden from the public eye; and 2) as 'sex/sexuality' has come to be a 'sacred' part of people's character, selling sex for money should be avoided (Muta 2001: 179). Moreover, society's ways of discussing and engaging in sex, let alone prostitution, is asymmetrical between men and women; while it is deemed permissible for men to talk publicly about 'sex,' women's 'sex/sexuality' has been relegated to the private sphere. Furthermore, there is a sexual double standard in which women are divided into 'mothers,' for whom 'sexuality' is reproduction, and who warrant protection, and 'whores' who are objectivized as targets of male sexual desire.

Examining the claims made by women's groups of the action conservative movement in relation to the comfort women issue from the perspective of the internalization of such male-centered values and sexual norms, we see that the assertion that comfort women were

186

highly paid is based on a prejudicial view of women working in the sex industry. Further, condemnation of comfort women's public revelations as 'shameful' can be interpreted as arising from a sexual norm dictating that it is not desirable to talk about sex, while the female activist's politely calling former comfort women 'grandmothers' instead of 'old hags' might be attributed to the perception that it is undesirable for women to speak roughly, thus violating 'feminine' norms.

It would be an oversimplification to attribute all the assertions made by conservative women's groups about the comfort women to the internalization of male-centered values and sexual norms, however. Such an interpretation cannot fully account, for example, for the appeal to women's human rights. If we apprehend the 'bashing' of comfort women by women's groups in the action conservative movement to be a manifestation of the internalization of male-centered values and sexual norms, then a campaign strategy of calling former comfort women 'whores' and differentiating them from their 'womanly' selves would have to be adopted. The roundtable discussion mentioned above acknowledges that feminists seek to make the comfort women issue a women's rights issue. To counter this, they might have attempted to argue that feminism should not appeal to women's rights, but instead, conservative women have adopted a strategy of appealing to 'women's human rights' from a different angle.

Another reason sexual discrimination by conservative women's groups cannot be fully explained in terms of the internalization of androcentric values and sexual norms is that discussing comfort women invariably alludes to wartime sexual violence, which means talking about 'sex,' which is a violation of their feminine norms. Moreover, aggressively attacking former comfort women and their supporters, and independently pursuing contentious issues rather than just following the lead of male groups would also mean departing from 'proper femininity.' In other words, if they were to obey male-centered values and sexual norms, and pursue their activism within those norms, their present movement would not be valid.

For those women's groups, former South Korean comfort women are 'other' in a context of ethnic discrimination, but not necessarily in a sexist context. For example, an orator at a Gentle Breeze streetside event mentioned the contemporary sex industry, as follows:

Chapter 6

> There are some attractive women walking there who are working in the so-called sex industry, I suppose. I, too, have wanted to have a go at working there myself, but as my use-by date has passed...[46]

Her statement 'I, too ... wanted to have a go at working there,' suggests that she perceives working in the sex industry as an extension of herself. In fact, conservative women activists have spoken positively about sexuality, apparently rejecting the sexual double standard and 'traditional' or 'proper' femininity. Although they claim to be opposed to the feminist movement, their appeal to the concept of 'women's human rights' indicates a recognition that the comfort women issue is a women's issue. In fact, as long as they are consciously engaged in developing women-centered organizations in the action conservative movement, they will not be able to avoid discussing the comfort women issue as a women's issue.

Thus, a different interpretation than the internalization of sexual norms can be given to the way conservative women's activist groups have expressed their uniqueness – without being smothered by male-centered groups – and have discovered the comfort women issue as a contentious issue about which they can speak and debate as women. The points on which they most severely criticize former comfort women and their support groups are that they regard former comfort women to have been 'highly-paid' in the past, and as now being supported both economically and spiritually by advocates and the government. These things are criticized by frequent use of the word 'shameful,' which is imbued with two meanings, one pointing to the fact of their having been comfort women, and the other to their having made public their past as comfort women. Underpinning their idea that these things are 'shameful' is the fact that, as 'women,' they recognize that women who have been sexually abused are stigmatized by society. Furthermore, there is perhaps also a perception that only former comfort women are being protected and supported by the governments of various countries and by advocates who include politicians and activists, as well as antipathy and objection towards that fact.

---

46 'Gentle Breeze [at] Hachiko Square. Female passers-by edition, 08/07.' (https://www.youtube.com/watch?v=USmakhHMcfA, Access: January 17, 2016).

Such antipathy can be interpreted as a reflection of the situation of women and women's sexuality in Japanese society, rather than a reaction by 'some extremists.' After all, women experiencing sexual violence in Japanese society are subjected both physically and mentally to great harm, and this harm is downplayed by society. For example, although there have been some amendments to the wording and punishments in Article 177 of the former Criminal Code, which determines the crime of rape, its basic legal principle had not changed for 110 years until its revision in June 2017. Rape is defined as '(sexual) assault or intimidation,' but unless a woman about to be raped can demonstrate that she 'vehemently resisted' through acts such as 'shouting in a loud voice,' or 'fleeing in search of help,' it is difficult to legally prove that there was no consent to the sexual intercourse (Tsunoda 2013). However, in many cases the perpetrators of rape are not strangers, but are known to their victims (Muta 2001), and as the victims share the same life sphere as the perpetrators, they cannot always resist. Due to revision of the former criminal law, the crime of rape (*gokan zai*), whose spelling included the symbol for 'female,' was amended to the crime of 'forcible sexual intercourse (*kyosei seiko to zai*),' and the acts it encompasses also expanded, but the structural condition of '(sexual) assault or intimidation' remains.

In the present situation, there continues to be a strong likelihood that a woman claiming to have been the victim of sexual violence will be subjected to further harm in the form of a metaphorical 'second rape.' When victims claim to have been sexually assaulted, the responses from both close acquaintances and society at large – whether implicit or explicit – suggest the victim's culpability, and minimization of her injury, as evidenced by comments such as: 'It's her fault for wearing such revealing clothing,' or 'She let a man into her room, so she intended to engage in sexual activity.' Moreover, faced with a prevailing 'rape myth' which suggests that rape is suddenly perpetrated by a stranger, or that the victim is somehow to blame, many women cannot bring themselves to report the sexual assaults they have endured.

If we take into account these responses to women's sexuality, and the contempt for women involved in the sex industry, then what links the hostility directed at former comfort women by conservative women activists is a logic that asks: 'Why do only comfort women, who were prostitutes, receive support from governments and organizations?' even though women are stigmatized by society if they are victims of sexual

Chapter 6

violence, regardless of whether they are working in the sex industry or not, and are almost never afforded any relief.

The hostility of conservative women activists towards former comfort women may be attributable to a situation in which women's rights are not adequately guaranteed in Japanese society, especially for those who have suffered from sexual violence. At the same time, because these women are embedded in the social institutions and social structures that denigrate women's sexuality in Japan, they cannot fully condemn the former comfort women in the way that many men do, and therefore display some sympathy for former comfort women in appealing to the concept of 'women's human rights.'

Chapter 7

Women who cannot sneer at comfort women: Interaction and gender in the action conservative movement

Interaction at the sites of activity

In the previous chapter, through analysis of videos posted on the Internet, I elucidated how conservative women's activist groups shifted their activities towards the comfort women issue. Even among the various conservative action groups that focused their efforts on Japan-residing foreigners, South Korea, China and North Korea, or the domestic left-wing, female-centered groups focused especially upon the issue of comfort women. Detailed examination of the discourse bashing former comfort women reveals that for these women's groups, the comfort women are not only a problem of historical recognition between Japan and South Korea, but also that the oppression of women's sexuality within Japan 'justified' conservative women's claims. In this chapter, based on my fieldwork with the conservative women's group, Association B, I will analyze micro-interactions among its members to highlight the complexities they face when grappling with the comfort women issue.

The central question in studies of Japanese conservative movements is why people participate in them. Higuchi (2014) proposes dividing the factors in participation into two phases: 1) the joining phase; and 2) the continuing phase, but research on the latter is scant. More recently, Kukiyama Kazuyuki has surveyed participants in offline gatherings of the conservative social networking service called 'myNippon,' and found that participants reported a sense of 'healing (*iyashi*),' 'relief from isolation,' and similar benefits from participating (Kukiyama 2015: 263). However, assuming that some participants in a conservative movement have anxiety, the process by which that anxiety may or may not be

Chapter 7

reduced through participating in a conservative movement has not been explored.

A gender perspective is essential for examining the continuity phase of participation. For female participants, especially, joining the conservative movement can open oneself to potential attack. Research on female participants in the conservative movement have reported stalking of women who joined demonstrations (Sanami 2013), and a female participant who 'could not bear being seen as a sex object' by the men in the group (Kitahara and Paku 2014: 146). Even though they might participate in the movement 'in the same way' as men, gender is a major factor in what they experience there.

In considering women in the conservative movement, one cannot overlook the sexism inherent in such a movement, or the (in)consistency of action with the values espoused by the movement. Kathleen Blee, who surveyed female activists in the U.S. extreme right movement for many years, says: 'In addition to espousing racial and religious superiority, racist groups promote ideas of individualism, anti-egalitarianism, nationalism, and traditional morality that are arguably harmful to, or at least problematic for, women' (Blee 2002: 31). She points to tensions not only in their relationships with male participants, but also between the ideas the movement touts and the female participants.

The survey methodology is also important. Blee identifies two main difficulties in surveying a racism-based extreme right movement. First, even where it is possible to elucidate an activist group's formally declared position by analyzing the newsletters and leaflets that the group produces, this sheds little light on activists' individual opinions, motivations or backgrounds. Furthermore, in interviews, activists tend to simply reiterate the group's stated position, making it hard to approach their inner selves. As we saw in Chapter Two, Blee used life-history interviews to overcome this problem, thinking it might be possible to reduce the intrusion of the group's position by encouraging the activists to tell their personal stories in chronological order, from before they joined the movement.

Previous studies of the Japanese conservative movement have generally been conducted using interviews. Yamaguchi, Saito and Ogiue (2012), who interviewed leaders of conservative groups opposed to gender equality, as discussed in Part II, and the study based on Blee's research by Higuchi (2014), who conducted life history interviews of members from Association of Citizens and activists of the action conservative movement are examples.

However, while interviews can yield data on activists' personal history and the circumstances of and motivation for joining the movement, there are inherent limitations to this survey method, namely that the way activists speak to an interviewer *differs from what they say in a movement activity*. We can see this clearly in the transcripts Higuchi (2012) published of interviews conducted with members from Association of Citizens and activists of the action conservative movement. What is most notable here is the gap between the violent words spat out during direct action, such as: 'Toss the Japan-residing Koreans into Tokyo Bay!' and 'Those whores are telling a pack of lies and trying to destroy Japan' and the much more measured words spoken to the interviewer, such as: 'They [i.e., Japan-residing foreigners] want to blend into Japan in their own way, too, and after all, they are resident foreigners in Japan. Well, I guess they are worried in their own way' (Higuchi 2012: 102).[1] The latter, more considerate narratives are perhaps because the relationship between the interviewer and the activists has influenced what was said.

In this chapter, I focus on the interaction between participants within a movement, which has not had much previous attention. Both the words uttered at sites of action and those said to interviewers are 'outward-directed,' so to speak. Whenever people in a social movement organization make assertions to people outside their movement, they emphasize clarity and correctness in order to claim that their assertion is justifiable. Yet, when protesting against foreigners, for example, they are vehement, declaring anger towards foreigners living in Japan.

Yet, we suspect that participants' internal communications differ from the messages conveyed to the outside world. Participants surely do not only communicate in terms of correctness and radicalism. Elements such as 'enjoyment' and 'interest' are also necessary to build relationships of

---

1   Yasuda, who compiled reports on Association of Citizens and conservative action groups, wrote his impression of Association of Citizens members, saying that 'most could only be described as "ordinary" once I actually met them,' and so 'I had nothing but let-downs after I had begun to gather material on Association of Citizens and the people connected with it' (Yasuda 2012: 315). To Yasuda, the possibility could not be discounted that members appeared 'ordinary' because they were behaving 'ordinarily' in front of Yasuda, an outsider.

Chapter 7

mutual trust, and to anchor new members in the movement. From here on, referring to Alan Fine's concept of 'idioculture' (Fine 1979; 1987), I shall describe and analyze the interaction of participants in women's groups in the action conservative movement. 'Idioculture' means 'a system of knowledge, beliefs, behaviors, and customs shared by members of an interacting group to which members can refer and employ as the basis of further interaction' (Fine 1979: 734). Incorporating a gender perspective, I will elucidate how participants in the action conservative movement interact, and on what basis that interaction is founded.

Target groups and an overview of the survey

Overview of the target group, Association B

The target of my survey was Association B, a female-centered group linked to the action conservative movement founded in 2009. Its office-bearers were a president and an advisor, both women in their sixties or so.[2] Its published membership comprised about 800, but only women could become full members of Association B, with men being treated as associate members. Full members numbered about 500, and associate members about 300.[3] Although the association's home page states that its members' ages range 'from their teens to their eighties,' I got the impression through my survey that the members who participated most frequently were in their fifties or above. Association B is mainly active in metropolitan Tokyo, but also has branches in Osaka and Hokkaido.

Association B engages in many and varied contentious issues. These include the comfort women and Yasukuni Shrine issues and promotion of security legislation, in addition to criticism of Japan-residing Koreans, China, North and South Korea, and the left wing in Japan. Its activities generally take the form of demonstration marches, protest action, and signature-gathering campaigns, but it also lobbies Diet members and

---

2   As it was not possible to obtain data relating to participants' basic attributes in this survey, the ages of participants mentioned hereafter were all approximated by the investigator.

3   Similar to what has been said about Association of Citizens' membership numbers, only a small proportion of Association B's were active, so it might be more appropriate to understand the published membership numbers as representing the number of registrants.

194

Women who cannot sneer at comfort women

regional assembly members, as well as making congratulatory visits to the Imperial Palace, and contributing votive lanterns to the 'Festival of Souls' at Yasukuni Shrine.

Overview of the survey

The data analyzed in this chapter is from participant observation that I conducted from April 2014 to January 2015 at Association B's non-demonstration activities consisting of 'cookery classes to support Tohoku revitalization,' lectures and post-lecture social gatherings, and interviews with Association B's president (female, sixties; hereafter, the president) and Mr. J (male, seventies), a regular participant in the cookery classes.[4] Since the Tohoku earthquake in 2011, Association B had been holding its 'cookery classes to support Tohoku revitalization' approximately every month or two. These originally began with the preparation of food whenever a grand *mochitsuki* (rice-pounding) event[5] was held, with the aim of promoting interaction among members. Ingredients produced in Tohoku were used at the cookery classes to support the quake-hit area. Initially, they had sourced oysters, vegetables and other foodstuffs from Tohoku, and sold them at the classes to support revitalization, but had ceased this practice by the time of my survey.[6] These cookery classes were open to non-members, and thus functioned both as a site for interaction among members and people belonging to other groups, as well as a site

---

4 I was granted permission by the president of Association B to conduct the survey. When I introduced myself to other members and participants at cookery classes or social gatherings, I announced that I was conducting academic research, and had been granted permission by the president.

5 *Mochitsuki* is a traditional Japanese winter event in which glutinous rice is pounded to make rice cakes. It is particularly popular among the elderly. Participants (mainly male) pound the rice rhythmically with the pestle in turn, often accompanied by chants and songs by females to keep the tempo. This event is a cultural and social gathering where family, friends and the local community bond through pounding.

6 However, the initial purpose of supporting the revitalization of Tohoku continued to be supported by regular participants, some of whom had gone to Tohoku as volunteers to support its revitalization and brought back local *sake* as a souvenir for the association.

Chapter 7

for introducing people to Association B for the first time.[7] There was an average of twenty participants in each class.

As Association B's principal activity comprises direct action, slippage is thought to exist between the cookery classes and the cohort that participated in those activities. Some people participate in both aggressive direct action and cookery classes, while others only participate in one or the other; cookery classes are often the first time people attend Association B's event. In this regard, when I reviewed videos of Association B's activities (on the Internet), I found that regular participants in the cookery classes, who could be seen to be full members, were also joining Association B's other activities, such as street speeches and marches. However, I was unable to identify any of the regular male participants in the cookery classes at direct action events. It was clear, though, that there was a higher proportion of males in the classes than at the association's main activities, and I was particularly interested in the influence this had on the interactions among participants. In what follows, citations from field notes are labeled as (FN [date]), and those from interviews as (IN [date]).

Two collective identities involving Association B

Women

First, let me confirm Association B's position in the action conservative movement. From its inception, Association B was intended as a women's group. Its president had been a member of Textbook Society and observed that it had few women. Through her participation in Textbook Society activities, she had 'resolved that women would have a voice' (IN 19 April 2014). She also thought that 'it would be nice if there were people who could act on an everyday basis,' like housewives, noting that the majority of activists in the Textbook Society were male, and many were

---

7   When I consulted Association B's president about beginning the survey, and sounded her out about participating in the cookery class (the most immediate event in the schedule), she replied that starting my survey from the cookery class would be 'the perfect answer' because it would be 'buzzing with lively discussion of cooking and politics' by 'conservative gents and ladies' who 'loved to talk' and 'loved looking after others.'

196

still employed, which limited the times of day that they could spend on activities (IN 19 April 2014).

The first task for the president and others was to develop a contact network among the female participants for exchanging information about events. Once the network was established, the numbers gradually increased, which led to the formation of Association B. Soon after its establishment, the association extended its activities to include political rallies, demonstrations, and so forth, similar to other groups affiliated with the action conservative movement. In its early political protests, with no set venue of its own, members practiced their speeches in private karaoke rooms, and said that their 'legs quaked with nervousness.' Their first event was at a major train station in Tokyo (IN 17 October 2014). Conservative movement activities are usually video recorded, live-streamed on the Internet, and the videos posted on YouTube and other sites. Association B wanted to do the same, but initially lacked the equipment, so it sent a call-out by word-of-mouth for people who could do the recording, editing and uploading (IN 17 October 2014). They later acquired the necessary equipment to do all this for themselves.

Association B's home page records its mission statement, as follows:

> We feel Japan is facing crisis because of the biased reporting in the mass media, the masochistic historical view in school classes, and suchlike.
>
> No more can we leave things up to men alone!
>
> We women are rising up to protect Japan.

Its mission is to differentiate the association from other, predominantly male conservative action groups by emphasizing that it is a group of women, led by women, as evidenced by the declarations that 'No more can we leave things up to men alone!' and 'We women are rising up.'

The 'left' and the 'right'

Ueno Yoko, who surveyed a regional branch of the Textbook Society, points out that its participants have numerous terms for referring to their 'enemies', such as China, South Korea, and the left-wing, but they have very few words for talking about themselves (Ueno 2003). A similar tendency can be seen in Association B. A newspaper article had described

Chapter 7

Association B as part of a 'Japanese women's conservative swing,' but the president was uncomfortable with this description, saying: 'We think we are in the center' (FN 22 June 2014). Although some participants at the cookery classes described themselves as conservative, and some expressed concerns about the future of the conservative movement, not everyone in the group identified as conservative, and many shared the president's discomfort about being labelled conservative or right-wing.

Nevertheless, Association B was a group for people who shared certain principles and political positions. While they might not be terms that members used to describe themselves, the words 'right' and 'left' were used to distinguish themselves from others. The following notes describe an exchange between Mrs. C and Mrs. D (female, around fifties) in an elevator on the way to an Association B lecture.

> On the way to the venue, the elevator stopped at a floor where a lot of notices were stuck on the wall.
>
> Straight ahead, there were two or three elderly men seated on a bench, playing a game of *go*. Mrs. C and Mrs. D, who until then had been having a lighthearted chat, suddenly fell silent, and a feeling of tension pervaded the air. In the end, when the elevator doors closed without anyone having got on, Mrs. C laughingly said to Mrs. D: 'I thought they were lefties.' She apparently had thought that the men playing *go* were 'leftist' activists. Mrs. D laughingly remarked: 'It's no good, is it, to regard everything with such an eye?' (FN 19 July 2014)

The venue was a labor hall in metropolitan Tokyo. Given that posters and leaflets relating to labor issues were stuck on walls everywhere throughout the building, and the people they saw were elderly men, Mrs. C and Mrs. D simply presumed they had to be lefties. Association B members rarely referred to themselves as 'the right,' but in calling people they perceived to be antagonistic to their movement 'the left,' they implicitly positioned themselves in opposition, on 'the right.'[8]

---

8 Some members may perceive their political position as a spectrum rather than a binary one, such as 'center-right.' As it was not possible to conduct interviews with members other than the president in this study, it is difficult to ascertain their exact political positions. However, as mentioned above, members' frequently spoke in terms of a left-right dichotomous scheme.

198

Interactions at the cookery classes

The scene at the cookery classes

Association B's cookery classes were held on weekends at a public facility in metropolitan Tokyo. Each class began at three-thirty in the afternoon and continued until six. When the food was ready, a social gathering was held in the same room, where the dishes that had been cooked were served, and the events wound up just after eight in the evening. The menus prepared at the cookery classes during the survey period are listed in Table 7.1. In these classes, a woman aged in her fifties or thereabouts, whom participants called '*Sensei* (teacher)' served as facilitator. Once most of the participants had arrived, the teacher would hand out the recipes for the menu to be prepared that day and explain the steps for cooking it. Participants would divide into groups of three or four, and cooperate with each other to do the cooking, discussing and allocating duties among themselves. At one event I observed participants expressing appreciation for the efforts of a woman who had dirtied her apron with potato starch, telling her it was 'evidence of her great job' (FN 17 October 2014).

In the early evening, before the food was served, more people arrived for the social get-together, including several who appeared to be on their way home from work. When the meals were ready, the latecomers joined in, with five or six people surrounding each of the four preparation stations, eating and sharing their impressions of the dishes, chatting while drinking the alcohol that they had brought along. Time was set aside for everyone to introduce themselves at the end of get-together. Participants introduced both themselves and topics that had provoked their interest or that they thought were dubious. These sometimes developed into a discussion.

As previously noted, these cookery classes were an open space, and non-members of Association B also attended. Women were in the majority, accounting for about seventy percent of participants, but five or six men also attended each session. There were also several non-members who were regulars at the cookery classes, and every session had at least one person who was participating in an Association B activity for the first time. Sometimes regional assembly members visited to say hello, and sometimes supporters would bring politicians along for introductions to the participants.

Chapter 7

Table 7.1 List of menus for cookery classes

Date of investigation	Menu
18th April	Meatloaf with spring onion; stir-fried devil's tongue jelly; hornwort kinpira; rice with bamboo shoots; clear soup with wakame seaweed; strawberry jelly
22nd June	Taiwan-style stir-fried rice vermicelli; summer vegetable salad; sushi rice with simple summery toppings; simmered summer vegetables; banana cake
17th Oct	Pork mince with sweet-and-sour sauce; beef and vegetables with gluten; mushrooms with citrus sauce; rice cooked with savory flavorings; clear soup with kelp and mitsuba; dessert

Ingredients were purchased by the teacher and advisor on the day. When they arrived at the facility with their purchases, the goods were carried to the cooking room, mainly by the male participants. One day, the buyers arrived a little late. While waiting for them, the participants were chatting with each other about the so-called 'sexist heckling incident' that occurred on 18 June 2014 at the Tokyo Metropolitan Assembly. When a female assembly member, Shiomura Ayaka, had posed a question to the assembly about support for women with problems related to pregnancy, childbirth, and infertility treatment, she was greeted by heckling from several male assembly members to the tune of: 'Shouldn't you hurry up and get married?' and 'Can't you have children?' One of the women at the cookery class had commented: 'I wonder if it was because she [Shiomura], too, started saying such things that she got taken for a ride by the femi-hags from the commos and the soci-dems' (FN 2 July 2014). The participants basically took a critical position vis-à-vis the female assembly member who became the target of the sexist heckling, but rather than criticizing Shiomura herself, their position appeared to have been rooted in their dislike of feminists and supporters of the feminists who criticized the heckling, as evidenced by their use of the terms 'commos,' 'soci-dems,' and 'femi-hags.'

This is a typical example of the cookery classes' discussions of the news and current affairs that stirred their nationalism and patriotic sentiments. Topics of discussion during my participation included cinema, as in: 'Did you see [the 2013 war drama film] "The Eternal Zero (*Eien no zero*)?"' (FN 18 April 2014); music or soccer, as in what they thought of singer Sheena Ringo's 'NIPPON,' the theme tune for national broadcaster NHK's soccer coverage when the World Cup was being held, or: 'Why is the Japanese soccer team so weak?' and 'The rising-sun mark can be seen in foreign countries, too, so [Japan] is popular, right?' (FN 22 June

200

2014). Furthermore, the advisor who had told several participants that she and the president had visited a museum devoted to the kamikaze suicide corps during a private trip brought along some green tea that she had bought at that time and served it to the class participants (FN 17 October 2014).

Participants basically enjoyed lighthearted conversation sprinkled with 'jokes' throughout the cookery classes and get-togethers. At first glance, such exchanges might be considered trivial, but participants' jokes should be seen as part of an idioculture that identifies these cookery classes with Association B, which is the leading group within the action conservative movement. Jokes serve a vital function of promoting and strengthening group identity and unity (Crawford 2003), so I will turn shortly to the jokes told at the cookery classes, and examine how they influence the participants. But first, I will elaborate on Association B's underlying – and generally explicit – attitudes to foreigners and their patriotic sentiments, and how these are expressed.

Korea-hating, China-hating, and patriotism

Higuchi focuses upon the opportunity structure of discourse as one of the factors in the rise of the antiforeign movement. From analysis of the 'right-wing critical forum' of publications such as *Seiron, Shokun!* and *WiLL*, Higuchi points out that 'the countries of East Asia became their biggest enemy' from the 2000s (Higuchi 2014: 153–4). 'Countries of East Asia' refers specifically to China, and South and North Korea. Rhetoric that is particularly hostile to South Korea and China is called '*ken-Kan* (hatred of things Korean)' and '*ken-Chū* (hatred of things Chinese),' respectively.

It is worth noting that Taiwan is not included in this grouping, nor in the hostilities. Despite the shadow of its colonial history, there is a discourse within the contemporary conservative movement – more broadly than just the action conservative movement – which discusses Taiwan in positive terms as being 'pro-Japanese,' as evidenced by comments such as: 'Many Japanese people worked selflessly for Taiwan's sake,' and 'Even now, its old people esteem [Japan]' (Hirano 2009: 275).

Association B holds these views about East Asia. At the cookery classes they could be seen in participants' interactions in a rather diffuse form, rather than a single coherent argument. Let me relay what

Chapter 7

happened when four of us – the president, member Mrs. E (female, in her fifties or so), Mrs. F (female, in her seventies or so) who was from another organization, and the investigator – were in the same group. Mrs. E conversed with the president, with whom she was on familiar terms, but had little occasion to speak with Mrs. F, whom she was possibly meeting for the first time. The menu for the day was 'meatloaf with spring onions.' The conversation below took place between Mrs. E and Mrs. F when they were preparing bell peppers for the vegetable sauté that would accompany the main dish.

> **Mrs. E:** 'Recently, all the red or yellow bell peppers are from South Korea.'
>
> **Mrs. F:** 'I wonder if it's because we can't grow them in Japan.'
> (FN 18 April 2014)

Mrs. E had negative feelings about the fact that the bell peppers sold at supermarkets were grown in South Korea, and when she expressed them, Mrs. F, who had seldom spoken until then, voiced her agreement. Mrs. E seems to have assumed that the bell peppers they used on that occasion were grown in South Korea, as there had not been any special remarks from the instructor about their origins.

Talk of South Korean-grown bell peppers continued at the next cookery class, as well. Below is an interchange between the teacher and the president when the former was explaining the preparation method.

> **Teacher:** 'Colored bell peppers are usually from South Korea, but…'
>
> **President:** 'That's very true.'
>
> **Teacher:** 'That's right, but today I had a proper search for Japanese-grown ones, and bought them, as I find South Korea abhorrent.' (FN 22 June 2014)

In the conversation between Mrs. E and Mrs. F, no further reference was made to where vegetables were grown. However, at the next class, the teacher herself alluded to where they were grown, and announced to the participants not only that the 'colored bell peppers were Japanese-grown,' but that she had made a special effort to search for them.

202

The menus at the cookery classes typically comprised Japanese cuisine, but once the menu was 'Taiwan-style stir-fried rice vermicelli.' Others might have called the same dish 'Chinese-style,' but Association B was very clear about using a 'Taiwan-style' cooking method instead of a 'Chinese-style.' Indeed, the teacher went further, explaining that she had made a special effort to find Taiwan-made vermicelli for this dish. In these examples we can see how a shared hatred of things Korean and Chinese was expressed in the form of sourcing ingredients and cooking methods.

At the same time, expressions of patriotism were embedded in the classes. The recipes handed out to participants in each class were printed on A4-sized paper. Each sheet featured a Japanese flag set below the title: 'Cookery class to support Tohoku revitalization.' Below the flag were the words: 'Japan, my beloved country.'

Participants' also expressed patriotic sentiments in the clothing and accessories they wore to the classes, as we can see in the following exchange between Mrs. C and Mrs. D about the triangular kerchief they wore on their heads.

> Mrs. C and Mrs. D came into the classroom in the middle of the teacher's step-by-step explanation of the recipe. After the two sat down, Mrs. D donned a triangular kerchief with a pattern of pink cherry blossoms on a black background. At the sight of this, Mrs. C whispered to Mrs. D: 'That's nice, isn't it?' and Mrs. D smilingly replied: 'I bought it at a 100-yen shop. It's autumn now, though.' (FN 17 October 2014)

Mrs. C had instantly noticed that Mrs. D had donned a kerchief with a cherry-blossom design, communicating shared knowledge that cherry blossoms are a motif that symbolizes Japan and patriotism.

These were all conversations between women. Where men were also involved, the hatred of Korean and Chinese things was expressed 'jokingly', based on the shared understanding of the participants. This occurred when the president, Mrs. E, Mr. O (male, sixties), and the investigator were in the same group. Mr. O attended Association C's cookery classes, which the teacher also ran, and had become acquainted with her there. According to the teacher, the other cookery class was 'not a "left" or "right" kind of place,' but Mr. O apparently had 'realized it was probably "that way" [right-leaning].' Association C's cookery

Chapter 7

classes were held at the same venue, so Mr. O. was quite at home with both the teacher and the environment, and was someone upon whom the other participants, both male and female, relied.

When the teacher and Mr. O were talking with the president about Association C, and said that Association C's participants were 'ordinary people,' Mrs. E asked in jest: 'Are there any from the extreme left (*kyokusa*)?' Mr. O replied laughingly: 'Probably not, as you might expect.' The teacher mentioned that there had for a time been a South Korean woman – who apparently had come to Japan due to her husband's work – at Association C's cookery classes, but after a while she had stopped coming, and it was clear that the teacher was happy about that. A female participant remarked jokingly: 'She came along expecting to be able to make *kimchi*, did she?' (FN 22 June 2014).

Although this conversation also involved men, the initiative belonged to the women. Having started with jokes relating to participants' ideology, such as 'right or left' or 'extreme left,' when the conversation turned to the teacher's description of the South Korean woman who stopped attending, a woman joined in, and hateful jokes about Koreans began to be voiced. It was clear that 'hatred of things Korean' was something that participants at Association B's cookery classes could mutually 'enjoy' in mixed company.

The function of jokes at the cookery classes

So, what does it mean for hateful jokes about 'things Korean,' 'things Chinese,' and for patriotic sentiments to be exchanged among participants? According to Alan Fine and Michaela Soucey (2005), jokes fulfill four functions in small groups, namely to: 1) smooth group interactions; 2) share affiliations; 3) separate the group from outsiders; and 4) generate and cement appropriate behavior for the group. Building on these insights, the jokes shared at Association B's cookery classes can be interpreted as having at least the following three roles.

First, participants smooth their interactions by exchanging jokes. It is hard to judge whether others share one's political views in everyday life. Hence, mentioning topics that have a certain orientation, such as hatred of specific others, or patriotism, can generate friction in the outside world.[9]

---

9   While the participants in Association B's cookery classes consider their po-

Association B is a place where such topics can be safely broached, and, as in the exchange between Mrs. E and Mrs. F about bell peppers, participants jokingly discuss these topics to smooth their interactions.

Second, such jokes function to help assess whether other participants share the same values as the joker. Non-members of Association B can join its cookery classes. Although there were some individuals, albeit a minority, that were encountering Association B for the first time, time for introductions was set aside at the end of each class. Joking about current issues that were of interest to the conservative community at the time opened possibilities to determine whether unfamiliar others were aware of the topic without disrupting the atmosphere. If the others laughed at the joke, they could be judged to have similar values as the joker. This is the second function suggested by Fine and Soucey of sharing affiliation, that is, the formation of a collective identity.

Third, jokes inferring hatred of things Korean and Chinese, and those expressing patriotism, serve to produce and reproduce the knowledge and conduct necessary for members to take part in Association B. In the example of South Korean bell peppers, antagonism towards South Korea was seen in a context specific to a cookery class: the source of the foodstuffs.

Initially, it was a conversation involving only two people, Mrs. E and Mrs. F, but at the next class, the teacher and president influenced how the cookery class was run by indicating in front of the whole class that they were using Japanese-grown bell peppers, and the other participants welcomed it with a smile. Thus, through the medium of jokes, attendees at the cookery class can generate and cement appropriate behavior for the group.

The jokes and conversations about hating Koreans and Chinese, and expressing patriotic values at Association B's cookery classes thus had a positive meaning for people within the group. However, one of the four functions of jokes posited by Fine and Soucey (2005) is the exclusionary character of creating boundaries between an in-group and an out-group. In the next section, I will examine a case in which the

---

litical position to be the center, they are aware that they are a social minority. When making their self-introduction, no small number of them confess that they are troubled because they cannot make others understand their views (FN 18 April 2014).

Chapter 7

usually calm atmosphere of Association B's cookery classes underwent a complete change.

On jokes about comfort women

Elderly men who ridicule comfort women

While it appeared that all participants could 'enjoy' jokes about Koreans, Chinese, and patriotism, reactions to jokes about comfort women at Association B's cookery classes were different. Association B had been energized by the comfort women issue. At the time of the survey the association's main focus was a campaign to remove a memorial to Korean victims of wartime forced relocation that had been erected in a park owned by a local government body. Association B's action was driven by a 'hatred of things Korean' and the very existence of the comfort women issue. For example, at an Association B lecture which reported on action to remove the memorial, someone commented that unless memorials to Koreans in Japan were removed, the removal of statues of young comfort women erected in the U.S. would be utterly impossible (FN 19 July 2014).

In its direct action, Association B assertively engaged in the comfort women issue, but at its non-demonstrative events the issue was rarely raised in conversation. During my participant observation, only once did participants talk about comfort women at a cookery class,[10] when the following exchange was observed. It began during the self-introductions at the end of the class when Mr. H (male, twenties) mentioned that he had taken part in a testimonial rally by former comfort women. Here, I quote at length from my field notes:

> Mr. H remarked that he had been to a testimonial rally by former comfort women, [using the respectful Korean term for 'grandmother,'] '*Halmoni.*' When he did so, the president immediately asked: '*Halmoni*?

---

10 Jokes about the comfort women were observed at lecture meetings. At the same time as the lecture by Association B discussed above, another lecture demanding resolution of the comfort women issue was being held at a different venue. When the president of Association B, who was serving as compere, mentioned in her initial greeting that 'there is a "rambling talk" today at XX University in the same timeslot, so…,' laughter erupted from the audience (FN 19 July 2014).

Of comfort women? Nothing but lies, right?' But Mr. H replied: 'Rather than it being all lies, it felt as if it was basically true, but a little embellished.' Mr. H seems initially to have attended the rally with a negative attitude towards comfort women, but as he listened to the testimonials, he gained a partially sympathetic impression. Other participants [in the cookery class] listened in silence to Mr. H, and for a while nobody said anything. Then, Mr. I (male, sixties) suddenly loudly demanded: 'So the comfort women were attractive women?' Mr. H did not reply, simply smiling ironically, and in the end Mr. H's introduction finished on a vague note. Next, it was the turn of Mr. J (male, seventies). When he rose from his seat and was about to speak, again Mr. I called out: 'Anyone who likes comfort women?' At this, Mr. J raised his hand and ingenuously replied: 'Yes, [me]!' Other participants were watching the interchange between the two with a smile, but nobody added to the interchange, or said anything else (FN 22 June 2014).

The young male, Mr. H, was attending the cookery class for the first time, while the elderly males, Mr. I and Mr. J were regular attendees. In the above scene, Mr. I and Mr. J made sexist jokes about elderly women with a history of having been forced to be comfort women – sexual objects. Considering that the conservative movement activists contend that 'comfort women were prostitutes,' this interchange both criticizes women who sell sex and affirms the men who buy women's sexuality.

If such jokes deepen connections among participants and keep people in the movement, this interaction over the comfort women also serves to exclude anyone the group regards as inappropriate. The exchange between the elderly Mr. I and Mr. J invalidated the views of the young Mr. H by ridiculing them.

Ridicule has the following characteristics: 1) it is for amusement; 2) it tinges the speaker who is doing the ridiculing and the words spoken with anonymity and universality by obscuring who is ridiculing; and 3) it severs the intentions of the person being ridiculed from their origins and places it in a different context (Ehara 1985). As the question: 'So the comfort women were attractive?' was for amusement, responsibility for those words was not questioned, and Mr. H's sympathy for former comfort women has been relegated to a context of individual sexual orientation relating to whether those women had been sexually attractive. Mr. I and Mr. J's jokes indicate to Mr. H that his display of empathy

Chapter 7

towards former comfort women was 'not appropriate' in the space that was Association B's cookery class. After this exchange, I did not see Mr. H again, but Mr. I and Mr. J continued to attend.

'Others' who are excluded and 'others' who cannot be excluded

However, this scene appears differently when we focus on the reactions of the female participants. In the series of exchanges starting with Mr. H's comment, the only woman to say anything was the president, whose utterance clearly expressed animosity and anger, as in: '*Halmoni*? Of comfort women? Nothing but lies, right?' After this comment, though, she remained silent, as did the other female participants.[11]

Nevertheless, differences of opinion among participants were rarely exposed at Association B's cookery classes. During introductions, once a speaker had finished, there were often responses from other participants. However, after the exchange above, there were no further discussions involving all participants for some time (FN 22 June 2014). It was only after a regular female participant, Mrs. D, spoke up that others also began to comment. Mrs. D's comment concerned the recent increase in Chinese residents in her neighborhood, their noisy outdoor conversations, and the way the rules for putting out the garbage had stopped being observed. In response, some of the men suggested that she should 'take photographs of the site if the garbage rules were not being obeyed' (FN 22 June 2014).

I can think of two possible reasons for the female participants in the cookery class greeting the jokes about former comfort women with silence. The first is their different stance vis-à-vis the comfort women issue. The president had alluded to that issue in our interview, but her opinion was closely tied to her own status as a woman. She remarked that South Korea 'should protect women's sexuality' within South Korea, rather than 'blaming Japan' for the comfort women issue, adding that 'as a woman, I wonder whether the human rights of prostitutes today

---

11 I was unable to ascertain what the female participants in this setting were thinking. Some of them agreed to an interview, and some of them abruptly cancelled the day before the survey. In those cases, they said they had become nervous at the thought of an interview and had become unwell. As I judged that interviews would be a mental burden for general female members, I decided not to proceed.

need not be protected, as well' (IN 19 April 2014). These remarks position the comfort women not only as an issue of historical recognition and diplomacy, but as a continuing issue for women. It seems that the president is grappling with that issue 'as a woman.'

Moreover, her views on the comfort women issue included criticism of men who bought sex. She stated: 'Prostitution will not disappear,' but immediately added: 'I am speaking from on high in thinking that [prostitution] will definitely not go away,' and 'the best thing would be for men to stop buying sex' (IN 19 April 2014). In contrast to the expression 'speaking from on high,' this constitutes a self-conscious statement of her status as a woman in a position where she does not need to sell sex.

However, in a later interview with Mrs. J, who had joined in banter about comfort women in the exchange initiated by Mr. H, she remarked that the comfort women issue was 'only to laugh at' (IN 15 November 2014). This form of expression springs from Mrs. J's perception that although wartime sexual violence occurs in every country, not only Japan, discussion of the comfort women is 'propaganda aimed at dragging Japan down' (IN 15 November 2014). For Mrs. J, that issue is far removed from her own sexuality.

The second reason was that the female participants found it hard to counter or object to the male attendees. During the research, I observed other instances of awkwardness in the air at Association B's cookery classes. Referring to the removal of Korean memorials, Mr. K (male, sixties) had provocatively declared in his introduction: 'Removal of the memorials will absolutely never be accomplished... I'll give them a million yen if they remove' them (FN 18 April 2014). Nobody responded to his face, but at the next class, in Mr. K's absence, the president read out blogs by female participants objecting to Mr. K, and the women present responded with applause (FN 22 June 2014). Thus, an indirect approach was employed to counter Mr. K. Even the president, who had the authority to manage the association's activities, found it difficult to directly object to male participants.

Of Fine and Soucey's (2005) four functions of jokes in small groups, jokes heard in Association B's cookery classes regarding the comfort women issue meet the criterion of separating the group from outsiders and maintaining boundaries. The ridicule directed at the young Mr. H made clear that showing empathy for former comfort women was not appropriate behavior in Association B. However, considering the female

Chapter 7

participants' silence in response to Mr. I and Mr. J, and the disparity between what the president and Mr. J each said about the comfort women, it appears that jokes that sexually objectified comfort women were also regarded as inappropriate behavior. However, on no occasion did women suggest that to the elderly males.

Even if the female participants were able to expel the young Mr. H from the group, they could not expel Mr. I and Mr. J, who had driven out Mr. H because, in addition to their difficulty in countering the arguments of the male attendees, the regulars, Mr. I and Mr. J at least shared the group's 'hatred of things Korean,' 'hatred of things Chinese,' and patriotism. The ideological opposition to the comfort women issue was a priority alongside patriotism and 'hatred of things Korean and Chinese' in Association B's cookery classes, rather than a gendered way of thinking about the comfort women, and while the men who had a different point of view about gender were not totally 'inside' the female-only Association B, the female participants could not drive them out, either.

Conclusion

The women's conservative movement in Japan: Its difficulties and prospects

In this book, I have analyzed the conservative women's movement by dividing it into two streams: one based on an identity as 'mothers,' and one as 'women.' In this concluding chapter, I reintegrate the two, and revisit the three issues set out in the Introduction, namely: 1) the social structure of the conservative women's movement; 2) the relationship between the conservative women's movement and male-centered activist groups and male participants; and 3) a perspective of the movement's leaders as 'women' rather than 'mothers.' In light of these points, I will consider the reasons for and the meaning of the appearance of the conservative women's movement in contemporary Japan. To that end, I will investigate the factors that triggered the rise of that movement from the perspectives of its surrounding social structure and its relationship with male-centered groups and male participants; and, after arguing that the conservative women's movement is an ambiguous presence for the conservative movement as a whole, I will attempt to reinterpret the conservative women's movement as a 'women's movement.' Finally, in closing this book, I will outline what this focus on the conservative women's movement can offer to conservative movement studies.

Factors that triggered the rise of the conservative women's movement

The nationwide organization of the conservative movement occurred from the 1970s and 1980s. Consequently, a grassroots conservative movement arose in the 1990s, with a form similar to traditional left-wing social movements. Japan Conference and the Textbook Society were both formed in 1997, followed in the 2000s by the appearance of the women's conservative movement. What factors were involved, then, in women becoming leading agents in the conservative movement?

Although differing in whether they position themselves as 'mothers' or as 'women,' conservative women's activist groups that campaign against gender equality have three shared characteristics in their organizational form and action strategy. First, groups composed solely of

Conclusion

women that engage in lively activity are small and grassroots. In both the campaign against gender equality and the action conservative movement, women participate on the fringes of the conservative movement, not the mainstream. Large organizations with branches and members across the nation, such as Japan Conference, Textbook Society, and Association of Citizens, take the initiative and lead the movement. The interactions of participants in Association B, which we examined in Chapter Seven, reveal that gender norms remain strong within the conservative movement, and female participants are often constrained by their male counterparts, unable to freely express their opinions. The emergence in the 1990s of a small-scale form of conservative activism conducted spontaneously by grassroots members, such as History Circle, facilitated women's entry into the conservative movement by enabling like-minded women to gather and conduct their activities while casually exchanging views.

Second, women-centered conservative groups emphasized 'femininity,' apparently due to their awareness of a need to strike a balance with male-centered conservative groups, and their audience outside of the conservative movement. Some women-centered groups had male office-bearers, like Association A, discussed in Chapter Five, but these men intentionally avoided coming to the forefront of the movement. Moreover, to make Association A a group 'that any kind of women would readily join,' it intentionally adopted a policy of not having a parent (male-centered) organization and its recruitment mainly targeted women. Similarly, the women's groups in the action conservative movement discussed in Chapter Six played up the fact that they were 'ordinary housewives,' or 'ordinary female office workers' and 'Japanese women' in their public activities, such as political propaganda events and demonstration marches. Association B, discussed in Chapter Seven, has also created a female-centered group to enable women to be 'more vocal.' In this way, both the movement opposed to the Basic Act for the Gender Equal Society such as Association A, and the action conservative movement emphasize 'femininity' in their organizational development and their public statements. Moreover, the conservative activist groups that emphasize being 'women' quite openly seek to appeal to women who would join the movement on that basis. Even if a group is formed with the above intentions, and the leader emphasizes 'femininity' and tries to mobilize women, the movement will not exist unless there are women who respond to the call in the first place.

Third, the state of gender-politics in Japan today makes it difficult for conservative male activists to directly address issues concerning the family and sexuality, which makes women's groups not only acceptable but strategically desirable within the conservative movement. Women's workforce participation and the comfort women issue are also difficult for male activists to criticize head-on. Opposition to the Basic Law on gender-equality, for example, is de facto opposition to women's workforce participation, and a defense of leaving women solely responsible for care in the household. Yet, as dual-income households have become the norm in contemporary society, it is difficult to win new support by vocally opposing these changes. Hence, as we saw in Chapter Five, male intellectuals argued that the traditional family system and gender norms should be preserved for the sake of the state and social order, without explicitly stating that 'women should remain at home.'

The comfort women issue is similarly fraught terrain for male activists. As we saw in Chapter Six, when male activists derided former comfort women as 'old hags' at a women-led activity, they were met with silence. The primary issues discussed by male-centered conservative action groups were Zainichi (Japan-residing) Koreans and diplomatic issues with countries of East Asia. The fact that all-male activities rarely address the comfort women issue probably stems from the recognition that the sex industry only exists because men 'buy' women's sexuality, and men aggressively disparaging former comfort women would highlight this situation.

Both the campaign against gender equality and the action conservative movement are able to dilute the antagonistic structure of 'men versus women' through female activists raising their voices and standing on the front lines of the movements. And not only men, but women, too, can take an oppositional stance towards gender equality or the comfort women issue. Through female participants speaking out against gender equality and the comfort women issue, male participants in the conservative movement, also, can unreservedly talk about these topics. The formation of groups for women by women in the conservative movement has been welcomed by male participants.

In light of the above, factors in the activation of the conservative movement by women can be summarized into the following four points:

213

Conclusion

1) the production of a style of activism comprising a grassroots-level conservative movement in the 1990s; 2) the entry of women into the conservative movement through the formation of new women-centered groups emphasizing 'femininity;' 3) the increasing demand for women to stand at the forefront of the conservative movement to address emerging contentious issues relating to the family and sexuality that were hard for male participants to handle; and 4) changes in social consciousness around women's sexuality, namely the social division of care and the comfort women issue, both within and outside Japan, which had become contentious issues for the conservative movement. The conservative women's movement was founded upon these factors.

Ambiguities in the conservative women's movement

The conservative movement has been discussed domestically as a driving force in the 'rightward drift' of Japanese society, but as I have elucidated in the various chapters in this book, if we focus attention on its female participants, it is clear that the conservative movement is not monolithic, especially in regard to gender-related topics. Compared to male-centered groups and male participants, the conservative women's movement is extremely ambiguous. Although these bodies share admiration for 'patriotism,' female-centered conservative groups are not wholly contiguous with the mainstream conservative movement, and in some ways conflicts with it.

In the case of the campaign against gender equality, female participants' views do accord with the conservative movement in general in their idealization of a family structure based on gender roles. However, as discussed in Part II, the way women talk about the family was very different from that of male participants. Women discussed the family with a focus on their own experiences, such as how their mother rejoiced at the brooch given to her on Mother's Day, or how they recognized their family members' respective food preferences and prepared meals accordingly so that members of different generations, from children to the elderly, could sit together round the dining table. Moreover, most narratives were emotional descriptions of interpersonal relationships connected through care. The 'housewife backlash' discourse which advocated the importance of the family even while spelling out feelings of frustration about the hardships of living as 'mothers,' 'wives,' 'daughters-in-law,'

214

The women's conservative movement in Japan

and 'housewives' covertly indicates that actual families do not fully conform to the stereotyped model in which the responsibility for care is fully borne by women. Their criticism of gender equality can also be read as an objection to the low social value afforded to care, as seen in their argument that the family only exists because of such care, although responsibility for care in the household is accompanied by suffering and pain.

If we take the women's movement against gender equality to be an objection to the social and political devaluation of such care work, their claims overlap with some important feminist themes. The 'feminist ethic of care,' which exposes the circumstances of anyone in a dependent position, and the political nature of the way care work is confined to the private domain and forgotten, is not antithetical to women in the conservative movement who act from the standpoint of mothers and wives.

As discussed in Chapter Four, since Gilligan's proposal of an 'ethic of care,' there have been repeated attempts, especially in feminist studies, to reconsider the modern independent/autonomous agent and the social structures built on the assumption of such agents from the perspective of care and dependency. U.S. feminist legal theorist, Martha Fineman, for example, having conceptualized the relationship between a giver and a receiver of care as the mother–child dyad,[1] argues that the focus of state protection should be shifted from the traditional family to the mother-child relationality (Fineman 1995). Eva Kittay also reexamines feminist theory with a focus on dependency and care, while contextualizing the critique of dependency alongside feminist critiques of equality. Kittay focuses on dependency because '[t]o incorporate the needs and values which women have attended to requires a transformation making equality truly inclusive' (Kittay 1999: 19).[2] Although relationships of dependency are experienced throughout life, liberal political theory, which discusses

---

1   Fineman recognizes that the 'mother-child dyad' is a metaphor, which does not necessarily depict the relationship between a mother and child. In their discussions of the 'ethics of care,' many writers have taken pains to avoid essentialism, and with similar qualifications, Fineman calls the relationship between those who provide care and those who receive care the 'mother-child dyad' in recognition of the historicity in which the pursuit called caring has mainly been the responsibility of women.

2   On Kittay's arguments, also see Kittay (2011) which contains records of Kittay's lectures in Japan and ample commentary.

215

freedom and equality from the perspective of the independent/autonomous individual, is criticized by both Gilligan and Kitay for having failed to take relationships of dependency into account.[3]

In Japan, too, the 'care' perspective has been examined not only in political thought, but also in philosophy, ethics, and sociology, in response to debate on a 'feminist ethic of care.'[4] Based on feminist theory that characterizes the idea of the modern free and equal agent as being androcentric, Okano Yayo (2005b) has pointed out that although any such agent is only possible through their receipt of care in the private domain, care had hitherto been seen as unworthy of discussion. Furthermore, through the concept of 'restorative feminism,' based on care, Okano has attempted to shake up the public/private dualism itself. Kanai Yoshiko, in turn, 'reflecting on the current position of feminism from the theme of "care,"' refers to the significance of reexamining feminist theory from that perspective,[5] saying: 'When we direct our "gaze towards care" at feminism, at that point, feminism's self-referent gaze which reflects on the subject matter that it has failed to address – couched in such terms as social engagement and participation, self-actualization, independence, and self-determination – cannot escape being questioned' (Kanai 2008: 120).

Globally, the most widely used definition of care is Berenice Fisher and Joan Tronto's, who argues that 'caring be viewed as a species activity that includes everything that we do to maintain, continue, and repair our "world"' (Fisher and Tronto 1990: 40; Tronto 2013). If we define 'care/caring' in this way, it seems to include most activities. Whether in the public or the private domain, such 'care' as housework, childrearing, and nursing would naturally be included, but it would also encompass activities such as roadworks, planting forests, or cleaning, in the sense of 'maintaining, continuing, and repairing our world.' Tronto acknowledges that this definition has been criticized as 'too broad,' but by defining

---

3   Brugére (2013) and LeBlanc (1999) also question the prevailing socio-political structure from the perspective of 'care' and an 'ethic of care.'

4   Ueno (2011b) examines the introduction of an 'ethic of care' to Japan, and its arguments.

5   Aruka (2011) and Okano (2012) also develop feminist theory based on 'care' or an 'ethic of care.' Interestingly, in men's studies, Hirayama (2017) critically examines masculinity from the perspective of the practice of 'care' and an 'ethic of care.'

'care/caring' with a wide scope, Tronto is striving to rethink the ways in which efficiency and productivity are socially and economically valued and to reforge democratic institutions by means of the practice of 'care.'[6]

Conservative women's assertions of the importance of care also resonate with a feminist ethic of care, but diverge in the way that gender roles were perceived. Gilligan's proposed 'ethic of care' or 'ethic of responsibility' has continued to be controversial in feminist studies, as well, though. The 'ethic of care' has been criticized as essentialist or perhaps being a reductive gender characterization. Especially in situations such as Japan's, where women's responsibility for and burden of care is still heavy, it is necessary to fully consider such a designation, regardless of the perspective from which an 'ethic of care' is discussed.

The feminist ethic of care and the thinking of women in the conservative movement about gender roles differ in the following respects. A feminist ethic of care expresses a social ideal in which the 'right to receive care' and *the right to perform care* are guaranteed for everyone, transcending differences in sex, age, ability, social class or race. In contrast, as discussed in Chapter Five, while women who actively oppose gender equality invoke the social significance of care, the 'care' that is imagined is that which they themselves have provided in the home as wives or mothers – it does not question gender roles. Although it overlaps with the feminist ethic of care in its valuation of the practice of care, women who participate in the conservative movement from the standpoint of mothers diverge from feminism on gender roles.

At the same time, the defense of gender roles by women who oppose the Basic Act for Gender Equal Society was different than the defense of the family by conservative intellectuals. From my interviews with regional women activists discussed in Chapter Five, it emerged that women with a history of discord in their relationships with parents-in-law and spouses had striven to smooth interpersonal relationships within the household by internalizing their role as wife or daughter-in-law. For these women, rather than gender roles being norms that people 'ought to obey,' they provided models for assimilating painful experiences connected with interpersonal relationships in the household, and for convincing themselves that such experiences are worthwhile.

---

6   See Okano (2015) for a Japanese study that considers democratic institutions from the perspective of an 'ethic of care.'

Conclusion

Nevertheless, their arguments had to coalesce with those of the conservative movement if they were to have broad appeal and raise awareness of the problem of the low social value of care in the home. From an international perspective, these were sluggish moves, but with falling fertility rates and a rapidly ageing society, the need to increase women's workforce participation in Japan became unavoidable, which in turn highlighted the need for society to bear responsibility for childrearing and nursing care. As the need for care to be conducted outside of the household intensified, so did scholarly interest in care, and the characteristics of the practice of care began to be more positively assessed. However, such reassessment is accompanied by fear that affirming the importance of care that women provide in the household would reinforce the gender norms that constrain women's independence and autonomy. The feminist ethic of care aims for all people, regardless of gender, to enjoy the right to receive care and the right to provide it. In contrast, conservative women activists who challenge the low social valuation of care from the perspective of wives and mothers conform to a conservative discourse because they do not challenge orthodox gender roles.

At the same time, underpinned by the social conditions that determine women's lives and sexuality, conservative women activists also share xenophobic sentiments towards Japan-residing foreigners and antagonism towards the countries of East Asia with the action conservative movement. As Higuchi Naoto (2014) points out, rather than remorse for its former colonial rule, or a willingness to offer adequate 'settlement' of its war responsibilities, Japanese society tends to express a wariness towards China and South Korea and attack resident-foreigners whose origins lie in those countries.

Nevertheless, conservative women activists display different reactions to the comfort women issue than their male counterparts. While the latter readily disparage former comfort women as 'prostitutes' or 'old hags (babā),' conservative women occasionally use the more polite word 'o-bāsan,' meaning 'grandmother' or 'elderly lady.' Additionally, while reproaching former comfort women and opposing the resolution of the comfort women issue, they do not joke about the former comfort women as the men do. These differences in response to the comfort women issue raise a series of questions: Why do they appear to be more sympathetic to the comfort women than the male participants? Why do they use the

The women's conservative movement in Japan

expression '*o-bāsan*' rather than '*babā*?' Why, while deeming prostitution to be shameful, do they allude to their own privilege in not having to resort to prostitution? Why do they regard the former comfort women as being socially and economically advantaged? And why do they assertively use the concept of women's human rights?

We might interpret the conservative women's more nuanced responses to the comfort women issue as an expression of the difficulties and hardships facing women in contemporary Japan. The reason that such women argue prostitution is shameful and embarrassing is that they know that working in the sex industry 'cannot be publicly revealed' because doing so would mean being socially stigmatized. Their view that former comfort women were 'receiving warm support, both socially and economically,' and their opposition to that, might be due to their recognition that once a person has been branded with the label of a sexual being in Japanese society, it would be impossible for that person to receive the kind of support that the conservative women believe former comfort women are 'enjoying;' and that 'disparity in treatment' seems to be 'unequal' in their eyes. Their inability to vilify now elderly former comfort women as 'old hags,' or to place them in a sexual context and ridicule them (see Chapter Seven), stems from their recognition of the likelihood that they, too, will be despised as 'old hags' someday.

Conservative women activists talk about the comfort women issue a lot more than their male counterparts, and, while sometimes seeming aggressive in their expression, they also sound somewhat sympathetic, because as women in Japan, they understand the kind of treatment people receive after being sexually abused. Their condemnation of foreign women who 'willingly or unwillingly engaged in prostitution' is inseparable from the widespread ethnic discrimination in Japanese society, even while acknowledging the continuing inequality and oppression of women in Japan.

Within the conservative movement, women's unique claims are not always acknowledged; there is a tendency for male participants to be prioritized, and for women's voices to be buried. However, as discussed, if we focus on the gender of participants in the conservative movement, it becomes clear that the movement is not monolithic. The conservative women's movement is ambiguous: while it advocates some of the same things as conservative men, it also conflicts in important ways.

Conclusion

Reading the conservative women's movement as a 'feminist movement'

Domestic feminist movements

When viewed in terms of its relationship with male-centered organizations and male participants, the conservative women's movement is ambivalent, despite differences in positionality, issues addressed and problem-consciousness, and regardless of whether its participants acted from the standpoint of mothers or women. In this book, I have positioned the conservative women's movement as a social movement connected with the wider conservative movement, but I suggest that if we focus on the ambiguity inherent in the women's movement and the ways in which it diverges from the mainstream conservative movement, it might be possible to interpret it as a feminist movement.

Women have developed social movements in various countries over many years. Social movements in which women have taken leading roles include consumer movements, mothers' movements, and feminist movements. Yazawa Sumiko defines a women's movement as a 'civic movement whose agents are women' (Yazawa 1999: 249) and cites 'equality, development, peace, environment, welfare, human rights, labor, participation (in the market, society and politics), violence, poverty, and oppression' as examples of issues that have mobilized women's movements (Yazawa 1999: 252). Following this definition, the women's conservative movement discussed in this book is clearly a women's movement. However, their movement diverges somewhat from traditional women's movements in that it does not appeal for equality, peace, or human rights.

If the conservative women's movement is also a feminist movement, what are its defining characteristics? Takemura Kazuko (2000)'s concept of 'domestic ideology' is useful here. According to Takemura, domestic ideology appeared along with the formation of the modern state, dividing human beings into men and women, and then assigning men to the public sphere and women to the private sphere. Takemura points out that the limitations of U.S. first-wave feminism was that it was based on such a 'domestic ideology.' Takemura goes on to describe domestic ideology drawing a dividing line between the inside and outside of the state at the same time, as follows:

> It [the modern state] is something that clearly divides people into men or women, relegating men to the public domain, and women to the private domain (domestic sphere), and further separates women into decent, domestic women and indecent women who work outside the home, or else respectable, domestic women and foreign women who need not be respected. (Takemura 2000: 12)

In the original text, Takemura spells out the English-derived pronunciation 'domestic' using Japanese words meaning 'inside the home (*katei no naka no*)' and 'inside the country (*kokunai no*),' respectively. Based on domestic ideology, women are not only separated into those inside and those outside the home, but also those inside and those outside the state. Furthermore, women in the domestic domain in both senses are deemed to be worthy of protection, while those outside the home or outside the country are taken to be 'indecent,' and 'not needing to be respected.'

The women's conservative movement that has emerged in Japanese society since 2000 could be called a domestic women's movement in the above two senses. Women who oppose the Basic Law for a Gender-Equal Society, which champions the realization of equal social participation of men and women, campaign from their position in the family as mother, wife, or housewife. Conservative women activists who oppose settlement of the comfort women issue – perceived as predominantly about South Korea – assume the position of being both Japanese and women. In this manner, regardless of any difference in positionality between mothers and women, I suggest that the women's conservative movement could be called a women's movement whose members choose to remain in the domestic (inside the home/inside the country) domain and emphasize being 'good mothers,' 'good wives,' and 'good Japanese women.'

Can there be such a thing as conservative feminism?

As I mentioned in the Introduction, recent U.S. studies have found feminists among right-wing women, referring to the growing number of women who self-identify as feminists within the right-wing movement, or who, even if they do not identify as feminists, nevertheless have a collective identity as women, and assert themselves politically as representative of women.

Conclusion

Such findings are not restricted to the U.S., either. Birgit Rommel-spacher discusses women in the German extreme right movement, using the term 'radical right-wing feminists' to refer to women who, tending to be excluded from right-wing activism accompanied by violence, call for equal participation with men in the movement (Rommelspacher 1999).

In the Japanese case, it is difficult to call the conservative women's movement feminist. However, if we view the conservative women's movement that has materialized since the 2000s from the perspective of a women's movement based on domestic ideology, it is conceivable that a trend calling itself feminist might emerge among these women in the future.

As mentioned, Takemura points out that U.S. first-wave feminism was limited because it was based on a domestic ideology. When women had no suffrage, and hardly any opportunity for higher education, first-wave feminism called attention to women's exclusion from the public domain. In demanding women's access to the public domain, they argued that women were endowed with 'piety, purity, and obedience, and were family-orientated,' and that these 'womanly elements were superior to those of men' (Kurihara 2009: 47). Moreover, partly due to the fact that suffrage was granted to African-Americans and male immigrants in the U.S. before women's suffrage was granted,[7] some activists advocated (educated) women's suffrage while harboring discriminatory attitudes towards race and social class (Aruga 1988; Blee 2018).[8]

U.S. first-wave feminism had to repeatedly demand the rights of women to advance into the public domain and to participate in politics against social and political institutional assumptions that the women's sphere of activity should be limited to the private domain of the home. To

---

7   Social reform movements such as that for the abolition of slavery were precursors to the formation of the first-wave feminist movement that sought women's suffrage in the U.S. Many women took part in the temperance movement as a social reform movement, which arguably led to 'the granting to women of a platform for training in public activity, and the provision of a support basis for the feminist movement from the late nineteenth century onwards' (Aruga 1988: 62). Women's participation in the militant movement for abolition of slavery led by William Lloyd Garrison was considered to have 'led to the rise of a radical feminist movement that transcended women's traditional place' (Kurihara 2009: 290).

8   However, such racial discrimination came to be criticized from 1905, mainly by suffragists in the northern U.S. (Kurihara 2009).

do so, it asserted women's innate moral superiority, which in today's eyes seems essentialist. However, in the present-day U.S., where women's suffrage is long established, doors to higher education have been opened to women, too, and it has become formally possible for women to build careers in both economic and political terms, it is no longer necessary for feminists to try to be 'good' women in the eyes of the state or of men.

In contrast, women participating in the conservative movement in contemporary Japan continue trying to be 'good' women in the domain of the home or the nation-state. However, their efforts to be 'good mothers' and 'good Japanese women' do not signify a simple internalization of androcentric values. While on the one hand a discourse of trying to broaden social responsibility for care has emerged, there remains a deep-rooted perception that such care work as housework, childrearing, and nursing should be women's responsibility in the household. Furthermore, it remains legally and socially difficult for women who have experienced sexual violence to report it, and many experience secondary victimization in the form of a 'second rape' when they do report what happened to them. In a context of tenacious sexism and oppression, the conservative women's movement is not striving to change the current situation, but rather to 'conserve' a place where they can be even a little safer in such a situation. For them, the conservative movement aims to enhance the position of women who aspire to remain in the domestic domain in the dual sense of being in the household and in Japan, without altering social institutions or social structures.

As long as the women's conservative movement maintains a collective identity as women, its relationship with conservative male activists will always be dogged by tension. Japanese women's lib took shape through raising objections to the sexism rampant in the new left-movement in the early 1970s. The conditions are there, now, for conservative feminism to emerge in Japan, triggered by an awakening to the sexism in the conservative movement. Discrimination and oppression towards women transcends race, ethnicity, social class, sexual orientation, ability, as well as various combinations of them. And across both the right and the left in terms of political ideology. When women who lie to 'the right' in political terms start to develop an independent movement as feminists, we may see pressure to reexamine such concepts as gender equality, the comfort women issue, or even feminism itself.

Conclusion

The conservative swing, and gender

When we focus on the conservative women's movement, we can see large-scale social changes in the gender underpinnings of the Japanese conservative swing. After the formation of the Textbook Society in the late 1990s, conservative activist groups began to form at a grassroots level. Until the appearance of the current action conservative movement, including Association of Citizens, both large nationwide organizations and local groups coexisted. The dynamics of the Japanese conservative movement began to be referred to as a 'rightward drift,' and numerous theories have been offered to explain why the conservative movement became so attractive. Explanations include growing anxiety about the increasing social liquidity and destabilization of employment that accompanies globalization (Oguma and Ueno 2003; Takahara 2006; Yasuda 2012); and geopolitical changes in East Asia due to the political and economic rise of East Asian nations, especially China and South Korea (Higuchi 2014).

The chapters of this book have demonstrated that gendered ideas and ideals about women's way of life are also significant factors in today's burgeoning conservative movement. Although there are problems such as the gender pay gap and the high proportion of women among non-regular workers, women's workforce participation is encouraged today, and many women have gained employment. Moreover, as women have begun to work, the allocation of care practices – housework, childrearing and caregiving – is no longer confined to the home, but has extended into the public domain; that is, private enterprise and public authorities. Care which previously had been the sole responsibility of women in the home has come to be demanded of men and the public domain. In response, people who had traditionally been able to avoid performing unpaid care work, as well as those who want to keep the cost burden of care low, oppose women's workforce participation. Furthermore, for women who have singlehandedly borne the responsibility for caring in the home, more extensive changes to Japanese social institutions and society, including the Basic Law, might seem to have overlooked the significance of the practice of care.

Moreover, there is a huge disparity between international and Japan's recognition of violence against women. The comfort women issue has surfaced as a problem of historical recognition and diplomacy between Japan and South Korea. One foundation for this is the globally shared view

224

that wartime sexual violence is a war crime. In Japan, there is insufficient general and institutional recognition of the harm of sexual violence, and when it is reported, the seriousness of the harm is underestimated. Given the present situation in Japan, pressure from the international community to resolve the comfort women issue – with its implied accusation of sexual violence perpetrated by the state – is perceived merely to be anti-Japanese, and has been resisted in the form of comfort-women bashing.

Focusing on the conservative women's movement highlights that international and domestic changes in women's workforce participation and women's sexuality have been factors in the rising conservative movement, the so-called Japanese conservative swing. In this context, the women's conservative movement is a mirror reflecting gender in Japan's 'drift to the right.'

Bibliography

Aiba, Juichi, 2000, 'Soron: Nihon seiji e no pureryudo' (Introduction: A prelude to Japanese politics), in Juichi Aiba (ed.), *Koza shakaigaku 9: seiji* (Course in sociology 9: Politics), University of Tokyo Press, 1–42.

Akamatsu, Katsumaro, 1952, *Nihon shakai undo shi* (A history of Japanese social movements), Iwanami Shoten.

Aoki, Osamu, 2016, *Nippon kaigi no shotai* (The true colors of the Japan Conference), Heibonsha.

Aoki, Satoshi, 1986, 'Kuroi seiryoku no "kyokasho" senryaku: "Nippon o mamoru kokumin kaigi" no shotai' (The black force's 'textbook' strategy: The true colors of the 'National Conference to Protect Japan'), *Bunka hyoron* (Cultural review), 305: 46–57.

Arai, Yoko, 2014, '"Shimin katsudo shiryo" senta to shimin undo o sasaeru shakai kyoiku' ('Materials on civic activities' centers and social education supporting civic movements), *Journal of Ohara Institute for Social Research*, 666: 53–66.

Araki, Naho, Nishikura, Miki, Fukushima, Yuriko and Horie, Yuri, 2012, 'Tokushu ni atatte' (On the occasion of a special issue), *Joseigaku* (Journal of Women's Studies Association of Japan), 20: 4–13.

Aruka, Miwako, 2011, *Feminizumu seigi ron: kea no kizuna o tsumugu tame ni* (A feminist theory of justice: For weaving the ties of care), Keiso Shobo.

Aruga, Natsuki, 1988, *Amerika feminizumu no shakai shi* (A social history of American feminism), Keiso Shobo.

Asai, Haruo, Kitamura, Kunio, Hashimoto, Noriko and Murase, Yukihiro, 2003, *Jenda furi, sei kyoiku basshingu: koko ga shiritai 50 no Q&A* (Gender-free and sex education bashing: 50 FAQs), Otsuki Shoten.

Bacchetta, Paola and Margaret Power (eds), 2002, *Right-Wing Women: From Conservatives to Extremists Around the World*, Routledge.

Blee, Kathleen M., 1991, *Women of the Klan: Racism and Gender in the 1920s*, University of California Press.

—— 1996, 'Becoming a Racist: Women in Contemporary Ku Klux Klan and Neo-Nazi Groups,' *Gender & Society*, 10(6): 680–702.

—— 2002, *Inside Organized Racism: Women in the Hate Movement*, University of California Press.

—— 2018, *Understanding Racist Activism: Theory, Methods, and Research*, Routledge.

Blee, Kathleen M. and Kimberly A. Creasap, 2010, 'Conservative and Right-Wing Movements,' *The Annual Review of Sociology*, 36: 269–86.

Bleich, Erik, 2011, *The Freedom to Be Racist? How the United States and Europe Struggle to Preserve Freedom and Combat Racism*, Oxford University Press.

Brugére, Fabienne, 2013, *L'éthique du care*, Presses Universitaires de France.

Burack, Cynthia and Jyl J. Josephson, 2003, *Fundamental Differences: Feminists Talk Back to Social Conservatives*, Rowman & Littlefield Publishers, Inc.

Burke, Edmund, 1790, *Reflections on The Revolution in France: and on the Proceedings in Certain Societies in London Relative to that Event in a Letter Intended to have been sent to a Gentleman in Paris*, https://socialsciences.mcmaster.ca/econ/ugcm/3ll3/burke/revfrance.pdf.

Clement, Grace, 1996, *Care, Autonomy, and Justice: Feminism and the Ethic of Care*, Westview Press.

Cohen, David S., and Krysten Connon, 2016, *Living in the Crosshairs: The Untold Stories of Anti-abortion Terrorism*, Oxford University Press.

Crawford, Mary, 2003, 'Gender and Humor in Social Context,' *Journal of Pragmatics*, 35: 1413–30.

Cudd, Ann E., 2002, 'Analyzing Backlash to Progressive Social Movements,' in Anita M. Superson and Ann E. Cudd (eds), *Theorizing Backlash: Philosophical Reflections on the Resistance to Feminism*, Rowman & Littlefield Publishers, Inc., 3–16.

Dworkin, Andrea, 1983, *Right-wing Women*, Perigee Books.

Ehara, Yumiko, 1985, *Josei kaiho to iu shiso* (The idea of women's liberation), Keiso Shobo.

—— 2007, '"Jenda fur" no yukue' (The direction of 'gender free'), in Tomoeda, Toshio and Yamada, Mamoru (eds), *Do! Soshioroji* (Do! Sociology), Yuhikaku, 171–96.

Eirei ni kotaeru kai (Society for honoring the glorious war dead), 1977, 'Kessei syuisho (Prospectus of formation),' in Eirei ni kotaeru kai (ed.), *Eirei ni kotaeru kai tayori* (Society for honoring the glorious war dead news), 1: 2.

Faludi, Susan, 1991, *Backlash: The Undeclared War against American Women*, Anchor Books.

Fine, Alan G., 1979, 'Small Groups and Culture Creation: The Idioculture of Little League Base Ball Teams,' *American Sociological Review*, 44(5): 733–45.

—— 1987, *With the Boys: Little League Baseball and Preadolescent Culture*, The University of Chicago Press.

Fine, Alan G. and Michaela Soucey, 2005, 'Joking Cultures: Humor Themes as Social Regulation in Group Life,' *Humor*, 18(1): 1–22.

Fineman, Martha A., 1995, *The Neutered Mother, the Sexual Family and Other Twentieth Century Tragedies*, Routledge.

Bibliography

Fisher, Berenice and Joan C. Tronto, 1990, 'Toward a Feminist Theory of Caring,' in Emily K. Abel and Margaret K. Nelson (eds), *Circles of Care: Work and Identity in Women's Lives*, SUNY Press.

Fujime, Yuki, 2015, *'Ianfu' mondai no honshitsu: kosho seido to Nihonjin 'ianfu' no fukashika* (The essence of the 'comfort women' issue: The licensed prostitution system and the invisibility of Japanese 'comfort women'), Hakutakusha.

Fujimoto, Kazumi and Suetsugu, Toshiyuki, 2011, *Ti Pati undo: gendai Beikoku seiji bunseki* (The Tea Party movement: An analysis of contemporary U.S. politics), Toshindo.

Fujioka, Nobukatsu, 1996, *Kingendai shi kyoiku no kaikaku* (Reform of modern and contemporary history education), Meiji Tosho.

Fujisawa, Hideo, 1977, 'Nihon shukyo hoso kyokai ga jissen shita yoron chosa "Yasukuni jinja mondai to yoron no doko" ni tsuite' (On the survey of public opinion conducted by the Japan Religious Broadcasting Corporation for the problem of the Yasukuni Shrine), *Nagasaki daigaku kyoyobu kiyo* (Bulletin of the Faculty of Liberal Arts, Nagasaki University), 17: 51–8.

Fujiu, Akira, 2017, *Dokyumento Nippon kaigi* (Document: Japan Conference), Chikuma Shobo.

—— 2018, *Tettei kensho jinja honcho: sono kigen kara naifun, hoshu undo made* (A thorough investigation into the Association of Shinto Shrines: From its origins to infighting and a conservative movement), Chikuma Shobo.

Funabashi, Kuniko, 2003, 'Jorei o meguru "kobo" kara miete kita mono: kongo o tenbo suru tame ni' (What has become visible from 'offense and defense' over ordinances: To survey the future), *Joseigaku* (Journal of Women's Studies Association of Japan), 11: 37–49.

—— 2007, 'Jenda byodo seisaku to bakkurasshu no haikei' (The background of gender-equality policy and backlash), *Tozai nanboku* (Bulletin of the Wako Institute of Social and Cultural Sciences), Wako daigaku sogo bunka kenkyujo, 18–29.

Gelner, Ernest, 1983, *Nations and Nationalism*, Blackwell Publishers.

Gender Equality Bureau Cabinet Office 2019. 'White Paper on Gender Equality 2019' (https://www.gender.go.jp/english_contents/about_danjo/whitepaper/pdf/ewp2019.pdf, Access: 8 August 2023).

Gender Equality Bureau, Cabinet Office 2019, 'Status of promotion of measures relating to the creation of a gender-equal society or women in local government bodies (2018–19),' (https://www.gender.go.jp/research/kenkyu/suishinjokyo/2018/report.html, Access: 8 August, 2023 in Japanese).

Gilligan, Carol, 1982, *In a Different Voice: Psychological Theory & Women's Development*, Harvard University Press.

Guido, Diane J., 2010, *The German League for the Prevention of Women's Emancipation: Antifeminism in Germany, 1910–1920*, Peter Lang Publishing, Inc.

Haidt, Jonathan, 2012, *The Righteous Mind: Why Good People are Divided by Politics and Religion*, Pantheon Books.

Hardisty, Jean, 1999, *Mobilizing Resentment: Conservative Resurgence from the John Birch Society to the Promise Keepers*, Beacon Press.

Hasegawa, Koichi, 1990, 'Shigen doin ron to "atarashii shakai undo" ron' (Resource mobilization theory and "new social movement" theory), in Shakai Undo Ron Kenkyukai (Association for social movement theory studies) (ed.), *Shakai undo ron no togo o mezashite: Riron to bunseki* (Toward an integrated social movement theory: Theory and analysis), Seibundo.

—— 1991, 'Shakai funso: naze genshiryoku o meguru goi keisei wa konnan ka' (Social conflict: Why is the formation of agreement around nuclear power difficult?), in Yoshida, Tamito (ed.), *Shakaigaku no riron de toku gendai no shikumi* (The mechanism of modernity, explained with sociological theory), Shin'yosha, 243–59.

Hashikawa, Bunzo, 1968, 'Nihon hoshu shugi no taiken to shiso' (Experience and thought in Japanese conservatism), in Hashikawa, Bunzo (ed.), *Sengo Nihon shiso taikei 7: hoshu no shiso* (The postwar Japanese thought system 7: Conservative thought), Chikuma Shobo, 3–43.

Hata, Nagami, 2002, 'Koizumi shusho Yasukuni sanpai no seiji katei: "kokka to irei" ni kansuru joron' (The political process of Prime Minister Koizumi's worship visit to Yasukuni: Introduction regarding 'the state and consolation of spirits of the war dead'), *Kikan senso sekinin kenkyu* (Quarterly report on war responsibility), 36: 10–8.

Hatano, Sumio, 2011, *Kokka to rekishi: sengo Nihon no rekishi mondai* (The state and history: History issues in postwar Japan), Chuo Koron Shinsha.

Higuchi, Naoto, 2012, 'Zaitokukai no ronri (6): warudo kappu ga kikkake to natta F-shi no baai' (The logic of Association of Citizens against the Special Privileges of resident-Koreans, 6: The case of Mr F, which became the impetus for the World Cup), *Shakai kagaku kenkyu* (Social sciences research), 25: 97–104.

—— 2014, *Nihon gata haigai shugi: Zaitokukai, gaikoku jin sanseiken, higashi Ajia chiseigaku* (Japanese-style exclusionism: Association of Citizens, foreigners' participation in politics and geopolitics in East Asia), Nagoya Daigaku Shuppankai (Nagoya University Press).

—— 2016, *Japan's Ultra-Right*, Trans Pacific Press.

Hirano, Kumiko, 2009, 'Taiwan ga aishita Nihonjin: ima yomigaeru "Torii Nobuhei" densetsu' (The Japanese whom Taiwan loved: The 'Torii Nobuhei' legend now reviving), *Seiron* (Sound argument), 443: 268–77.

Bibliography

Hirayama, Ryo, 2017, *Kaigo suru musukotachi: danseisei no shikaku to kea no jenda bunseki* (Sons who care: The blind spot of masculinity and the gendered analysis of care), Keiso Shobo.

Hirschman, Albert O., 1991, *The Rhetoric of Reaction, Perversity, Futility, Jeopardy*, The Belknap Press of Harvard University Press.

Hobsbawm, Eric and Terence Ranger (eds), 1983, *The Invention of Tradition*, The Press Syndicate of the University of Cambridge.

Hori, Yukio, 2000, *Zoho sengo no uyoku seiryoku* (Enlarged edition. Postwar right-wing forces), Keiso Shobo.

Horiuchi, Kaoru (ed.), 2006, *Kateika saihakken: kizuki kara manabi ga hajimaru* (Rediscovering home economics: Learning begins from realization), Kairyudo.

Hosoya, Makoto, 2005, 'Danjo byodoka ni taisuru kinnen no hando wa naze okiru no ka?' (Why has the backlash against moves to gender equality occurred in recent years?), *Sekai* (The world), 738: 96–105.

Ida, Hiroyuki, 2006, 'Bakkurasshu no haikei o saguru' (Investigating the background of backlash), in Nihon josei gakkai jenda kenkyukai (ed.), *Q&A danjo kyodo sankaku/jenda furi basshingu: bakkurasshu e no tettei hanron* (Q&A on gender equality and gender-free bashing: A thoroughgoing counterargument towards backlash), Akashi Shoten, 176–86.

——— 2005, 'Kazoku no arikata to jenda furi basshingu: mondai no kaiketsu o saguru giron o' (The configuration of the family and gender-free bashing: Calling for discussion to search for solutions to the problem), in Kimura, Ryoko (ed.), *Jenda furi toraburu: Basshingu gensho o kensho suru* (Gender-free trouble: Investigating the bashing phenomenon), Hakutakusha, 117–43.

Iguchi, Kazuki, 1981, 'Yasukuni jinja no "ronri"' (The 'logic' of the Yasukuni Shrine), in Yamaguchi, Keiji and Matsuo, Shoichi (eds), *Sengo shi to hando ideorogi* (Postwar history and backlash ideology), Shinnihon Shuppansha, 118–41.

Iiyama, Masashi, 2008, *Amerika no shukyo uha* (America's religious right), Chuo Koron Shinsha.

——— 2013, *Amerika fukuinha no hen'yo to seiji: 1960 nendai kara no seito saihensei* (The transformation and politics of American evangelicals: Political party reorganization from the 1960s), Nagoya Daigaku Shuppankai (Nagoya University Press).

Imai, Isamu, 2002, 'Senbotsusha izoku undo no keisei to sengo kokka e no saitogo: senso giseisha izoku domei bunretsu o megutte' (The formation of the war-bereaved families movement and its reintegration into the postwar state: Around the breakup of the War-Bereaved Families League), *Nenpo Nihon shiso* (Annual journal of Japanese historical studies) 2002: 83–108.

— 2003, 'Sengo kokka to no kankei kakuritsu o motometa senbotsusha izoku undo: senryoka no tenkai to "aikokushin" mondai' (The war-bereaved families movement that sought the establishment of a relationship with the postwar state: The development of the movement and the issue of 'patriotism'), *Nenpo Nihon shiso* (Annual journal of Japanese historical studies) 2003: 115–34.

— 2017, *Sengo Nihon no hansen, heiwa to 'senbotsusha': izoku undo no tenkai to Miyoshi Juro no keisho* (Postwar Japan's anti-war, peace and 'war dead': The development of the bereaved families' movement and Miyoshi Juro's alarm bell), Ochanomizu Shobo.

Ino, Kenji, 2005, *Nihon no uyoku* (Japan's right-wing), Chikuma Shobo.

Ino, Kenji (ed.), 2006, *Uyoku, kodo no ronri* (The logic of the right-wing and action), Chikuma Shobo.

Ito, Kimio, 2002, 'Danjo kyodo sankaku shakai no mitorizu: bakkurasshu (gyakuryu) o koete' (Blueprint for a gender-equal society: Transcending backlash), *Toshi mondai kenkyu* (Journal of municipal problems), 54(3): 17–29.

— 2003a, '"Danjo kyodo sankaku" ga toikakeru mono: gendai Nihon shakai to jenda poritikusu' (What 'gender equality' questions: Contemporary Japanese society and gender politics), Inpakuto Shuppansha.

— 2003b, 'Bakkurasshu no kozu' (The composition of backlash), *Joseigaku* (Journal of Women's Studies Association of Japan), 11: 8–19.

Josephson, Jyl J. and Cynthia Burack, 1998, 'The Political Ideology of the Neo-traditional Family,' *Journal of Political Ideologies*, 3(2): 213–31.

Jomaru, Yoichi, 2011, *'Shokun!' 'Seiron' no kenkyu: hoshu genron wa do hen'yo shite kita ka* (A study of *Shokun!* (Everyone!) and *Seiron* (Sound argument): How has conservative discourse transformed?), Iwanami Shoten.

Joshita, Ken'ichi, 2012, 'Senryoki no Nihon izoku kosei renmei no katsudo to sono seiji-teki eikyoryoku' (The activities of the Japan Bereaved Family-Welfare Federation in the Occupation period and its political influence), *Ritsumeikan daigaku jinbun kagaku kenkyujo kiyo* (Research bulletin of the Institute of Humanities, Human and Social Sciences, Ritsumeikan University), 97: 91–114.

Kabashima, Ikuo and Takenaka, Yoshihiko, 1996, *Gendai Nihonjin no ideorogi* (The ideology of the contemporary Japanese), University of Tokyo Press.

Kaino, Tamie, 2006, 'Nihon ni okeru josei no jinken seisaku kadai' (Issues in women's human rights policy in Japan), *F-GENS janaru* (F-GENS journal), Ochanomizu joshi daigaku nijuisseki COE puroguramu: 'Jenda no furontia' (Ochanomizu Women's University 21st century Center of Excellence program: 'Frontiers of gender studies'), 5: 81–5.

Kaizuma, Keiko, 2005, 'Taiko bunka toshite no 'han "feminachi"': Nihon ni okeru dansei no shuenka to bakkurasshu' ('Anti-"feminazis"' as counterculture: Men's marginalization and backlash in Japan), in Kimura, Ryoko (ed.), *Jenda furi toraburu: Basshingu gensho o kensho suru* (Gender-free trouble: Investigating the bashing phenomenon), Hakutakusha, 35–53.

—— 2017, 'Nihon ni okeru josei hoshu seijika no gunji kyoko shugi to jenda no hen'yo' (Female conservative politicians' military hard-lining and the transformation of gender in Japan), *Jenda-ho kenkyu* (Gender-law studies), 4: 91–110.

—— 2018, 'Feminizumu no shimai, hoshu to riberaru no kimaira: gunji kyoko shugi-teki josei hoshu seijika no shiji kakutoku kozo to imeji kino' (The chimera of the feminist sisters, conservative and liberal: The structure of gaining support by military hard-liner female conservative politicians and imaging function), *Gendai shiso* (Contemporary thought), 46(2): 135–49.

Kanai, Yoshiko, 1990, 'Uman ribu tojo kara hachiju nendai ronso made' (From the appearance of Women's Lib until the 1980s controversy), in Bessatsu Takarajima Henshubu (eds), *Wakaritai anata no tame no feminizumu nyumon* (Introduction to feminism for those who want to understand), 52–61.

—— 2008, *Kotonatte irareru shakai o: joseigaku/jenda kenkyu no shiza* (A society in which we can be different: The perspective of women's studies/ gender studies), Akashi Shoten.

Kanbara, Hajime, 2014, *Heito supichi ni kosuru hitobito* (People who challenge hate speech), Shinnihon Shuppansha.

Kano, Mikiyo, 2012, 'Tojishasei to ichidai shugi' (Stakeholdership and one-generationism), *Joseigaku* (Journal of Women's Studies Association of Japan), 20: 16–24.

Kashima, Takashi, 2018, 'Danjo kyodo sankaku no aratana suteji: seibetsu yaku-wari buntan ishiki no kaisho o chiho jichitai kara kangaeru' (A new stage for gender equality: Consideration from local authorities about the elim-ination of consciousness of the gendered division of labor), in Dokuritsu Gyosei Hojin Kokuritsu Josei Kyoiku Kaikan (NWEC) (ed.), *NWEC jissen kenkyu* (National Women's Education Center practical research), 8: 6–23.

Katagiri, Shinji, 1995, *Shakai undo no chuhan'i riron: shigen doin ron kara no tenkai* (Middle-range theory in social movements: Expanding from resource mobilization theory), University of Tokyo Press.

Kawasoe, Keiko, Katsuragi, Nami, Akao, Yumi and Kaneshi, Erika, 2014, *Kokubo joshi ga yuku: nadeshiko ga kuni o omou te nani ga warui* (National defense women on the go: What is wrong with dianthus flowers [Japanese women] loving their country?), Bijinesusha.

Kawasoe, Keiko and Sugita, Mio, 2016, *'Rekishi-sen' wa onna no tatakai* (The 'history wars' are a women's fight), PHP Kenkyujo.

Kimura, Ryoko, 2005, 'Kyoiku ni okeru "jenda" no shiten no hitsuyosei: "Jenda furi" ga mondai na no ka' (The necessity for a 'gender' perspective in education: Is 'gender free' a problem?), in Kimura, Ryoko (ed.), *Jenda furi toraburu: Basshingu gensho o kensho suru* (Gender-free trouble: Investigating the bashing phenomenon), Hakutakusha, 75–94.

Kimura, Yukihiko, Sono, Shion and Yasuda, Koichi, 2013, 'Teidan: minzoku wa fikushon da' (Tripartite talk: Ethnos is fiction), in Kimura, Yukihiko, Sono, Shion and Yasuda, Koichi (eds), *Nashonarizumu no yuwaku* (The allure of nationalism), Korokara, 9–79.

Kinjo, Tamayo, 2012, 'Shorai e no fuan to bosei kara "kuni o mamore": ukeika suru joshi no "seigi"' ('Protect the country' from anxiety towards the future and motherhood: The 'righteousness' of right-leaning women), *AERA*, 25(52): 10–3.

Kinoshita, Hanji, 1951a, '(Shiryo) Sengo kyoku-u seito no seitai' ((Materials) The ecology of postwar far-right political parties), *Shakaigaku hyoron* (Japanese sociological review), 2(1): 29–43.

—— 1951b, 'Shinsei uyoku undo o tsuku: Nihon-ban "nashonarizumu" no mebae' (Prodding the new right movement: The germination of Japanese-style 'nationalism'), *Kaizo* (Reconstruction), 32(11): 71–9.

—— 1965, 'Nihon no uyoku/sekai no uyoku: sono keifu to shiso-teki haikei' (Japan's right-wing/the world's right-wing: Their genealogy and ideological background), *Asahi janaru* (Asahi journal), 7(35): 12–9.

—— 1976, 'Tenkanki ni tomen suru uyoku undo (ge): Rokkido jiken o megutte' (The right-wing movement facing a turning point (part 2 of 2): Focusing on the Lockheed incident), *Gekkan shakai to* (Socialist party monthly), 234: 123–30.

—— 1977, *Nihon uyoku no kenkyu* (Studies in the Japanese right-wing), Gendai Hyoronsha.

Kinoshita, Naoko, 2017, *'Ianfu' mondai no gensetsu kukan: Nihonjin 'ianfu' no fukashika to genzen* (The discursive space of the 'comfort women' issue: The invisibility and visibility of Japanese 'comfort women'), Bensei Shuppan.

Kitada, Akihiro, 2005, *Warau Nihon no 'nashonarizumu'* (Laughable Japanese 'nationalism'), Nippon Hoso Shuppan Kyokai.

Kitagawa, Kenzo, 2000, *Sengo no shuppatsu: bunka undo, seinendan, senso mibojin* (Postwar departures: The cultural movement, youth associations and war widows), Aoki Shoten.

—— 2005, 'Senso mibojin to izokukai, mibojinkai' (War widows and the Japan War-Bereaved Families Association and Widows' Association), in Hayakawa, Noriyo (ed.), *Senso, boryoku to josei 3: shokuminchi to senso sekinin* (War, violence and women 3: Colonies and war responsibility), Yoshikawa Kobunkan, 155–74.

Kitahara, Minori and Paku, Suni, 2014, *Okusama wa aikoku* (The wife is a patriot), Kawade Shobo Shinsho.

Kitajima, Manji, 1987, '*Shin Nihon shi* o meguru rekishigaku jo no mondai ten: gendai rekishigaku no kadai ni yosete' (Problematic issues in history around the *New Japanese History* textbooks: On the pretext of questions in contemporary history), *Rekishi hyoron* (Review of Japanese history), 444: 12–29.

Kittay, Eva F., 1999, *Love's Labor: Essays on Women, Equality, and Dependency*, Routledge.

Kittay, Eva F., Okano, Yayo and Muta, Kazue (comp. and trans.), 2011, *Kea no rinri kara hajimeru seigiron: sasaeau byodo* (A theory of justice begun from the ethics of care: Mutually-supportive equality), Hakutakusha.

Klatch, Rebecca E., 1987, *Women of the New Right*, Temple University Press.

—— 2001, 'The Formation of Feminist Consciousness among Left- and Right-wing Activists of the 1960s,' *Gender & Society*, 15(6): 791–815.

Kodama, Yuji, 2009, *Sei kyoiku saiban: Nanao yogo gakko jiken ga nokoshita mono* (The sex education trial: The legacy of the Nanao Special Needs School incident), Iwanami Shoten.

Koizumi, Akiko, 2011a, 'Kazoku no kachi to wa nani ka (1): shukyo uha to doseikon' (What does 'family values' mean? (1): The religious right and same-sex marriage), *Hogaku ronso* (Kyoto law review), 170(1): 62–79.

—— 2011b, 'Kazoku no kachi to wa nani ka (2, kan): shukyo uha to doseikon' (What does 'family values' mean? (2, final): The religious right and same-sex marriage), *Hogaku ronso* (Kyoto law review), 170(2): 65–89.

—— 2015, '"Kazoku no kachi" ga imi suru mono: Amerika ni okeru doseikon sosho' (What 'family values' means: Same-sex marriage lawsuits in America), in Ochiai,Emiko and Tachibanaki, Toshiaki (eds), *Henkaku no kagi toshite no jenda: rekishi, seisaku, undo* (Gender as a key to change: History, policy and movements), Minerva Shobo, 165–82.

Koshiba, Hisako, 2008, 'Tokuseiron ni motozuku danjo kyodo sankaku jorei seitei to sono go no gyakuten: Ube-shi no jirei' (The establishment of gender equality ordinances based on trait theory, and its later reversal: The case of Ube city), *Joseigaku* (Journal of Women's Studies Association of Japan), 16: 53–67.

Köttig, Michaela, Renate Bitzan and Andrea Petö (eds), 2017, *Gender and Far Right Politics in Europe*, Palgrave Macmillan.

Ku, Yujin (Koo, Yoojin), 2009, '"Atarashii rekishi kyokasho o tsukuru kai" no *exit, voice, loyalty*: Higashi Ajia kokusai kankei e no gan'i o chushin ni' (Exit, voice and loyalty in the Japanese Society for History Textbook Reform: Centering on implications for East Asian international relations), *Sokan shakai kagaku* (Komaba studies in society), 19: 18–38.

Kubo, Fumiaki and Tokyo Zaidan 'Gendai Amerika' Purojekuto (Tokyo Foundation [for Policy Research]) (eds), 2012, *Ti pati undo no kenkyu: Amerika hoshu shugi no hen'yo* (Research on the Tea Party movement: The transformation of American conservatism), NTT Shuppan.

Kukiyama, Kazuyuki, 2015, '"Aikoku komyunit" ni tsudou hitobito no raifu sutori: sono ba ga motsu imi to ayausa' (Life stories of people who gather in 'patriotic communities': The meanings and risks those situations carry), *Nihon oraru hisutori kenkyu* (Japanese oral history research), 11: 253–67.

Kurahashi, Kohei, 2018, *Rekishi shusei shugi to sabukarucha: kyuju nendai hoshu gensetsu no media bunka* (Historical revisionism and subcultures: The media culture of '90s conservative discourses), Seikyusha.

Kurihara, Ryoko, 2009, *Amerika no dai-ippa feminizumu undo shi* (A history of the American first-wave feminist movement), Domesu Shuppan.

LeBlanc, Robin, 1999, *Bicycle Citizens: The Political World of the Japanese Housewife*, University of California Press.

Luker, Kristin, 1984, *Abortion and the Politics of Motherhood*, University of California Press.

MacKinnon, Catharine, 2005, *Women's Lives, Men's Law*, Harvard University Press.

Maeda, Akira, 2013, *Zoho shinpan heito kuraimu: zoo hanzai ga Nihon o kowasu* (Enlarged edition. Hate crimes: Hate crimes destroy Japan), San-Ichi Shobo.

Maeda, Akira (ed.), 2013, *Naze, ima heito supichi na no ka: sabetsu, boryoku, kyohaku, hakugai* (Why hate speech now? Discrimination, violence, intimidation and persecution), San-Ichi Shobo.

——2016, *'Ianfu' mondai/Nikkan 'goi' o kangae: Nihongun seidorei sei no inpei o yurusanai tame ni* (Pondering the 'comfort women' issue and Japan–South Korea 'agreement': So as not to forgive coverup of Japanese military sexual slavery), Sairyusha.

Mannheim, Karl, 1927, Das konservative Denken: soziologische Beiträge zum Werden des politisch-historischen Denkens in Deutschland, *Archiv für Sozialwissenschaft und Sozialpolitik*, Bd. 57, I.S. 68–142, II, S. 470–95.

Mansbridge, Jane J., 1986, *Why We Lost the ERA*, The University of Chicago Press.

Maruyama, Masao, 1957, 'Hando no gainen' (The concept of backlash), *Iwanami koza gendai shiso 5: hando no shiso* (Iwanami course in contemporary thought 5: Backlash thought), Iwanami Shoten, 3–31.

Miyachi, Masato, 1981, 'Hando-ka ni okeru Yasukuni mondai no ichi' (The position of the Yasukuni issue in the trend toward backlash), in Yamaguchi, Keiji and Matsuo, Shoichi (eds), *Sengo shi to hando* (Postwar history and backlash), Shinnihon Shuppansha, 91–117.

Momota, Michihiro, 1987, '"Shita kara no gunji-ka" no senpei: kaiken o enshutsu suru "Nihon o mamoru kokumin kaigi"' (The vanguard of 'militarization from below': The 'National Conference to Protect Japan' directing constitutional amendment), *Gekkan shakai to* (Socialist party monthly), 376: 64–74.

Moriwaki, Takeo, 1997, 'Rekishi kyoikugaku no kakuritsu no tame ni: Fujioka Nobukatsu-shi no teigen o megutte' (For the establishment of a pedagogy of history: Focusing on the proposals of Professor Fujioka Nobukatsu), in Nara-ken Rekishi Kenkyukai (ed.), *Sengo rekishigaku to 'jiyu shugi shikan'* (Postwar history and the 'liberalist historical view'), Aoki Shoten, 39–71.

Morooka, Yasuko, 2013, *Heito supichi to wa nani ka* (What is hate speech?), Iwanami Shoten.

Munson, Ziad W., 2008, *The Making of Pro-Life Activists: How Social Movement Mobilization Works*, The University of Chicago Press.

Murai, Atsushi, 1997, *Rekishi ninshiki to jugyo kaikaku* (Historical recognition and instructional reform), Kyoiku Shiryo Shuppankai.

Muta, Kazue, 1996, *Senryaku toshite no kazoku: kindai Nihon no kokumin kokka keisei to josei* (The family as strategy: The formation of the modern Japanese nation-state and women), Shin-yo-sha.

—— 2001, *Jissen suru feminizumu* (Feminism in practice), Iwanami Shoten.

—— 2006, *Jenda kazoku o koete: kingendai no sei/sei no seiji to feminizumu* (Transcending the gendered family: Present-day sexual/gender politics and feminism), Shin-yo-sha.

Nagayoshi, Kikuko, 2019, 'Netto uyoku to wa dare ka: netto uyoku no kitei yoin' (Who are the Internet right-wingers? The specified requirements of the Internet right-wingers), in Higuchi, Naoto, Nagayoshi, Kikuko, Matsutani, Mitsuru, Kurahashi, Kohei, Fabian Shäfer and Yamaguchi, Tomomi (eds), *Netto uyoku to wa nani ka* (What is the Internet right-wing?), Seikyusha, 13–43.

Nakajima, Michio, 1981a, 'Seiji hando ni okeru shukyo kyodan no yakuwari' (The role of religious organizations in political backlash), in Yamaguchi, Keiji and Matsuo, Shoichi (eds), *Sengo shi to hando ideorogi* (Postwar history and backlash ideology), Shinnihon Shuppansha, 142–82.

—— 1981b, 'Konnichi no tenno ideorogi no toraekata' (How to apprehend today's emperor ideology), in Yamaguchi, Keiji and Matsuo, Shoichi (eds), *Sengo shi to hando ideorogi* (Postwar history and backlash ideology), Shinnihon Shuppansha, 70–90.

Nakajima, Takeshi, 2013, *'Riberaru hoshu' sengen* ('Liberal conservative' declarations), Shinchosha.

Nakamasa, Masaki, 2014, *Seishinron nuki no hoshu shugi* (Conservatism without idealism), Shinchosha.

Nakamura, Kazunari (Ilson), 2014, *Rupo Kyoto Chosen gakko shugeki jiken: 'heito kuraimu' ni koshite* (Report on the attack on the Kyoto North Korean school: Against 'hate crimes'), Iwanami Shoten.

Nakamura, Momoko, 2007, *'Onna kotoba' wa tsukurareru* ('Women's language' is constructed), Hitsuji Shobo.

Nakano, Koichi, 2015, *Ukeika suru Nihon seiji* (Rightward-drifting Japanese politics), Iwanami Shoten.

Nakano, Toshio, Itagaki, Ryuta, Kimu, Chanroku, Okamoto, Yuka and Kimu, Puja, 2017, *'Ianfu' mondai to mirai e no sekinin: Nikkan 'goi' ni koshite* (The 'comfort women' issue and responsibility towards the future: Defying the Japan–South Korea 'agreement'), Otsuki Shoten.

Nakayama, Toshihiro, 2013, *Amerikan ideorogi: hoshu shugi undo to seiji-teki bundan* (American ideology: The conservative movement and political division), Keiso Shobo.

Nara-ken rekishi kenkyukai (ed.), 1997, *Sengo rekishigaku to 'jiyu shugi shikan'* (Postwar history and the 'liberalist historical view'), Aoki Shoten, 39–71.

Narita Satoshi 1982, 'Kaiken-ha no aratana sakudo: "Nihon o mamoru kokumin kaigi" no "genjitsu-teki" senryaku' (New maneuvers by the constitutional amendment faction: The 'National Conference to Protect Japan'), *Zen'ei* (Vanguard), 476: 188–99.

Nihon josei no kai (ed.), 2007, *Kazoku no kizuna o mamoru tame ni: josei mo genki ni kuni-zukuri hito-zukuri* (For protecting family bonds: Women, too, energetically build the nation and build people), Nippon Kaigi Jigyo Senta.

Nippon izokukai, 1974, 'Haha no zo yotei dori shunko' (Construction of the mother's statue begins as scheduled), *Nihon izoku tsushin* (Japanese Bereaved Families' newsletter), 287.

—— 1977, 'Eirei ni kotaeru kai, issenman nin shomei stato, koshiki sanpai, Yasukuni jinja de yobikake' (Society for Honoring the Glorious War Dead, start gathering ten million signatures, official visits to Yasukuni Shrine, calling at the shrine), *Nihon izoku tsushin* (Japanese Bereaved Families' newsletter), 322.

—— 2006, 'Junkai tokubetsu kikaku ten: Akita, Gifu-ken de kaisai. Showakan' (National Showa Memorial Museum touring special project exhibition opens in Akita and Gifu prefectures), *Nihon izoku tsushin* (Japanese Bereaved Families' newsletter), 670.

Nippon izokukai (ed.), 1987, 'Nippon izokukai no yonju nen' (Forty years of the Japan War-Bereaved Families Association), Zaidan hojin Nippon izokukai.

Nippon izokukai fujinbu (ed.), 1995, *Fujinbu yonju nen* (Forty years of the women's division), Zaidan hojin Nippon izokukai fujinbu.

Nippon izoku kosei renmei, 1949, *Nippon izoku kosei renmei kaiho 1* (Family-Welfare Federation's inaugural bulletin 1)

Noda, Yasuhisa (ed.), 2010, *Hoshu shugi to wa nani ka* (What is conservatism?), Nakanishiya Shuppan.

Nozaki, Yoshiko, 2008, *War Memory, Nationalism and Education in Postwar Japan, 1945–2007: The Japanese History Textbook Controversy and Ienaga Saburo's Court Challenges*, Routledge.

Ochiai, Emiko, 2004, *Nijuisseiki kazoku e, dai-san-ban: kazoku no sengo taisei no mikata/koekata* (Towards the twenty-first-century family, third edition: How to view and transcend the family's postwar order), Yuhikaku.

Ochiai, Emiko and Joshita, Ken'ichi, 2015, 'Rekidai shusho no kokkai hatsugen ni miru "Kazoku" to "josei": "ushinawareta nijunen" no ideorogi-teki haikei' ('Families' and 'women' as seen in national parliamentary speeches of successive prime ministers: The ideological background of the 'lost twenty years'), in Ochiai, Emiko and Tachibanaki, Toshiaki (eds), *Henkaku no kagi toshite no jenda: rekishi, seisaku, undo* (Gender as a key to change: History, policy and movements), Minerva Shobo, 207–34.

Ochiai, Hitoshi, 1987, *Hoshu shugi no shakai riron: Haieku, Hato, Osutin* (The social theory of conservatism: Hayek, Hart, Austin), Keiso Shobo.

Ogino, Miho, 2001, *Chuzetsu ronso to Amerika shakai: shintai o meguru senso* (The abortion debate and American society: The war over the body), Iwanami Shoten.

Oguma, Eiji, 2002, *'Minshu' to 'aikoku': sengo Nihon no nashonarizumu to kokyosei* ('Democracy' and 'patriotism': Nationalism and publicness in postwar Japan), Shin-yo-sha.

Oguma, Eiji and Ueno, Yoko, 2003, *'Iyashi' no nashonarizumu: kusa no ne hoshu undo no jissho-teki kenkyu* (A nationalism of 'healing': An empirical study of the grassroots conservative movement), Keio Gijuku Daigaku Shuppankai.

Oka, Makiko, Yamamoto, Yumiko et al., 2013, 'Dai zadankai: Iza yukan! Ianfu mondai ni joseitachi no koe o (Soryoku daitokushu: Kankoku no "sei dorei" netsuzo o yurusu na!)' (Big roundtable: Now let's go! Add women's voices to the comfort women issue (Full-scale bumper special feature: Do not allow fabrication of South Korean 'sex slaves')), *WiLL*, 105: 222–31.

Okamoto, Masataka, 2013, 'Nihon ni okeru heito supichi kakudai no genryu to Korianofobia' (The source of expansion of hate speech in Japan and Koreanophobia), in Komai, Hiroshi (sup. ed.), Kobayashi, Masao (ed.), *Imin, diasupura kenkyu 3. Reishizumu to gaikokujin ken'o* (Migration and diaspora studies 3. Racism and xenophobia), Akashi Shoten, 50–75.

Okano, Yayo, 2000, 'Kazoku to seiji' (The family and politics), *Ritsumeikan hogaku* (Ritsumeikan law), 3, 4: 854–889.

—— 2005a, 'Jenda no seiji: nani ga miushinawarete iru no ka' (The politics of gender: What is being missed?), in Kimura, Ryoko (ed.), *Jenda furi toraburu: Basshingu gensho o kensho suru* (Gender-free trouble: Investigating the bashing phenomenon), Hakutakusha, 55–74.

—— 2005b, 'Tsukuroi no feminizumu e' (Towards a feminism of reparation), *Gendai shiso* (Contemporary thought), 33(10): 80–91.

—— 2012, *Feminizumu no seijigaku: kea no rinri o gurobaru na shakai e* (The politics of feminism: Bringing an ethic of care to global society), Misuzu Shobo.

—— 2015, *Senso ni kosuru: kea no rinri to heiwa no koso* (Opposing war: The ethic of care and the conceptualization of peace), Iwanami Shoten.

—— 2016, 'Feminizumu rinrigaku kara kangaeru Nikkan goi' (Japan–South Korea agreement considered from feminist ethics), in Maeda, Akira, (ed.), *'Ianfu' mondai/Nikkan 'goi' o kangae: Nihongun seidorei sei no inpei o yurusanai tame ni* (Pondering the 'comfort women' issue and Japan–South Korea 'agreement': So as not to forgive coverup of Japanese military sexual slavery), Sairyusha, 54–64.

—— 2018, 'Dotoku-teki sekinin to wa nani ka: Nikkan goi to "heiwa no hi" o megutte' (What is moral responsibility? Around the Japan–South Korea agreement and 'peace memorials'), in Muta, Kazue (ed.), *Kakyo suru feminizumu: Rekishi, sei, boryoku* (Feminism that bridges the gap: History, sex, violence), Osaka University Knowledge Archive, http://doi.org/10.18910/67844.

Okin, Susan M., 1989, *Justice, Gender, and the Family*, Basic Books.

Oku, Kentaro, 2009, 'Sangiin zenkokuku senkyo to rieki dantai: Nippon izokukai no jirei bunseki' (Upper house national constituency elections and interest groups: A case analysis of the Japan War-Bereaved Families Association),' *Senkyo kenkyu* (Japanese journal of electoral studies), 25(2): 67–82.

Obinata, Sumio, 2009, 'Senso no taiken, kioku, ninshiki to jenda' (Experiences, memories and recognition of war, and gender), in Yoneda, Sayoko, Obinata, Sumio and Yamashina,Saburo (eds), *Jenda shiten kara sengo shi o yomu* (Reading postwar history from the perspective of gender), Otsuki Shoten, 171–200.

Osawa, Kimiko, 2015, 'Traditional Gender Norms and Women's Political Participation: How Conservative Women Engage in Political Activism in Japan,' *Social Science Japan Journal*, 18(1): 45–61.

Osawa, Mari, 2002, 'Josei seisaku o do toraeru ka' (How do we understand women's policy), in Osawa, Mari (ed.), *Kaitei ban. Nijuisseiki no josei seisaku to danjo kyodo sankaku shakai kihon ho* (Revised edition. Twenty-first-century women's policy and the basic law for a gender-equal society), Gyosei, 2–26.

Otake, Hideo, 2005, *Saigunbi to nashonarizumu: sengo Nihon no boei kan* (Rearmament and nationalism: Postwar Japanese views of defense), Kodansha.

Otomo, Yuko, 2006, 'Boshi setai no tojisha soshiki no ishiki to rekishi-teki tenkai: Nihon ni okeru shuyo no tojisha soshiki o jirei to shite' (The consciousness and historical evolution of single-mother-household stakeholder organizations: With the main stakeholder organizations in Japan as examples), *Shakai fukushigaku hyoron* (Review of social welfare studies), 6: 47–59.

Otsuji, Hidehisa, 1988, 'Bokkemon jinsei 4' (An audacious life, 4), *Nihon Izoku Tsushin* (Japan Bereaved Families newsletter), Nippon izokukai, 456.

Otsuki, Takahiro, 2000, *Atashi no minshu shugi* (My democracy), Mainichi Shimbunsha.

Ouchi, Hirokazu, 2003, 'Kyoiku genba kara Ehime "Tsukuru kai" kyokasho saitaku to kyoku-u no taito' (From the chalkface: the Ehime 'Japanese Society for History Textbook Reform' textbook selection and the rise of the extreme right), *Sekai* (The world), 709: 264–270.

Power, Margaret, 2002, *Right-Wing Women in Chile: Feminine Power and the Struggle Against Allende, 1964–1973*, Pennsylvania State University Press.

Ridgeway, James, 1991, *Blood in the Face: The Ku Klux Klan, Aryan Nations, Nazi Skinheads, and the Rise of a New White Culture*, Thunder's Mouth Press.

Rommelspacher, Brigit, 1999, 'Right-Wing "Feminism": A Challenge to Feminism as an Emancipatory Movement,' in Nira Yuval-Davis and Pnina Werbner (eds), *Women, Citizenship and Difference*, Zed Books Ltd, 54–64.

Ruoff, Kenneth J., 2001, *The People's Emperor: Democracy and the Japanese Monarch, 1945–1995*, Harvard University Asia Center.

Sanami, Yuko, 2013, *Joshi to aikoku* (Women and patriotism), Shodensha.

Sano, Wataru, 2010, 'Hadoikku Ronzuri to nashonaru torasuto' (Hardwicke Rawnsley and the National Trust), in Noda, Yasuhisa (ed.), *Hoshu shugi to wa nani ka* (What is conservatism?), Nakanishiya Shuppan, 182–204.

Sasaki, Takeshi, 1993, *Amerika no hoshu to riberaru* (America's conservatives and liberals), Kodansha.

Sasanuma, Tomoko, 2004, *Josei kaiho no ningen sengen: Ehime-ken no danjo kyodo sankaku suishin jorei hihan* (Women's liberation's humanity declaration: Criticism of Ehime prefecture's gender equality promotion ordinance), Sofusha Shuppan.

Sato, Fumika, 2006, 'Feminizumu ni iradatsu "anata" e: "ikari" wa doko e mukau beki na no ka' (To 'you' who are irritated by feminism: Where should that 'anger' head?), *Ronza*, 131: 212–7.

Sato, Tatsuya, 1982, 'Ugomeki hajimeta "kusa-no-ne" kaiken undo: "Nihon o mamoru kokumin kaigi" no kaiken senryaku to senjutsu' (The 'grassroots' constitutional reform movement that has started to squirm: The constitutional reform strategy and tactics of the 'National Conference to Protect Japan'), *Gendai no me* (Contemporary eye), 23(5): 227–35.

Schreiber, Ronne, 2008, *Righting Feminism: Conservative Women and American Politics*, Oxford University Press.

Seki, Katsura, 2016, *Jenda bakkurasshu to wa nan datta no ka: shi-teki sokatsu to mirai e mukete* (What was the gender backlash? Toward a historical review and the future), Inpakuto Shuppankai.

Shakai undo ron kenkyukai (Association for social movement theory studies) (eds), 1990, *Shakai undo ron no togo o mezashite: riron to bunseki* (Aiming for an integration of social movement theory: Theory and analysis), Seibundo.

Shin, Ki-young, 2004, 'Danjo kyodo sankaku jorei no settei to sono bakkurasshu taisaku de watashitachi wa nani o mananda no ka: Futatsu no kesu' (What did we learn from the establishment of gender equality ordinances and their backlash measures? Two cases), *Kuni, jichitai no jenda seisaku: wakate kenkyusha, NGO chushin-gata wakushoppu hokokusho* (National and local government gender policies: Report on young researchers and NGO-centric workshops), Ochanomizu joshi daigaku nijuisseki COE puroguramu (Ochanomizu Women's University 21st century Center of Excellence program: 'Frontiers of gender studies' project A1 'Research relating to gender policies in Asia and their appraisal), 45–55.

Shiokawa, Nobuaki, 2008, *Minzoku to neishon* (Ethnos and nation), Iwanami Shoten.

Somusho (Ministry of Internal Affairs and Communications). 2009. 'Heisei nijuichnen tsushin riyo doko chosa (2009 Survey on communications usage trends).'

Sugano, Tamotsu, 2016, *Nippon kaigi no kenkyu* (Research on the Japan Conference), Fusosha.

Sugita, Mio, 2014, *Nadeshiko fukkatsu: josei seijika ga dekiru koto* (The revival of Nadeshiko: What female politicians can do), Seirindo.

Suzuki, Ayaka, 2019, 'Uncustomary Sisterhood: Feminist Research in Japanese Conservative Movements,' in Emmanuele Toscano (ed.), *Researching Far-Right Movements: Ethics, Methodologies, and Qualitative Inquiries*, Routledge, 84–101.

Suzuki, Ayaka, Seki, Megumi and Hori, Akiko, 2014, 'Josei undo to gyosei no kyodo ni kansuru ichi kosatsu: Nuita Yoko to danjo kyodo sankaku bijon ni chakumoku shite' (A consideration of the cooperation between the women's movement and the authorities: Focusing on Nuita Yoko and visions of gender equality), *Joseigaku kenkyu* (Women's studies review), Osaka Furitsu Daigaku Joseigaku Kenkyu Senta, 120–41.

Bibliography

Suzuki, Yuko, 1997, *Senso sekinin to jenda: 'jiyu shugi shikan' to Nihongun 'ianfu' mondai* (War responsibility and gender: The 'liberalist historical view' and the Japanese military 'comfort women' issue), Miraisha.

Taka, Fumiaki, 2015, *Reishizumu o kaibo suru: Zainichi Korian e no henken to intanetto* (Dissecting racism: Japan-residing Koreans and the Internet), Keiso Shobo.

Takahara, Motoaki, 2006, *Fuan-gata nashonarizumu no jidai: Nik–Kan–Chu no netto sedai ga nikumiau honto no riyu* (The age of unstable nationalism: The real reason for mutual hatred among the Japanese, Korean and Chinese Internet generations), Yosensha.

Takemura, Kazuko, 2000, *Feminizumu* (Feminism), Iwanami Shoten.

Takenobu, Mieko, 2005, 'Yappari kowai? Jenda furi basshingu' (Scary, after all? Gender-free bashing), in Kimura, Ryoko (ed.), *Jenda furi toraburu: basshingu gensho o kensho suru* (Gender-free trouble: Investigating the bashing phenomenon), Hakutakusha, 19–34.

Tamashiro, Fukuko, 2022, *Okinawa to sekushuariti no shakaigaku: posuto-koroniaru feminizumu kara toinaosu Okinawa sen, Beigun kichi, kanko* (The sociology of Okinawa and sexuality: The Battle of Okinawa, U.S. military bases and tourism questioned anew from postcolonial feminism), Jinbun Shoin.

Tanaka, Mitsu, 2001, *Inochi no onnatachi: torimidashi uman ribu ron* (Women with life: A disorderly theory of women's liberation), Pandora.

Tanaka, Nobumasa, 1995, 'Izoku no hanseiki' (The bereaved families' half-century), in Tanaka, Nobumasa, Tanaka, Hiroshi and Hata, Nagami (eds), *Izoku to sengo* (Bereaved families and the postwar), Iwanami Shoten, 1–79.

—— 1997, *'Senso no kioku' sono inpei no kozo: kokuritsu senso memoriaru o toshite* (The hidden structure of 'war memory': Through national war memorials), Ryokufu Shuppan.

Tawara, Yoshifumi, 2008, *'Tsukuru kai' bunretsu to rekishi gizo no shinso: shonenba no rekishi kyokasho mondai* (The fragmentation of the 'Japanese Society for History Textbook Reform' and the depths of historical falsification: The crucial history textbook issue), Kadensha.

Tominaga, Kyoko, 2015, 'Shakai undo no hen'yo to arata na "senryaku": kaunta undo no kanosei' (Transformation in social movements and new 'strategy': The potential for counter movements), in Yamazaki, Nozomu (ed.), *Kimyo na nashonarizumu no jidai: haigai shugi ni koshite* (The age of bizarre nationalism: Challenging chauvinism), Iwanami Shoten, 113–138.

Tronto, Joan, 2013, *Caring Democracy: Markets, Equality, and Justice*, New York University Press.

Tsuji, Daisuke, 2017, 'Keiryo chosa kara miru "netto uyoku" no purofiru: 2007-nen, 2014-nen webu chosa no bunseki kekka o moto ni' (Profile of the 'Internet right-wing' seen from quantitative surveys: Based on the analytical results of 2007 and 2014 web surveys), *Nenpo ningen kagaku* (Human science annual report), 38: 211–24.

Tsuji, Daisuke and Fujita, Tomohiro, 2011, 'Netto uyoku'-teki naru mono no kyojitsu: chosa deta kara no jissho-teki kento (The falsehoods and truths of something like the 'Internet right-wing': An empirical examination from survey data), in Kotani, Satoshi, Doi, Takayoshi, Haga, Manabu and Asano, Tomohiko (eds), *Wakamono no genzai: Seiji* (Young people's present day: Politics), Nihon Tosho Senta, 131–57.

Tsukada, Hotaka, 2015, *Shukyo to seiji no tentetsuten: hoshu godo to seikyo itchi no shukyo shakaigaku* (The junction of religion and politics: A sociology of religious movements promoting conservative alliances and religio-state regimes), Kadensha.

Tsukada, Hotaka (ed.), 2017, *Tettei kensho: Nihon no ukeika* (Thorough investigation: Japan's rightward swing), Chikuma Shobo.

Tsunoda, Yukiko, 2013, *Sei to horitsu: kawatta koto, kaetai koto* (Sex and the law: What has changed, what we want to change), Iwanami Shoten.

Tsuruta, Atsuko, 2005, 'Kateika kyokasho basshingu o kensho suru: kogeki no ito wa nani ka' (Investigating home economics textbook bashing: What is the aim of attack?) in Kimura, Ryoko (ed.), *Jenda furi toraburu: Basshingu gensho o kensho suru* (Gender-free trouble: Investigating the bashing phenomenon), Hakutakusha, 145–64.

Tuttle, Lisa, 1986, *Encyclopedia of Feminism*, Longman Group.

Ueno, Chizuko, 2011a, *Fuwaku no feminizumu* (Feminism at forty), Iwanami Shoten.

—— 2011b, *Kea no shakaigaku: tojisha shuken no fukushi shakai e* (Sociology of care: Towards a welfare society with stakeholder sovereignty), Ohta Books.

Ueno, Yoko, 2003, '"Futsu" no shimintachi ni your "Tsukuru-kai" no esunografi' (Ethnography of the "Tsukuru-kai" by "ordinary" citizens) in Oguma, Eiji and Ueno, Yoko, 2003, *'Iyashi' no nashonarizumu: kusa no ne hoshu undo no jissho-teki kenkyu* (A nationalism of 'healing': An empirical study of the grassroots conservative movement), Keio Gijuku Daigaku Shuppankai, 69–186.

Uno, Shigeki, 2016, *Hoshu shugi to wa nani ka? Han-furansu kakumei kara gendai Nihon made* (What is conservatism? From opposition to the French Revolution to contemporary Japan), Chuko Shinsho.

Wada, Yu and Inoue, Emiko, 2010, *Sankei Shimbun* ni miru jenda bakkurasshu no hasso to ronri (The conception and logic of gender backlash seen in the Sankei newspaper), *Inpakushon* (Impaction), 174: 72–80.

Waldron, Jeremy, 2012, *The Harm in Hate Speech*, Harvard University Press.

Watanabe, Hideki, 1999, 'Sengo Nihon no oyako kankei: yoiku ki no shitsu no hensen' (Parent–child relationships in postwar Japan: Qualitative changes in parent–child relationships in the child-rearing period), in Meguro, Yoriko and Watanabe, Hideki (eds), *Koza shakaigaku 9: Kazoku* (Course in sociology 9: The family), University of Tokyo Press, 89–117.

Yamaguchi, Tomomi, 2006, '"Jenda furi" ronso to feminizumu undo no ushinawareta junen' (The 'gender-free' controversy and the feminist movement's lost decade), *Bakkurasshu!* (Backlash!), Sofusha, 244–82.

—— 2013a, 'Xenophobia in Action: Ultranationalism, Hate Speech, and the Internet in Japan,' *Radical History Review*, 117: 98–118.

—— 2013b, 'Feminizumu no shiten kara mita kodo hoshu undo to "ianfu" mondai' (The action conservative movement seen from the perspective of feminism, and the 'comfort women' issue), *Journalism*, 282: 81–91.

——2016, 'Kanmin-ittai no "rekishisen" no yukue' (The direction of the 'history wars', a united effort between government and people), in Yamaguchi, Tomomi, Nogawa, Motokazu, Tessa Morris-Suzuki and Koyama, Emi (eds), *Umi o wataru 'ianfu' mondai: uha no 'rekishisen' o tou* (The 'comfort women' issue goes overseas: Questioning the right-wing 'history wars'), Iwanami Shoten, 97–136.

——2019, 'Netto uyoku to feminizumu' (The Internet right-wing and feminism), in Higuchi, Naoto, Nagayoshi, Kikuko, Matsutani, Mitsuru, Kurahashi, Kohei, Fabian Shäfer and Yamaguchi, Tomomi (eds), *Netto uyoku to wa nani ka* (What is the Internet right-wing?), Seikyusha, 164–95.

Yamaguchi, Tomomi, Nogawa, Motokazu, Tessa Morris-Suzuki and Koyama, Emi (eds), 2016, *Umi o wataru 'ianfu' mondai: uha no 'rekishisen' o tou* (The 'comfort women' issue goes overseas: Questioning the right-wing 'history wars'), Iwanami Shoten.

Yamaguchi, Tomomi, Saito, Masami and Ogiue, Chiki, 2012, *Shakai undo no tomadoi: feminizumu no 'ushinawareta jidai' to kusa-no-ne hoshu undo* (The disorientation of social movements: Feminism's 'lost age' and grassroots conservative movements), Keiso Shobo.

Yamamoto, Yumiko, 2014, *Josei ga mamoru Nihon no hokori: 'ianfu mondai' no shinjitsu o uttaeru nadeshiko katsudo roku* (The pride that a woman keeps of Japan: A chronicle of activities of the Nadeshiko Action group that invokes the truth of the 'comfort women issue'), Seirindo.

Yamazaki, Masahiro, 2016, *Nippon kaigi: senzen kaiki e no jonen* (The Japan Conference: Sentiments towards a return to the prewar), Shueisha.

Yamazaki, Nozomu, 2015, 'Kimyo na nashonarizumu?' (Bizarre nationalism?), in Yamazaki, Nozomu (ed.), *Kimyo na nashonarizumu no jidai: haigai shugi ni koshite* (The age of bizarre nationalism: Challenging chauvinism), Iwanami Shoten, 1–28.

Yasuda, Koichi, 2012, *Netto to aikoku: Zaitokukai no 'yami' o oikakete* (The Internet and patriotism: Pursuing the 'iniquity' of the Association of Citizens against the Special Privileges of resident-Koreans), Kodansha.

——2015, *Heito supichi: 'aikokusha' tachi no zoo to boryoku* (Hate speech: The hatred and violence of 'patriots'), Bungei Shunju.

Yazawa, Sumiko, 1999, 'Onnatachi no shimin undo to enpawamento' (Women's civic movements and empowerment), in Kamada, Toshiko, Yazawa, Sumiko and Kimoto, Kimiko (eds), *Koza shakaigaku 14: jenda* (Course in sociology 14: Gender), University of Tokyo Press, 249–89.

Yazawa, Shujiro (ed.), 2003, *Koza shakaigaku 15: Shakai undo* (Course in sociology 15: Social movements), University of Tokyo Press.

Yoshii, Hiroaki, 1999, *Hihan-teki esunomesodoroji no katari: sabetsu no nichijo o yomitoku* (Discourses in critical ethnomethodology: Decoding routine discrimination), Shin-yo-sha.

Yoshihara, Reiko, 2013, *Amerika no dainiha feminizumu: 1960 nendai kara gendai made* (America's second-wave feminism: From the 1960s until the present), Domesu Shuppan.

Ziegler, Mary, 2013, 'Women's Rights on the Right: The History and Stakes of Modern Pro-life Feminism,' *Berkeley Journal of Gender, Law, and Justice* 28: 232–268.

Appendix

Translations of organization names in this book

English	Japanese	Abbreviation
Aichi Prefectural Residents' Council	Aichi kenmin kaigi	
All-Campus Joint Struggle Committee	Zenkyoto	
Alliance of Diet Members for Promotion of Imperial Era-name Legislation	Gengo hoseika sokushin kokkai giin renmei	
Alliance of Families of War Victims	Senso giseisha izoku domei	
All-Japan Council of Patriotic Organizations	Zen Nippon aikokusha dantai kaigi	
All-Japan Federation of Military Pensioners' Associations	Gun'on renmei zenkoku rengokai	
Association for Self-Cultivation and Sincerity	Shuyodan	
Association for Self-Cultivation Youth Division	Shuyodan seinenbu	
Association of Citizens against the Special Privileges of resident-Koreans	Zainichi tokken o yurusanai shimin no kai	Association of Citizens
Association of Consumer Organizations	Shufuren	
Association of Former Naval Officers	Suikokai	
Association of Shinto Shrines	Jinja honcho	
Bereaved Families' Council of Diet Members	Ikazoku giin kyogikai	
Bracing Wind Yamato	Rinpu Yamato	
Buddhist Prayer Society	Bussho gonenkai kyodan	
Central Nogi Association	Chuo Nogi kai	
Church of World Messianity	Sekai kyusei kyo	
Citizens' Group that will not Permit Invasion of Japan	Nippon shinryaku o yurusanai shimin no kai	
Citizens' Group to Protect Japan	Nippon o mamoru shimin no kai (Nichigokai)	
Company of Fighting Women on the Brink	Tatakau josei gakeppuchi tai	
Confederation of Greater Japan Patriotic Organizations: Council for Countermeasures to the Current Situation	Dai Nippon aikokusha dantai rengo: Jikyoku taisaku kyogikai	
Council for a New Japan	Shin Nippon kyogikai	
Democratic Liberal Party	Minji-to	
Democratic Socialist Party	Minsha-to	
Ehime Branch of the National Association for the Rescue of Japanese Kidnapped by North Korea	Rachi higaisha o sukuu kai Ehime	Rescue Association
Era Name Law	Gengo-ho	
Federation of Women's Groups	Kakushu josei dantai rengokai	
Gathering to Study the Eastern Thought of Yasuoka Masahiro	Zenkoku Shiyu Kyokai	

Conclusion

English	Japanese	Abbreviation
Greater Japan Imperial Banner Association	Dai Nippon kinki kai	
Greater Japan Nationalist Party	Dai Nippon kokumin-to	
Guard	Shin'eitai	
Hiroshima Prefectural Residents' Council for Protecting Japan	Nihon o mamoru Hiroshima kenmin kaigi	
History Circle	Fumi-no-kai	
House of Growth	Seicho no ie	
Institute of Moralogy	Moraroji kenkyujo	
Japan Association	Nippon kai	
Japan Bereaved Family-Welfare Federation	Nippon izoku kosei renmei	
Japan Business Federation	Keidanren	
Japan Community Friends' League	Goyuren (Nippon goyu renmei)	
Japan Conference	Nippon kaigi	
Japan Conference League of Local Assembly Members	Nippon kaigi chiho giin renmei	
Japan Council	Nippon kyogikai	
Japan First Party	Nippon Dai-ichi To	
Japan Heroic Spirits' Support Association	Nippon eirei hosankai	
Japan Policy Institute	Nihon seisaku kenkyu senta	
Japan War-Bereaved Families Association	Nippon izokukai	Bereaved Families Association
Japan Women's Group Gentle Breeze	Nihon josei no kai Soyokaze	Gentle Breeze
Japan Wounded Soldiers' Association	Nippon shoi gunjinkai	
Japan Youth Council	Nihon seinen kyogikai	
Japanese Society for History Textbook Reform	Atarashii rekishi kyokasho o tsukuru kai	Textbook Society
Japanese Women for Justice and Peace	Nadeshiko Action	Justice and Peace
Japanese Women's Association	Nihon josei no kai	
Japanese women's study group 'Let's rebuild Japan'	Tatenaoso Nippon josei juku	
Japanism Federation	Nippon shugi rengo	
Learning from Japanese History Group	Nihon no rekishi ni manabu kai	
"Let's protect the imperial house" Okayama prefectural residents' group	Koshitsu o mamoro Okayama kenmin shukai	
Lion's Society	Shishi no kai	
Military Club	Kaikosha	
Military Pensioners' Association	Gun'on renmei	
Modern Dianthus Club	Gendai nadeshiko kurabu	

248

Appendix

English	Japanese	Abbreviation
National Conference to Protect Japan	Nihon o mamoru kokumin kaigi	
National Congress for the Establishment of an Autonomous Constitution	Jishu kenpo seitei kokumin kaigi	
National Convention for Realizing State Support for Yasukuni Shrine	Yasukuni-jinja kokka goji kantetsu kokumin kyogikai	National Convention for Yasukuni
National Council for Achievement of Legalization of Imperial Era Names	Gengo hoseika jitsugen kokumin kaigi	
National Foundation Day	Kenkoku kinen no hi	
National Protection Corps	Gokokudan	
Nationwide War Comrades' Association	Zenkoku sen'yukai	
New Buddhism Religious Organization	Shinsei bukkyo kyodan	
New Edition Japanese History	*Shinpen Nihon shi*	
New Liberal Club	Shin jiyu kurabu	
New Society for Expelling Foreigners	(Shin joi undo) Haigaisha	
NPO Movement to Eradicate Foreigner Crime	NPO gaikokujin hanzai tsuiho undo	
Original Gospel Bible Seminary	Kirisuto no makuya	
Patriotic Women's Gathering Flower Clock	Aikoku josei no tsudoi Hanadokei	Flower Clock
Pillar of the Nation Society	Kokuchukai	
Prefectural Residents' Council	Fumin kaigi	
Regimen Society	Yojokai	
SDF Friendship Association	Taiyukai	
Shinto Political Alliance	Shinto seiji renmei	
Shinto Youth Association	Shinto seinenkai	
Society for Honoring the Glorious War Dead	Eirei ni kotaeru kai	
Society for the Protection of Japan	Nihon o mamoru kai	
Society to Seek Restoration of Sovereignty	Shuken kaifuku o mezasu kai	
Tokyo Japan–Korea Friendship Association	Tokyo Nik–kan shinzen kyokai	
Ube Women's Group to Think about Gender Equality	Danjo kyodo sankaku o kangaeru Ube josei no kai	
Unification Church, now renamed the Family Federation for World Peace and Unification	Toitsu kyokai	
War Victims' Relief Association	Senso giseisha engokai	
Women's Group for Thinking about 'Gender-Free'	Jenda furi o kangaeru Osaka josei no kai	
Women's society that denies the lie of the military comfort women	Jugun ianfu no uso o yurusanai josei no kai	
Yamaguchi Women's Forum Ube	Yamaguchi josei foramu Ube	
Young Men's Association for Japanese Reconstruction	Nippon kenseikai	

249

Index

Subjects

2channel, 161

abortion, 9, 56, 72, 126
action conservative movement, 3–8, 13, 15, 58, 60–61, 149–150, 152–153, 155–157, 159–165, 170, 176, 181–184, 186–188, 191, 193–194, 196–197, 201, 212–213, 218, 224
active agent, 11–12, 148
activists, 3, 6, 8, 10–12, 15, 67, 129, 143, 149–150, 153, 157, 162–165, 168–170, 174, 176–177, 179, 182, 184–185, 188–190, 192–193, 196, 198, 207, 213, 217–219, 221–223
affirmative action, 11
agency, 12
agent, 1, 11–12, 102, 148, 152, 211, 215–216, 220
All-Campus Joint Struggle Committee, 32
Alliance of Diet Members for Promotion of Imperial Era- name Legislation, 46
androcentric, 7, 32, 117, 216
androcentric values, 187, 223
animosity, 5, 58, 156–157, 208
antagonism, xii, 111, 115, 205, 218
antagonistic, 4, 198, 213
anti-feminist movement, 7–8
anti-foreign movement, 3, 201
anti-Japanese sentiment, 184
anti-militarism, 34
anti-nuclear power movement, 13, 132
anxiety, 2–3, 8, 54, 75, 100, 134, 149, 191, 224
Article Nine, 21, 175–176
Asama Sanso Incident, xi
ashamed, 182, 185
Asian Women's Fund, 152
Asia-Pacific War, 1, 53, 89

Association A, 102–103, 112, 121, 123, 126–130, 132–137, 140, 143–145, 212
Association B, 191, 194–199, 201, 203–206, 208–210, 212
Association of Citizens, 3–6, 58–60, 149, 152, 156–159, 162, 193–194, 212, 224
Association of Citizens against the Special Privileges of resident-Koreans, *see* Association of Citizens
Association of Consumer Organizations, 149
Association of Shinto Shrines, 31, 40–41, 43, 45–46, 48, 130–131, 144
autonomy, 118, 218

backlash, 2, 22–23, 44, 55–57, 67–68, 72, 98–102, 104–111, 114–116, 118–119, 121, 128, 139, 214
Basic Act, *see* Basic Act for Gender Equal Society
Basic Act for Gender Equal Society, 5, 212, 217
Basic ordinance for the wholesome development of children, 124
behavior, 10, 63, 160, 186, 194, 204–205, 209–210
bell peppers, 202, 205
bereaved families (war-bereaved families), 33–38, 74, 76, 81, 84, 88, 92–93
big government, 10
boundaries, 26, 205, 209
breadwinner, 15, 33–34, 86, 97
Breath of Japan, 49, 73, 101–102, 104, 111
Buddhist, 43, 60

Cabinet Office, 58, 68, 122, 148
campaign, 42–43, 48, 50, 53, 57, 60–61, 75, 80, 84, 121–123, 139, 143, 150, 156, 170, 176, 178, 187, 194, 206, 211–214, 221
caravan, 45–46, 48

251

care, 10, 15, 29, 73, 81, 93, 95, 99, 107, 110, 114–119, 121, 134, 141–142, 145, 148, 213–218, 223–224
care work, 116–117, 121, 215, 223–224
care-versus-justice debate, 117
Channel Sakura, 7, 161
chauvinistic nationalism, 3
cherry blossoms, 203
child rearing, 62, 73, 93, 95, 99, 107, 112–114, 216, 223–224
  by breastfeeding, 114
children, 8, 12–13, 15, 35, 52, 56, 61, 72–95, 97, 103, 106–107, 112–113, 116, 118, 122, 124, 128–129, 135, 139–141, 149, 158, 173–176, 183, 200, 214
China, xii–xiii, 2–3, 24–25, 53, 85, 134, 150–151, 156–157, 161, 184–185, 191, 194, 197, 201, 218, 224
Choices for Tomorrow, 71, 101–102, 104, 112
Christian evangelicals, 10
civic activities, xi
civic groups, xiii, 45, 124, 162
civil rights, 22
Cold War, 2, 23
collective action, xi
collective identity, 1, 205, 221, 223
colonialism, 4, 151
comfort women issue, 15–16, 62, 151–153, 163, 176–178, 180, 183–188, 191, 206, 208–210, 213–214, 218–219, 221, 223–225
comfort-women bashing, 13, 152–153, 225
common sense, 139–140
commonality, 104, 115
communism, 10, 27, 29, 46
Communist Party, 34
Concerned Women for America (CWA), 11
conservatism, 1, 10, 14, 19–22, 24, 72, 100, 148
conservative faction, 2, 57, 67, 72, 153

conservative movement, 1–10, 12–16, 19, 21–25, 28–29, 31–33, 38–39, 44, 50–51, 54–56, 58, 60–63, 66, 68–69, 71–74, 95, 97–100, 119, 121–124, 143–144, 149–150, 152–153, 155–157, 159, 160–165, 170, 176, 181–184, 186–188, 191–194, 196–198, 201, 207, 211–215, 217–221, 223–225
conservative swing, xiii, 2, 198, 224
conservative women's movement, 66, 211, 214, 219–220, 222–225
constitution, 41, 49, 174–176
constitutional reform, 21, 24, 48–50, 175
Convention on the Elimination of all Forms of Discrimination against Women, 66
conversation, 201–206, 208
cookery classes, 195–196, 198–201, 203–206, 208–210
counterculture movement, 59
coup d'état-orientation, 29
Criminal Code, 189
cyberspace, xiii

defense, 4, 6, 24, 48, 72, 116, 119, 149, 213, 217
democratic, 1, 33, 36, 46, 166, 169–170, 172, 217
Democratic Party, 166, 169–170, 172
demonstrations, 3, 7, 158, 162–166, 170, 177, 192, 197
  marches, 58, 60, 62, 156, 173, 186, 194, 212
dependence, 117, 119
deviant behavior, 160
diplomacy, 4, 49, 58–59, 209, 224
discourse, 13, 15, 21–22, 58, 67–68, 71–74, 78, 83, 86, 88, 90–95, 97, 104, 106, 108, 111, 113, 115–116, 119, 128, 133, 143, 149, 152–153, 157, 161, 181–182, 185, 191, 201, 214, 218, 223
discriminatory sentiment, 59, 150
dissatisfaction, 3, 141

domestic, 7, 21, 23, 85, 89, 95, 121, 125, 163, 191, 214, 220–223, 225
   feminist movements, 220
   ideology, 220–222
   violence, 85, 95, 125
drifting to the right, xii

East Asia, 2–4, 6, 24, 27, 53, 150, 156, 201, 213, 218, 224
economic growth, 23, 34, 82, 85, 93
education, 12, 21, 28, 44, 48–53, 55–56, 62, 71, 73, 91, 103–104, 106, 109–110, 112–114, 121–122, 128, 131, 133, 139, 144, 148–149, 161, 222–223
Ehime Prefecture, 57, 102, 123–124, 128, 143
empathy, 136, 182, 207, 209
emperor, 2, 24, 26–27, 34, 39, 43, 47–49, 54, 116
environmental movement, 1
equal pay, 11
equality, 5, 7–8, 11, 13, 15–16, 23–24, 55–57, 61, 63, 66–69, 71–72, 89, 91, 97–105, 107–110, 112–113, 115–117, 119, 121–129, 133, 136–140, 143–145, 157, 192, 211–217, 220, 223
era names, 43–47, 50
   era-name legislation, 31, 43, 46–47, 50, 63
   era-name movement, 45
essentialist, 117, 217, 223
ethic of care, 15, 115, 117–119, 121, 215–218
ethnic
   discrimination, 184–185, 187, 219
   minorities, 1, 4, 58
ethnocentrism, 58
Everyone! (Shokun!), 98, 101, 110–111, 113
exclusivism, 4
expert, xiii, 111
extreme right, xiii, 192, 222

facilitator, 199
family, x, 12, 15, 24, 34, 49, 55, 66–69, 71–76, 78, 82, 85–86, 88, 90–95, 97, 99, 103–116, 118–119, 122, 125, 128–129, 133, 135, 140–145, 148–149, 153, 157, 172, 195, 213–215, 217, 221–222
   image, 15, 85, 108
   values, 15, 55, 67, 71–74, 88, 90–95, 97, 103–105, 108, 111–112, 115–116, 119, 145, 148
   -state ideology, 116
fascism studies, 1
female activist, 6, 8, 10, 12, 15, 150, 163, 168, 174, 176, 179, 182, 185, 187, 192, 213
female intellectuals, 111–115, 119
female participants, 6–7, 66, 149, 153, 173, 179–180, 182, 192, 197, 208–210, 212–214
female-centered conservative groups, 14, 214
femi-hags, 200
femininity, 55, 62, 67, 71–72, 97, 112–123, 128–129, 160, 186–188, 212, 214
feminism, 7, 10, 13, 55, 61, 67–69, 97–100, 113, 150–151, 161, 184, 187, 216–217, 220–223
   first-wave, 220, 222
   theory of care, 15
fieldwork, 14–15, 69, 123, 149, 191
Flower Clock, 5, 61–62, 149–151, 159, 162, 164–165, 167–168, 170–178, 181–184
Foreign Ministry, 62, 167, 176–177
framing, 145
French Revolution, 19–21

gender, 1, 5–9, 13, 15–16, 24–25, 32, 55–57, 61, 63, 66–69, 71–72, 89, 91, 97–105, 107–13, 115–119, 121–129, 133–134, 136–140, 142–145, 153, 191–192, 194, 210–215, 217–219, 223–225

equality, 5, 8, 13, 15–16, 56, 63, 66–69, 71–72, 89, 91, 97, 99–105, 107–110, 112–113, 115–117, 119, 121–129, 133–134, 136, 137–140, 144–145, 192, 211–212, 214–215, 217, 223
equality ordinance, 5, 56–57, 61, 98, 105, 122–126, 143
equality policy (gender equality policies), x, 5, 55, 66–67, 98, 127, 137
gap, 7, 148
identity, 7, 100
perspective, 6–9, 32, 192, 194
role, 66, 68, 72, 97, 99, 111, 140, 142, 145, 214, 217–218
division of labor, 24, 66, 72, 108, 110–111, 118
structure, 13
gender-free, 55–56, 67–68, 71, 101, 103–104, 109–110, 122–123, 128–129, 139–140
education, 56, 71, 103–104, 110, 122
Gentle Breeze, 5, 61–62, 150, 159, 162, 164–166, 168–170, 174, 176–183, 187–188
geopolitical structure of East Asia, 3
GHQ, 35, 78
globalization, 2, 224
grandmothers (obāsan), 182, 183, 187
grassroots, 2, 9, 15, 33, 48, 50–51, 57–58, 60–61, 63, 66, 69, 89, 98, 100, 102–103, 121–123, 127, 129, 134, 143, 211–212, 214, 224
grassroots women, 9, 63, 69, 98
grassroots women's conservative movement, x, 69

hate speech, 58–59, 158–159, 165, 180
Hate Speech Law, 158
hatred, xiii, 5, 58, 180, 201, 203–206, 210
heroic spirits, 8, 34–35, 37, 40, 87, 92, 94
heterosexual, 72–73, 95, 97
historical revisionism, 2, 33, 52–53, 67, 119, 185

History Circle, 2, 4, 54, 123–124, 143, 212
history education issues, 133
history textbook, 2, 25, 51, 53, 85, 133–134, 143, 157
homemakers (shufu), x, 12, 15, 100
hostility, xii, 3, 54, 108, 150, 161, 184–185, 189–190
House of Growth, 25, 27, 31–32, 40, 44–45, 48, 130–131, 133, 135–136, 144
human rights, 15, 55, 67, 69, 151, 157, 166, 183–184, 187–188, 190, 208, 219–220
husband, 15, 33–34, 38, 79–80, 86, 92–94, 97, 106–107, 109–110, 113, 128, 138–142, 204

ideas, 10, 28, 104, 110, 124, 145, 160, 192, 224
identity, 7–8, 54, 119, 149, 201, 211
ideology, 3, 19–24, 44, 51, 100, 105, 116, 159–160, 204, 220–223
idioculture, 194, 201
image of the suffering mother, 15, 71, 82, 84, 86, 89–90, 92–95
Imperial Rescript on Education, 73, 149
improvement, 20, 38, 74
Independent Women's Forum (IWF), 11
Indonesia, 185
Institute of Moralogy, 44, 130–131, 133, 136, 142, 144
intellectuals, 24, 28, 91, 102, 111–115, 119, 128, 143, 213, 217
interaction, 15, 113–114, 135, 139, 141, 191, 193–196, 201, 204–205, 207, 212
interest group, 33, 37
internalization, 186–188, 223
Internet, xi–xii, 3, 14–15, 54, 58, 63, 123, 155, 157, 160–162, 191, 196–197
interpersonal relationships, 107–108, 116, 118, 121, 142, 214, 217
intersection, 184–185
interviews, 3, 6, 10, 14–15, 39, 121, 123, 129–130, 137, 158, 192–196, 198, 208, 217
izokukai, 14, 35–38, 42, 74–75, 84–85, 91

Index

\Japan Bereaved Family-Welfare Federation, 34, 74, 76, 78, 81

Japan Conference, 31–32, 47, 49–52, 56–57, 60–61, 63, 89, 98–99, 101, 114, 121, 130–131, 133–135, 143–144, 211–212

Japan Conference's Osaka Women's Division, 61

Japan Current Review, 57, 101–102, 104, 109

Japan Socialist Party, 33, 89

Japan War-Bereaved Families Association, 14–15, 31–34, 69, 74–76, 78, 95, 97

Japan Women's Group Gentle Breeze, *see* Gentle Breeze

'Japanese', 7

anti-foreigner movement, 3

conservative swing, 85, 224–225

flag, 149, 203

imperial era names, 43

military, 2, 53, 63, 151–152, 178, 181, 185

mothers, 87–88, 172

society, 49, 63, 112, 152, 158, 168, 186, 189–190, 214, 218–219, 221

Society for History Textbook Reform, *see* Textbook Society

women, 6, 62, 174, 177, 182, 198, 212, 221, 223

Japanese Women for Justice and Peace (Nadeshiko Action), *see* Justice and Peace

Japanese Women's Association, 61, 98, 114, 121

Japan-residing Koreans, 3, 58, 155–156, 159, 180, 184–185, 193–194, 213

Japan–South Korea relations, xii–xiii, 134

Japan–U.S. Security Treaty, xi, 23–24, 27

jokes, 15, 201, 204–210

justice, 8, 117–118, 149

Justice and Peace, 5, 61–62, 150–151, 162–166, 174, 176–177, 184

Kaiho, 76, 78–81, 83, 87–88, 93

kamikaze suicide corps, 201

Kanagawa Prefecture, 2, 54, 123

ken-Chū (hatred of things Chinese), 201

ken-Kan (hatred of things Korean), 201

kimono, 170

Kono Statement, 152

Korea, 2–6, 24–25, 40, 53, 58–59, 62, 85, 134, 149–152, 155–156, 158–159, 161, 163–164, 166, 172, 175, 177–178, 180–185, 187, 191, 193–194, 197, 201–206, 208–210, 213, 218, 221, 224

University, 158

War, 78

Kudan kaikan (Kudan hall), 34

Kyoto North Korean Number One Elementary School, 158

labor movement, 1

laissez-faire conservatives, 10–11

Law for Relief of War Victims and Survivors, 36

LDP, 33–34, 36–37, 44, 46–47, 82, 86–89, 91, 95, 122, 126–127, 166

leader, 11, 26, 29, 32, 44, 47, 74, 98–99, 111, 132, 136, 143, 159, 169, 172, 192, 211–212

left ('the left'), 198

leftists, 23, 157

-wing, 27, 29, 32, 45, 54, 157, 162, 184, 191, 194, 197, 211

movement, xi, 27, 29

legislation, 31, 43–47, 50, 63, 66, 126, 194

liberal, 8, 21–23, 51–52, 72, 85, 215

Liberal Democratic Party, *see* LDP

life history, 3, 10, 192

life history interviews, 3

local government, 5, 56–57, 102, 122, 128, 206

magazine, 8, 14–15, 33, 52, 67–68, 97–98, 100–103, 108, 111, 128, 133, 137, 149, 151, 184

mainstream, 101–102, 104–112, 114–116, 118–119, 128, 212, 214, 220

255

Women on the Right

male counterparts, 176, 179, 212, 218–219
male participants, 6–7, 61, 160, 165, 168–170, 179–180, 182, 188, 192, 196, 200, 209, 211, 213–214, 218–220
male-centered groups, 5, 12, 14, 62, 168, 170, 211, 214
male-centered value system, 186
Marxism, 23
masculinity, 11, 55, 67, 71–72, 97, 112, 123, 128–129, 216
masochistic historical view, 51, 62, 197
maternal, 8, 66, 88
maternity, 8, 113
Matsuyama City ordinance, 127, 134, 137, 143
members, 28, 32, 34–36, 38, 41–42, 45–47, 49–50, 52, 56, 58, 61–62, 73–76, 78, 81, 83–84, 87, 89–90, 93, 95, 98, 107, 111, 118, 121, 123, 125–130, 132–133, 136–137, 142–145, 148, 150–151, 159–164, 169, 171–172, 180–181, 183–184, 191, 193–198, 200, 205, 208, 212, 214, 221
message boards, 161
methodology, 13, 25, 39, 76, 129, 160, 192
military comfort women, 51–53, 63, 150–152, 157, 166, 178, 180–182, 185, *see* comfort women
mixed- sex class rolls, 139
mobilize, 13, 29, 36, 66, 74, 78, 100, 136, 144, 161, 163, 213, 220
motherhood, 8, 12, 149
mother-in-law, 106–107, 140–141
mothers, 8, 12–13, 15, 66, 69, 78–81, 83–90, 92–93, 97, 103, 107, 110, 133, 141–142, 145, 148–150, 168, 172–174, 176, 178, 184–186, 211, 214–215, 217–218, 220–221, 223
movement, 13, 149, 220
motivation, 34, 119, 135–136, 192–193
myNippon, 191

nadeshiko, 6, 61

Nadeshiko Action, 5, 61
Nanking massacre, 2, 51, 53, 155
narratives, 10–11, 14, 74, 76, 84, 86, 93, 106–107, 110, 118–119, 132, 137, 142–143, 145, 193, 214
National Conference to Protect Japan, 25, 47–49
National Convention for Yasukuni, 37–39
national movement, 41, 49–50, 60
national rally, 37, 45–46
nationalism, 2–3, 22, 24–25, 51, 116, 192, 200
nativist movement, 4
neo-liberal, 12, 72–73, 100
Net right-wing, 161
Netherlands, 185
New Civics Textbook, 53
new conservatism, 24, 72, 100
New History Textbook, 53
New Right, 10
new right-wing movements, 26
new social movements, 1
newsletters, 14, 68, 76, 79, 97, 100–101, 160–161, 192
NGOs, xi, 7, 157
NHK, 171, 200
Niconico video, 162–163
non-demonstration activities, 15, 195
non-members, 195, 199, 205
non-political, 103
North Korea, 24, 62, 130, 150, 156, 158, 172, 182, 184, 191, 201
NPOs, xi, 157
nuclear armaments, 156
nuclear power generation, 174–175

Okinawans, 169
old regime, 23
opinion magazines, 14–15
ordinary citizens, 54, 123, 145
organs, 14, 69, 100–101, 128, 138
Original Gospel Bible Seminary, 130–131, 136, 144
Osaka Prefecture, 5, 61

Index

Osprey, 166, 168–169, 178–179
outward-directed, 193

participant observation, 195, 206
participation, 5–6, 9–10, 12, 23–24, 32,
	54, 68, 99–100, 105, 108, 113, 121,
	123, 129, 132, 136, 145, 148–149,
	191–192, 196, 200, 213, 216, 218,
	220–222, 224–225
patriarchal family, 99
patriotic woman, 149
Patriotic Women's Gathering Flower
	Clock, *see* Flower Clock
patriotism, 3, 6, 8–9, 13, 21, 24, 43–44,
	58, 62, 71, 90, 92–93, 116, 161, 201,
	203–206, 210, 214
peace, 34–35, 44, 91, 169, 220
perpetrators, 184, 189
Philippines, 134, 185
political
	awareness, 22–24
	claims, 68, 116
	organization, xiii, 158
	party, 127, 168, 183
	propaganda activity, 150, 164–165,
		169–172, 179
	protest, 62, 156, 171, 197
	role, 160
	socialization, 3
	system, 21, 22, 33
politicians, xiii, 6, 35–36, 38–39, 60, 62,
	91, 111, 119, 128, 188, 199
positionality, 148, 220–221
postwar
	configuration of the family, 84
	era, 1
	Japan, 1, 4, 14, 23–24, 31–33, 40, 53,
		60–61, 82
potential supporters, 160
poverty, 35, 78, 80–81, 87–88, 95, 220
prime minister, 2, 29, 35, 38–39, 43–44,
	50, 85–86, 157
print media, 160–162, 165
private domain, 94, 117, 119, 215–216,

221–222
problem-consciousness, 63, 69, 220
progressive movements, 1
progressivism, 19–20, 46
pro-Japanese, 201
pro-life feminist, 11
propaganda, 25, 40, 150, 158, 163–167,
	169–172, 175, 179, 181, 183, 209, 212
proper femininity, 67, 97, 112, 123,
	128–129, 160, 186–188
proper Japanese-ness, 21
proposal for separate surnames for
	married couples, 112, *see also* separate
	surnames for married couples
prostitutes, 151–152, 181–182, 185, 189,
	207–208, 218
protest, 3, 5, 29, 59–60, 62–63, 134, 149,
	152, 156–159, 162–166, 168–171,
	173, 176–183, 186, 193–194, 197
	action, 29, 60, 168, 177, 194
	march, 3, 168
public domain, 11, 69, 221–222, 224
public/private dualism, 216

quantitative analysis, 14, 165

racism, 19, 58, 192
racism-based extreme right movement, 192
racist, 10, 192
radical right-wing feminists, 222
rally, 5, 36–39, 45, 79– 80, 83–84, 90, 98,
	152, 157, 176, 206–207
rape, 9, 189, 223
rape myth, 189
reactionary, 21
reactionism, 19, 21–22
Reagan administration, 55, 67
recruit, 39, 144, 160–162, 212
recruiting, 144, 160
reproduction, 125–126, 186
reproductive health and rights, 125–126,
	128
Rescue Association, 130–131, 137
resident Koreans, 3–6, 58, 155, 158–159

257

resource mobilization theory, 3
responsibilities, 1, 55, 80, 118, 218
reverse course, 23
rhetoric, 22, 69, 95, 201
right to perform care, 217
rightist, 8–9, 11, 156
rights, 1, 7, 15, 22, 55, 58, 66–67, 69,
    114, 117–118, 125–126, 128, 140,
    151, 156–157, 166, 170, 183–184,
    186–188, 190, 208, 219–220, 222
rightward swing, 44
right-wing, xi, 1–2, 4, 9, 10–12, 14, 19,
    25–29, 32, 44–46, 60, 119, 161, 185,
    198, 201, 221–222
    civic movement, x–xiii
    student movement, 32, 45
    women, 9–12, 221

Sankei Shinbun, 52, 55, 57, 67, 98
school, 2, 48, 53, 56, 61, 83, 86, 103, 106,
    109, 131, 133, 135, 138–139, 143,
    155–159, 197
Second Basic Plan for Gender Equality, 68
second rape, 189, 223
Second World War (World War II), 8, 14,
    25, 31, 43, 69, 74, 151
second-wave feminist movement, 7, 12,
    148
Seiron (Sound Argument), 33, 52, 55, 67,
    98, 102, 130, 201
self-confidence, 7, 100
self-determination, 1, 125–126, 128, 216
self-identify, 21, 221
self-liberation, 12
Senkaku/Diaoyu Islands, 157
separate surnames for married couples,
    63, 104–105, 113, 166–167, 172–173
separation of church and state, 38
sex/sexuality, 186
    education, 56, 113, 121, 128, 139
    object, 192
    -class system, 9
sexism/sexist, 7, 13, 72, 148, 151,
    184–187, 192, 200, 207, 223

sexual
    discrimination, 7, 187
    harassment, 125
    norms, 186–188
    violence, 151–152, 189–190, 223, 225
sexuality, 125–126, 153, 186, 188–191,
    207–209, 213–214, 218, 225
shame, 81, 92, 182–183, 186
shameless, 185
Shinto, 43, 131
Shokun! (Everyone!), 33, 52, 55, 67, 71,
    98, 102, 201
signature-gathering campaigns, 194
silence, 156, 207–208, 210, 213
single-female-parent households, 80–81
sit-in, 38
small groups, 159, 204, 209
Social Democratic Party of Japan (SDPJ),
    33
social
    conservatives, 10–11, 72
    get-together, 199
    institutions, 21–22, 82, 117, 190,
        223–224
    issue, 23, 63, 72, 95, 161
    justice, 1
    media, xii, 161
    minority, 1, 205
    movements, xi, xiii, 1, 11–12, 22, 24,
        32, 56, 99, 160–161, 211, 220
    norms, 12, 110, 113, 124
    participation, 5, 121, 148, 221
    structures, 9, 11–13, 116, 129, 190,
        211, 215, 223
soci-dems, 200
societal changes, 98
Society for Honoring the Glorious War
    Dead, 38–39, 41, 45–48, 50
Society for the Protection of Japan,
    43–47, 49, 73
Sound Argument (Seiron), 33, 98, 101,
    103–105, 111–114, 130–131, 133

Index

South Korea, xii–xiii, 2, 25, 58–59, 85, 134, 150–151, 156, 161, 163–164, 166, 172, 175, 177–178, 180–183, 185, 187, 191, 194, 197, 201–202, 204–205, 208, 218, 221, 224
special privileges for Japan-residing' Koreans (Zainichi tokken), 3
standpoint, 4, 12–13, 53, 79, 112, 148, 175–176, 184, 215, 217, 220
STOP ERA campaign, 9
street parade, 38
streetside speeches, 3, 45, 60, 62, 158, 162
student movement, xi, 1, 32, 45
suffering mother, 15, 71, 78, 82, 84–86, 88–90, 92–95
suffrage, 166, 222–223
Suiheisha, 152
Suiheisha History Museum, 152

Taiwan, 151, 185, 200–201, 203
Takeshima/Dokdo Island, 58, 156
Tea Party movement, 11
teasing, 68
terrorism, 28–29
Textbook Society, 2–4, 6, 52–54, 56–57, 60, 67, 89, 98, 121, 123, 130–131, 133, 135, 143–144, 152, 196–197, 211–212, 224
textual analysis, 165
tradition, 26, 28, 72–73, 86, 91
traditional, 2, 9, 21, 43–44, 55, 63, 67–68, 71–73, 86, 94, 98–99, 113, 124, 128, 140, 188, 192, 195, 211, 213, 215, 220, 222
traditionalist, 19
Tsuruhashi, 5, 155–156, 159
Tsushin, 39, 42, 76–77, 79–80, 82–84, 86–87, 89–94

Ube Women's Group to Think about Gender Equality, 5, 61, 98
ultraconservatism, x
ultranationalist groups, 26
United Nations, 7, 47, 62
Ustream, 162–163

values, 11, 15, 54, 71–72, 91–95, 114, 116, 129, 136, 186–187, 192, 205, 215
vested interests, 99–100, 119
victim, 9–11, 51, 81, 175, 184, 189, 206, 223
videos, 14–15, 160, 162–165, 168–170, 172, 174, 176–177, 179, 181, 185, 191, 196–197
violence, 9, 25, 29, 68, 85, 95, 125, 151–152, 187, 189–190, 209, 220, 222–225
voluntary participation, 54, 123
volunteerism, xi

war criminals, 26
war widows, 34–35, 74–75, 77–82, 87, 92–93
wartime sexual violence, 151, 187, 209, 225
Wednesday Demonstration, 62, 166, 177
welfare, 22–24, 35–36, 44, 74, 81, 131, 220
welfare state, 22
whiteness, 11
widow, 34–36, 74–82, 85–87, 92–93
WiLL, 151, 184, 201
women of the Japanese conservative movement, 6
women's
    division, 38, 61, 74, 78–83, 135
    groups, 5, 7–8, 13–15, 61, 81, 150, 153, 160, 168, 174, 184–187, 191, 194, 212–213
    human rights, 15, 67, 69, 151, 183–184, 187–188, 190, 219
    independence, 218
    liberation, 7, 12–13, 68, 148, 161, 223
    life-choices, 8
    movement, 1, 11–12, 15–16, 50, 55, 61, 66, 121, 137, 148, 211, 214–215, 219–225
    oppression, 7
    sexuality, 153, 189–191, 207–208, 213–214, 225
World Cup, 58, 200

Women on the Right

xenophobia, 4, 19, 119

Yamaguchi Prefecture, 5, 41, 57, 61, 98, 101, 105, 123
Yasukuni
mothers, 8
Shrine, 2, 8, 22, 24–25, 33–35, 37–40, 42–43, 50, 63, 75, 79, 84–85, 87, 157, 194–195

Shrine Bill, 37–38, 75
wives, 82, 93
young adults' division, 75,78, 86–87
youth division, 38, 40, 75, 82, 84, 86
YouTube, 156, 162–163, 168–172, 175, 177–183, 188, 197

Personal Names

Akamatsu, Katsumaro, 1
Bagehot, Walter, 21
Blee, Kathleen, 9–10, 192
Burke, Edmund, 20–21
Clement, Grace, 117–118
Creasap, Kimberly, 9–10
Cudd, Ann, 67, 99
Dworkin, Andrea, 9–11
Ehara, Yumiko, 7, 68, 100
Faludi, Susan, 55, 67
Fine, Alan, 194, 204–205, 209
Fineman, Martha, 215
Fisher, Berenice, 216
Gellner, Ernest, 24–25
Gilligan, Carol, 117–118, 121, 215–217
Hardisty, Jean, 11
Hasegawa, Koichi, 1, 132
Hayek, Friedrich, 21
Higuchi, Naoto, 3–4, 6, 162, 185, 191, 193, 201, 218
Hirschman, Albert, 21–22
Hori, Yukio, 25, 28–29, 31
Hume, David, 21
Ida, Hiroyuki, 7, 56, 72, 100–101, 121
Ino, Kenji, 27–29
Ito, Kimio, 67, 71, 99–100
Joshita, Ken'ichi, 36, 86
Kabashima, Ikuo, 23–24
Kanai, Yoshiko, 123, 148, 216
Katagiri, Shinji, 1
Kim, Hak-sun, 151, 178
Kinoshita, Hanji, 26, 28–29

Kitahara, Minori, 7, 149–150, 192
Kittay, Eva, 119, 215
Klatch, Rebecca, 10–11
Kobayashi, Yoshinori, 53, 133
Mannheim, Karl, 19–20
Maruyama, Masao, 22
Nakajima, Takeshi, 21
Nakayama, Toshihiro, 22–23, 72
Oguma, Eiji, 2–3, 6, 54, 63, 123
Okano, Yayo, 98, 116, 164, 216–217
Oku, Kentaro, 37, 75–78
Otsuki, Takahiro, 4
Pak, Suni, 7, 150
Rommelspacher, Birgit, 222
Ruoff, Kenneth, 31, 45
Sanami, Yuko, 6–7, 62, 149, 192
Schlafly, Phyllis, 9
Schmitt, Carl, 21
Schreiber, Ronne, 11
Soucey, Michaela, 204–205, 209
Sugita, Mio, 6, 62–63
Takemura, Kazuko, 220–222
Takenaka, Yoshihiko, 23–24
Tanaka, Nobumasa, 34–35, 37
Tocqueville, Alexis de, 21
Tronto, Joan, 216–217
Ueno, Yoko, 2, 4, 6, 54, 63, 123, 197
Yamamoto, Yumiko, 6, 62, 163, 184
Yamatani, Eriko, 56, 71, 111–114, 128
Yasuda, Koichi, 3, 5, 58, 60, 149, 159, 165, 193
Yazawa, Sumiko, 220